JUDE

Liz Trotta

JUDE

A PILGRIMAGE

TO THE

SAINT OF

LAST RESORT

HarperSanFrancisco
A Division of HarperCollinsPublishers

HarperCollins books may be purchased for educational, business, or sales promotional use. For information please write: Special Markets Department, HarperCollins Publishers, Inc., 10 East 53rd Street, New York, NY 10022.

HarperCollins Web Site: http://www.harpercollins.com

HarperCollins®, 📖®, and HarperSanFrancisco™ are trademarks of Harper-Collins Publishers Inc.

FIRST HARPERCOLLINS PAPERBACK EDITION PUBLISHED IN 2005

Library of Congress Cataloging-in-Publication Data
Trotta, Liz.
    Jude : a pilgrimage to the saint of last resort / Liz Trotta.
    ISBN 0–06–075697–7 (pbk.)
1. Jude, Saint—Cult. 2. Jude, Saint—Legends. 3. Trotta, Liz. 4. Middle East—Description and travel. 5. Italy—Description and travel. 6. United States—Description and travel. I. Title.
BT693.T76   1998
226'.092—dc21   96–50997

05 06 07 08 09 RRD 10 9 8 7 6 5 4 3 2 1

To my parents, who had the story first.

"The natural flights of the human mind are not from pleasure to pleasure, but from hope to hope."

—Dr. Samuel Johnson
The Rambler
March 24, 1749

CONTENTS

ACKNOWLEDGMENTS

IT IS TRULY STARTLING HOW EVERYONE WITH WHOM I CAME into contact in this quest eventually felt Jude's touch, especially those who did not seek it. No bright lights, no whirling skies, just a chain of unexpected events that invariably bore his trademark.

Besides to Jude himself—the benefactor and moving presence of this book—I am profoundly indebted to so many loyal and learned friends and colleagues who have each in their own way led me into his undiscovered territory. Thank you to all who took my hand, especially:

Deborah Schneider, my agent, for a quiet endurance that rescued the project more than once.

Barbara A. Lee for general brilliance, and especially her Italian ear.

Jim Benenson for practical editorial advice, rare discernment, and easy humor.

Luz de Castro of New York for translations of Spanish material and Susan El-Hage of Beirut for similar work in Arabic.

Professor Richard Gordon for the zeal of his belief and the grace of his life.

Kate Skattebol for watchfulness in the world of English Judeana.

Jack Hartigan for a shrewd legal mind and red tape–cutting skills when it counted.

George and Hoda Montgomery for intrepid reporting from the trail in the Middle East.

John Keene for being "Semper Fi" in the tradition of the Corps.

Last but most notably, Timothy Dickinson for bringing discipline, wisdom, and incomparable editing skill to the manuscript as well as an unshakable faith that Jude's story would be told.

PROLOGUE

I HAVE NO JUDE STORY. NOR HAVE I EVER TAKEN OUT space in the classified columns to petition or thank him. Any vague feeling or sense of his presence emerges entirely from hazy childhood memories of the green and white letters that arrived at our home from an array of St. Jude shrines. My mother, you see, was a serious enthusiast, and my family passed more than one evening studying the enclosed lists of impossible causes matched with little boxes to mark for special prayers.

The day came soon enough when, like youth hostels and gardenia corsages, holy helpers seemed to be something I had outgrown. A hard-driving career in television network news left little time or energy for spiritual matters, except, perhaps, to cover a Vatican pageantry or the occasional reports of visions of the Blessed Virgin in somebody's backyard.

A few years ago, when I remarked to a friend that St. Jude seemed to have gone very high profile, and might be worth an editorial look, he observed that, without realizing it, I had made a life out of risk, operating in Jude's territory all along, but without ever acknowledging his presence. A sobering thought, indeed. If he was right, then, living within that magnetic field, something had been hectoring me to a recognition: Jude did seem to be a continuing presence, the everywhere saint who had faded for awhile, only to reappear with a fantastic claim, the patron of last resorts, lost causes, the impossible, the man to summon as the ship goes down. Was he a story? If anything, Jude's fabled obscurity, not to mention his reputation for actually performing the impossible, seemed "raw meat" enough for anyone even remotely interested in news. Suddenly, the mystery of his longevity and obscurity began to fuel my sense of being a reporter as well as a Catholic. No, I did not want to go home again, nor did I expect this journey to return me to my mother's kitchen table. Didn't it make a different kind of sense to see if I had a Jude story? Hagiographers, biblical scholars, pamphleteers—all have had their say. It was time to hunt the man down.

BALTIMORE

> *"And of some have compassion,*
> *making a difference:*
> *And others save with fear, pulling*
> *them out of the fire . . . "*
>
> The Epistle of Jude, first century

> *"I want to thank St. Jude*
> *for hearing my prayers.*
> *I had no place else to*
> *turn . . . "*
>
> R. S., 1997

VINCENZO PULLARA, A PLUMP STUBBY MAN, wears the smoldering expression of one who harbors dark secrets. Vincenzo and his group are setting out to make a novena at the shrine of St. Jude, patron saint of impossible causes. By his own admission, Mr. Pullara is on good terms with "the guys who hang around the coffee shops"—and he doesn't mean Starbucks. He and his friends are the stuff of Hollywood miniseries: their frighteningly childlike nicknames whisper along the mean corridors of New York's criminal courts. The FBI once described him as a lieutenant in the Gambino family.

One stormy day in May, he and forty of his friends and family are hurtling through the rain and fog in a Greyhound bus bound for Baltimore. They are pilgrims. Within hours, they will be kneeling at the foot of an almost diagnostically unimpressive statue, which will, indeed, throw the intensity of their gratitude and devotion into deeper relief.

And here I am, too—not really sure why. Perhaps to satisfy a longtime reporter's hunch that there is something in the air about a man named Jude, something deeply believed, strangely and repeatedly justified, but never explored. In a Catholic childhood, very representative of a time, and now astonishingly remote in retrospect, he stood motionless among other saints, only murkier and more plastery than they, yet credited with a vast if vague power to rescue and redeem the most lost of causes. Shadowy indeed, but massed into the shadow of a mountain by the intense conviction and devotion of so many of his followers.

In adult life, he became impersonally more real to me. He persisted in the background, his devotees and strange achievements turning up in unexpected places. Repeatedly, I was bumping into stories of how this Unknown Soldier of the spirit was drawing countless new souls, people frantic for hope in an ever more desperate world. But why—and how? I ask Vincenzo.

"You know, I didn't use to believe," he says, "but now I see that things happen when I ask his help. And I have to say thank you."

And a big thank you it should be. In 1987, two hard-charging federal prosecutors in the Justice Department—Louis Freeh, now director of the FBI, and Rudolph Giuliani, now mayor of New York City, were hot on the trail of some of the aforementioned coffee shop crowd involved in a heroin importing ring that operated out of several Brooklyn pizzerias and reached all the way to Sicily. The tenacious duo eventually won seventeen convictions in the notorious "Pizza Connection" case. Charged as a fugitive in a murder-for-hire scheme, Vincenzo was linked to the shooting of one of the defendants on a busy Greenwich Village street, only to be mysteriously saved when a key government witness reneged on his agreement to testify and the authorities were compelled to drop charges. His wife's supplications to St. Jude, he is convinced, kept him out of prison. He beams over at her, flashing his diamond pinkie ring.

Jerry Pullara is handing out Twinkies and hard Sicilian sausage, brushing her hair back to show off fourteen-carat-gold St. Jude earrings. She likes nothing better than to lead guests to the five-foot statue of Jude in her Queens living room. "I talk to him as I go around the house each day. I don't know what I'd do without him. I consult him on everything." Now the children are singing in a Sicilian dialect; the men are poring over *Oggi,* an Italian newspaper, and a lady in black faces the crowd, intoning, *"In nomine Patris, et Filii et Spiritu Sancti . . ."*

The pilgrims have begun their journey.

Seventy years ago, G. K. Chesterton observed that "America is a nation with the soul of a church."

Shrewd then, this observation can now be seen as downright prescient, for as the second Christian millennium draws to its fulfillment, America is caught up in one of the most fervent religious revivals in its history, no mere parade of dreamy-eyed angels and clamor of New Age vibrations but a stirring of spirits, a yearning of hearts, and, in a deeper sense, a chorus of bewilderment and desperation from a people long seen as the most blest among nations: best, brightest, richest, prettiest, smartest, most resiliently optimistic. And now, perhaps, the most desperate. Peace, prosperity, triumph, and justification in the Cold War—the hard-won goals of all the demanding years since the breaking of the Axis—are leaving us the time and sense of anticlimax to turn our spirits inward, to explore the emptiness that no American military or political victory seems able to fill, that no material gain or scientific milestone can dispel.

Once our triumphs, intellectual and technical, fed our legendary American optimism, our "can do" outlook as the leader of the free—and, implicitly—the decent world. Small wonder that those conditioned to treat these accomplishments as the prerequisites to happiness, purpose, and self-respect found themselves feeling small, belittled, and desperate in the very moment of victory. As we discovered that a small poverty-stricken Southeast Asian nation could humble us and that "Made in Japan" was no longer a cheap imitation, as a nation and individually, we were brought face-to-face with our own vulnerability, or, as the theologians say, "creatureliness." The fitting recourse to this sense of loss must be hope, for without it, desperation waits to fill the void.

So many of our answered prayers have left us more wanting in an endless letdown of finite achievement after triumph, however mighty, in the material world. Graduates of the "Me generation," those who sought to be "Masters of the Universe," seem to have discovered in their middle age, at last, that they are not lords of their own destiny. It is a time of internal transformation, a hunger for personal experience of a higher power. Prayer—the final sensation—is back in fashion. Might we one day turn to a TV talk show and find an unctuous host quizzing a panel of "People Who Hope Too Much"?

Therapy, offering a curiously flat optimism, a glassy acceptance of those who like to talk endlessly about themselves, and smug panaceas for infinite agonies, has long lost its glitter. Even sex—embarrassingly the touted cure-all of the last thirty years—has not delivered. Instead of inner peace, there is fragmentation; rootlessness; divorce; friction among cultures; racial hatred; drug, alcohol, and child abuse; and out of this hollowness, an unnamable craving.

After defining the "big payoff" in worldly terms, we discover that this world offers none large enough to crowd out its dark and barren horizons. We got the Mercedes we prayed for and found that it carries the freedoms of the heart no further than do our own two feet. So long feeling itself "the chosen country," America now wallows in cultural and spiritual self-rejection, while desertion and discredit threaten church and state alike. Darkness overarches belief as the shared certainty that things will work out, that the future belongs to the country that God has chosen, dissolves into formless unease. With this self-doubt, *sancta simplicitas*—simple holiness—has been diminished in our lifetime. All forms of belief, even in science, are threatened, and half-baked theories of the spirit rush to fill the gaping wound.

- Psychics and UFO-sighters are telling their stories to more sympathetic ears than ever before.

- Reports of apparitions of the Blessed Virgin and weeping icons reach an all-time high.

- Talk of millennialism—whether as the endgame of history or rebirth into an unfathomable New Age—adds urgency and sometimes terror to the spiritual debate.

- A cult commits mass suicide to hitch a ride on a comet.

It comes as no surprise that Gregorian chant soars up out of the past to score repeatedly on the pop music charts. Or that a TIME/CNN poll conducted by Yankelovich Partners indicates that 82 percent of 1,004 people questioned believe in the healing power of personal prayer. Hope, the last rallying point in common between secular and religious visions, and operating between presumption and despair, assumes that we can somehow work our way through the rubble to carry on. Or, to put it more bluntly: we are dealing with a "fallen" human race whose hope must in the end be sought beyond this creation. "Hoping against hope" we say, an unconscious admission that rational, ordinary hope must be transcended by a higher, if not irrational, hope.

Standing back from material access to the ordinary offices of religion in this world, St. Jude Thaddeus beckons, ready to soar beyond earthly solutions and harbor us in the territory of last resort. In the end, weariness forces us to his undemonstrative but total consideration. The exhausted find that it is worth hanging on—there *is* a recourse. Solitary, walking a secret highway wholly apart from the millennial crowd of signs and searches, he waits for the righteous and the far-wandered alike to call his name. Unlike a great historically established figure, he is an abnormal saint for an abnormal age, picking his time and place for intervention as subversively as he intervenes. We can understand a world war or depression driving the masses into Jude's camp of irregulars, as they have in the past. But when people turn to him in a time of peaceful prosperity, then we must face the daunting prospect that the treacherous consequences of moral emptiness may be more disastrous than those of persecution and war.

St. Jude Thaddeus, least known of the Twelve and yet renowned worldwide for his specific works, has woven himself in and out of history from the moment a carpenter's son summoned him to his side. Returning today, he casts his shadow at the very center of the endless struggle between hope and despair, back with greater force than ever before. Energized by a very special vision, Jude—and Judeans—has emerged from the spiritual aridity that seems to parch the whole world into an awakening of hope. Not the clear-edged specific virtue but an inchoate upwelling in hearts world over, souls stretched to extremity but finding a last helper before they snap. They do not entertain the hope of faith, just the hope of hope.

Most puzzling of all, there is the impalpable ubiquity of this mysterious man who, without historical or theological proof, has been delegated the amazing burden of retrieving lost causes. They call him a saint, but is he more? And even if "just" a saint, a saint like which other? Contentious Jerome? Passionate Augustine? Theresa? Joan? He slips away from such comparisons, as he has always. In pursuing Jude, one finds his presence and his story on the street, where news gets out ahead of any journalist or talk-show host. It explodes into the lives of ordinary people with the speed and sophistication of a stealth aircraft, leaping from mouth to mouth, heart to heart, pushing the boundaries of witnesses to his works. These stories of hope rewarded do not add up to hard evidence (scientific roof or church approval) of spiritual interventions. Unbounded in their economic and geographic reach, consistent in their desperation, they weave a luminous cloak of compelling clues, high-speed hints, that Jude—farmer, apostle, preacher, martyr, saint, ubiquitous presence—has emerged as one of the most potent figures in spiritual America.

Midwestern farmers raise roadside shrines to him. New York trendsetters wear St. Jude necklaces. Keychains bearing the supplication "St. Jude Protect Me" adorn the most well cut vests. Hospital patients go to surgery with St. Jude medals pinned to their gowns. Worshipers and the curious throng Jude novenas throughout the country. His name is overheard in a hotel lobby, an unemployment office. A young boy in a Korean grocery collects money for his winning ticket in a state lottery, telling his friend that one day he will name his son Jude. Gypsy fortune-tellers keep statues of Jude in their eerie parlors. T-shirt wearers blazon his name across their chests. A golf tournament takes its name from him. As does a bowling league. And a bicycle club. His oldest and most recognized presence in this country surfaces more regularly in the classified columns of daily and weekly newspapers of cities great and small. The publication of petitions for his help and the formula thank-you prayers for help received are central to the Jude devotion.

Pseudo-Judeana, a kitschy subculture of superstition and bad taste, comedy and tragedy, thrives, driven in part by Jude's status as the "Invisible Man." Unseen but eminently accessible, this no-frills Jude comes complete with private ritual and his very own deal, substituting form for substance. Mass mailings of chain letters girdle the world like satellites ("Good luck will come to you within four days if you send copies of this letter to twenty people. If you break the chain, then prepare for bad luck"). Jude home pages crackle along the impulses of the Internet, among them these very same chain letters and a motivational handbook based on the intimate details of Jude's life as disclosed by an Italian "visionary" (On his childhood: "Jude's family lived down the street from Jesus." On his married life: "Their home, a rented two-story stone building, was shared with another couple").

We are, in short, witnessing a Jude explosion, a return to a saint who, although a mystery, has marshaled the despairing and the lonely, believers and doubters, into taking that extra step toward him as he awaits their call. He seems to be standing just behind the door at those stark moments in everyone's lives when the heart can only cry out "Why me?"—when even God Himself seems remote from those who believe, and impossible to those who do not. Despair is never selective, roaming the world with democratic devastation: roads of escape run out, support systems shut down, faith shutters, and hope itself, the final defense, dries up and seems to wither away. In the mortal and eternal duel between hope and despair, this perplexing figure from the byways of Galilee walks dustily among the exhausted souls of the modern world, that rabble of the desperate grabbing for his hands only as they go down for the third time. To them, Jude Thaddeus is the rescuer of Everyman, of those left only with ancient words from David's great psalm—*Eli, Eli, lama sabachthani?* ("My God, my God, why hast thou forsaken me?")— words that Jesus Himself uttered in the final extremity of the cross.

As the murmurs of the inconsolable gather into an anthem, we can see that the crosses carried in Jude's army are of infinite variety. The tales epitomizing these burdens often end unexpectedly, as did that about the late Jimmy Hoffa. After the strange twisted giant of the Teamsters disappeared, his wife, Josephine, in shock and facing cataract surgery, spent much of her time praying before a shrine of St. Jude in their home. Hoffa had given it to her just before he vanished.

More often hope is rewarded, though not always immediately. The stories pour in from everywhere.

Mrs. L. C. writes from Tampa: "I dreamt of a small statue of St. Jude. He was on top of the VCR in my bedroom speaking to me, but upon waking I could not recall what had been said. This strange drama occurred two nights in a row . . . I had never heard of St. Jude . . ."

L. C. mentioned the dream to her mother, who explained that he was the saint of lost causes, and then forgot about him. A week later she stepped over a discarded Jude novena pamphlet on her way into church. Not facing any hopeless quandary, she filed it away. Only when she lay on her bed facing a miscarriage did she begin to pray the Jude novena and promised to name a healthy child after the saint. Her doctors told her to expect the worst—but she brought forth a robust boy. "We call him 'Jude.'"

Mr. P. M., an army veteran, remembers that at fourteen he had rheumatic fever complicated by heart problems that confined him to bed for four years. The doctors' predictions of a life of limited physical activity seemed to close the door on his twin dreams of becoming a boxer or an actor. But a friend passed on word of Jude and "I began to pray very hard." When he went for his army physical, no trace of the disease could be found, nor did it surface when he endured even more rigorous training to join the fabled 82nd Airborne Division. Once out of the service, he became an amateur boxer and, at age sixty-seven, still trains and works out six days a week. "I guess I'm not going to become a famous actor," he chuckles, adding that each day he thanks St. Jude for his "great miracle of health."

To best explain what Jude *is,* we must consider what he is not. No standard myth prevails, no elaborate imagery bathes him in celestial light, no great Jude story or association catches our attention—only hushed wonders told and retold from friend to stranger to eavesdropper. Oddly enough, no one ever seems to have claimed a vision of him. Jude statues are not seen weeping. He is not even to be found on the curricula of religious schools. Yet when all else fails, when, if you will, all the "assigned specialists" have fallen down on the job, you know that Jude lurks in the wings. And only late in the day do most people realize that this presence is Jude. They are backed into Jude. They do not come forward in the ordinary highly organized manner of the church, asking, "To whom do I go to for this?" There is the Roman bureaucratic specialist approach—and then there is Jude, a revered apostle of Jesus and at the same time utterly non-Roman, un-organizational, un-bureaucratic. People reach out to him, often not knowing whether he's man or woman, Jew or Gentile. Only in the end is it clear that it is Jude they've been seeking.

Appeals to him do not resemble those to the saints of air travel, the battlefield, or cabdrivers. The realm of impossible causes embraces a much wider range of humanity and so, by definition, demands an intermediary of special powers. Being an apostle and probable cousin of Jesus should certainly underline Jude's standing as a true insider, and yet those very facts are so often unknown to his followers. Instead, he arrives as an anonymous holy helper, a bulge in the curtain. The impalpability of Jude is the essence of his appeal.

For an age preoccupied with heavy-hitter celebrity saints, this is a singularly apt contrarian shade, extreme in spareness of outline, not gussied up with spectacular miracles like the sun spinning in the sky at Fatima, or glitzy shrines adorned with the crutches of the crippled as at Lourdes. He is not one's life companion, as the Virgin is perceived, or even the now-cashiered St. Christopher. Michelangelo never captured him in marble. Jude does not command attention. He is almost passive, the saint of shadows who travels light.

In a time of utter identification with the sound bite, he stands in silence, mythless: Jude the Deliberately Obscure, the guerrilla operating unseen in the mist, an apparition over the horizon, the farthest out, remote—yet hearing the weakest, most desolate cries. There is an ESP quality about it all, as though people vaguely feel they are connected to hope—to Jude. Was it by accident that the Beatles turned that perception into the biggest-selling single of their fabulous career, "Hey Jude"? Mention the saint to anyone who doesn't know him, and prepare to hear a few bars of this unforgettable tune, an anthem to hope. For years, many assumed that the mop-haired pipers of the '60s heroes might have been under the spell of the saint of the impossible, some going so far as to read a subconscious invocation into that haunting melody. But John Lennon and Paul McCartney have always defended the song's unhallowed origin, shrewdly debunking psychological analyses and tea-leaf readings of alleged hidden lyrics. Not an unexpected attitude from a group whose Liverpool charm essentially flowed from their innate hatred of pretension and an insistence that there is always less than meets the eye.

Most accounts of the song's evolution begin with McCartney driving his Aston-Martin from London to Weybridge to return John's five-year-old son, Julian, to his mother, Cynthia. At the time, 1968, the Lennons were near divorce and Yoko Ono was very much a fixture in John's life. McCartney, seeking to comfort Julian, began singing, "Hey Julian," which evolved into "Jules" and later "Jude." How is not really explained, although some speculate it seemed a better fit historically and melodically. The popular explanation is that Lennon liked the song and thought that Paul had subconsciously directed it to him because of his affair with Yoko, as though McCartney were saying "Hey, John." As for the song's puzzling suggestion that a "movement" is needed on one's (Jude's or John's) shoulder, Lennon is often quoted as having heard it as a message from McCartney: "The angel in him was saying 'Bless You.'"

They made the recording in the Apple Boutique on Abbey Road, a clothing store the Beatles had bought and turned into a recording studio. The night before the Jude session, someone had whitewashed the window and scrawled "Hey Jude" across it. Shopkeepers went into an uproar, scenting anti-Semitism, and someone smashed the window with a brick. Never mind. Two days later, they did a revision in one take, seven minutes of hope set to music. The song was released on August 30, 1968. McCartney was afraid it wasn't any good, but it became a hit within two weeks. Although much of the song was "nah, na-na-nah," millions heard the sound of hope, the sound of Jude. Tim Riley writes of "Hey Jude" in his book *Tell Me Why:* "The genius lies in the way he includes the listener in the same pilgrimage."

And a journey of prayer it is, one that cautions against fear, or playing it too cool, for these things stand in the way of home or hope, that which makes all things better. A song itself can, it would seem, remake the sad music of life.

But what do we really know about Jude? As muted a figure as can be imagined, he moves in and out of the Gospel story with less impact than any of a dozen minor characters, including the three Marys who were not Jesus' mother—obscure in their own way, for they have not been specifically identified—as well as Martha, Lazarus, Simon of Cyrene, and the good and the bad thief.

There is virtually no study of him, either in the scholarly or popular sense, so it is logical that no one really knows how or when so obscure an apostle became so closely associated around the world with impossible causes. A little known but lyrical novena of Spanish origin, dated 1702, makes no reference to any such connection. But the Jesuit authors of the *Acta Sanctorum,* the supreme compendium of saints' lives, speak in Tome 12 (October volumes) of their 1863 commentary of an "amazing" devotion to Jude "in certain regions." They cite a "Little Office of St. Jude" published in 1826 that specifically describes him as "the special advocate of the unfortunate and well-nigh hopeless." The question of why Jude was "neglected" evokes an oft-repeated theory: a similarity between Jude's name and that of the traitor Judas Iscariot confused and even frightened people away. Who finally cleared up the confusion, and why, is not explained. Lacking hard evidence, we can only suspect that

Jude's effective intercession on behalf of those in hopeless straits established his reputation for rescue.

The relative length of entries about Jude compared to those of other saints in the great *Acta Sanctorum* underscores his obscurity. For example, in a sampling of the Jude and October volumes—spanning a period of more than two hundred years—material on St. Norbert totals 107 pages; St. Anselm of Canterbury, 89; St. Brigid of Ireland, 87; St. Agatha, 63; while Jude—an apostle of the Lord—staggers in last with 39 pages.

What we know about him, then, derives chiefly from three sources: the gospels, the writings of the church fathers, and tradition. Legend, too, has embroidered an unusually large part of what little story he has. This is the gist of it: he is the eleventh named of Jesus' twelve apostles. In John's Gospel he is called "Judas, not the Iscariot," probably in an attempt to distinguish him from the traitor. In Matthew and Mark, he is called "Thaddaeus" (or "Lebbaeus"), and in Luke and Acts, "Judas the brother of James." This "James" (James the Less), thought to have been the son of Alphaeus (Cleophas), became the first bishop of Jerusalem. Both James and Jude are identified as the "brothers" of Jesus, that is, His kinfolk, as the contemporary meaning of the word and other scholarly evidence of the time dictates.

Some sources, following an interpretation by St. Jerome and other church fathers, reason that Jude and his three brothers—James (the Less); Simeon, or Simon (the second bishop of Jerusalem); and Joses (Joseph)—were first cousins of Jesus through their mother, Mary of Cleophas, thought to have been the Blessed Mother's sister. Some sources add Matthew, or Levi, a customs official and the patron saint of bankers, to the list of Jude's brothers. Others, subscribing to the interpretation of the Apocryphals and most of the Greek fathers, contend that Jude was a stepbrother of Jesus because Joseph married twice, first Mary of Cleophas, who bore him four sons and died, and then Mary the Blessed Mother. Hegesippus names all four sons as first cousins of Jesus on the side of their father, Alphaeus, who was Joseph's brother. And finally, and generally discredited, the formidable Tertullian ("It is certain because it is impossible") holds that Jude was a real brother of Jesus, a son of Mary and Joseph, but too many historical objections preclude any claim to the validity of this theory. In any case, a family tie to Christ—probably cousinhood—is widely believed to be one of the sources of Jude's special power and has shaped an iconographical tradition emphasizing the saint's physical resemblance to Jesus.

The name that today is translated as Jude, Judas, and Judah was originally one Hebrew word, *yehudhah,* literally meaning "praised by the Lord" or "I will praise the Lord"—thus, the English translation of this Hebrew name is "Judah," also written "Juda," while the diminutive form is "Jude." Jude, or Judas, was a popular name among Jews and early Christians. As with all the apostles, we know nothing about this Jude's physical appearance, although one can derive a sense of his physique and personality from his other names—Thaddeus, from the Aramaic, and Lebbaeus, from the Hebrew, both meaning chesty, hearty, courageous, bighearted.

Jude's iconography, his appearance in art traditions, generally pictures him as an old man of a Jewish and patriarchal cast, with a long or short beard. There are modern exceptions, such as the movie star version set in brightly colored square tiles on the outside wall of the Jude shrine in San Diego. A Franciscan shrine in Mt. Vernon, New York, presents two impressions of Jude in their mailings: a snowy-haired old man with a matching long beard dressed in muted brown and green, or a young man of beatnik demeanor wearing bright red and blue. Traditionally, Jude wears combinations of green, white, red, and brown, and his feet are bare or in sandals. Green, the color of hope in church liturgy, is Jude's color. Chrysoprase, a gem of golden-green beryl or apple-green chalcedony, is associated with Jude as a symbol of wisdom and recalls the foundation stone of the golden and heavenly city that St. John saw in a vision.

In some representations of St. Jude, a tongue of fire, marking him as one of the Twelve, hangs over his head, and in others a gold nimbus, the mark of a saint. Often he holds a closed or open book, intended to be his Epistle, grips a halberd, the type of battle-ax his assassins wielded to murder him. Other symbols associated with Jude include an anchor, a boat held in his hand, a child holding a boat, a boat hook, an oar, a lance, loaves and fishes, a club, a long cross, an inverted cross, and a carpenter's square. Frequently he wears the Medallion of Jesus on his breast, a disc depicting the face of Christ; sometimes it sits in the palm of his hand. In an English church window, Jude is holding a scroll bearing the words *Carnis Resurrectionem* ("the Resurrection of the Body"), the penultimate phrase of the Apostles' Creed. According to tradition, the apostles, before separating, composed this declaration of faith, of which each one furnished a sentence or proposition. Usually, however, it is the last line, *Et vitam aeternam* ("And life everlasting") that is cited as belonging to Jude Thaddeus.

What people see—or imagine—as they pray to Jude varies. The bearded fatherly figure is what some conjure up, but more often than not Jude is an unfilled space, a white circle in their consciousness. One man who came to Jude through the classified ads said, "I don't see a statue, but I am closest to seeing certain virtues and characteristics: peace, wisdom, and compassion. I don't see a face. It's a kind of meditation."

Some commentaries divide St. Jude Thaddeus into two separate saints, or they distinguish Jude the apostle from

Thaddeus, a disciple (a follower of Christ). Consequently, feast days differ: in the Eastern rites, for example, the Syrian calendar celebrates St. Thaddeus on May 14 and the apostle Jude on May 19 or December 18. Usually, the feast days are grouped in May or December, but the Latin church sets aside October 28 for Jude and Simon; both, significantly, are apostles and, quite possibly, brothers.

Jude lived and died in the first century. The traditional material about his ministry and martyrdom is not reliable, but much of its general story line has come down unchanged almost from his lifetime. He may have come from Galilee, though the Syriac *Doctrine of Addai* names as his birthplace Paneas, an ancient Syrian city where people once worshiped Pan. This is the Caesarea Philippi of the New Testament, today called Baniyas.

His strange and largely undocumented story unfolds after the Ascension. Bereft of their Master, the apostles had to face the thorny problem of incorporating Gentiles into a church formed by Jews. The revolt against Roman rule and the destruction of Jerusalem and the Second Temple must have been agonizing for those disciples who lived to see it. But the whole ordeal of the early missionary church is hard to imagine. The surviving words of St. Paul tell of the always dangerous and often brutal conditions that Jude and the rest of the apostles had to overcome daily as they spread the word of Christ:

> ". . . Thrice was I beaten with rods, once was I
>   stoned,
> thrice I suffered shipwreck, a night and a day I have
> been in the deep;
> In journeyings often, in perils of waters,
> in perils of robbers, in perils by mine own
>   countrymen,

in perils by the heathen, in perils in the city,
in perils in the wilderness, in perils in the sea,
in perils among false brethren;
In weariness and painfulness, in watchings often,
in hunger and thirst, in fastings often, in cold
and nakedness . . ."

2 Cor. 11:25–27

Basically, three renditions of Jude's journeys arise from the works of those who recorded the fragments of his history: Eusebius, often referred to as the father of church history, recorded the earliest extant account of the best-known story in the third century, relating how after an exchange of letters between Christ and King Abgar of Edessa, Jude journeyed to that kingdom and cured and converted Abgar on behalf of the risen Christ. A sixth-century writer we only know as Pseudo-Abdias chronicled Jude's journeys to Persia, providing the only account in which St. Jude and St. Simon travel, proselytize, and die together. Last, medieval historian Păwstos Buzand recorded Jude's founding of the church of Armenia (Armenians claim this was the first of all national Christian churches) and his death there by order of the king.

Eusebius, a Greek Christian historian, draws Jude's missionary itinerary over many lands in his *Ecclesiastical History,* while the Roman Breviary mentions only Mesopotamia and Persia. After the Ascension, it is believed that Jude set out to reach up and down Judea, Samaria, Idumea, and Syria, but especially in Mesopotamia and Greater Armenia. Like St. Simon, Jude may have been one of the Zealots, the Jewish nationalist party annihilated in the catastrophic rebellion of 70 A.D. Legends surviving from the fourth century credit Jude and Simon with missionary work crowned by their martyrdom in Persia between 64 and 69 A.D. Fortunatus and other

Western martyrologies support these legends; for this reason, the two saints have been commemorated together since the eighth century. Some traditions say that Jude may have returned temporarily to Jerusalem after the martyrdom of his brother, St. James the Less, bishop of Jerusalem, in 62 A.D., and assisted at the unanimous election of his successor, St. Simon, another of Jude's brothers.

Jude's central tradition is symbolized by a standard portrayal in which he wears a picture of Jesus on his chest, a reference to the legend of Abgar, the king of Edessa (now modern Urfa in eastern Turkey). On hearing of Jesus' miracles, the leper king sent a messenger begging Him to come, only to be told that he should have faith and wait to be visited by one of Jesus' disciples. One version of the story says that so compelling was the messenger's description, Abgar immediately dispatched the court painter to portray Christ, and so overcome was this painter by the divine face that he was unable to paint. But Jesus, moved by compassion, pressed a cloak to His face, imprinting His features upon it. Abgar's messenger returned with the cloth and the king kept it in his palace. After the Crucifixion, Jude journeyed to the tiny kingdom and cured the king of his leprosy by applying the holy cloth.

The most popular rendition of this persistent tale, however, differs in minor details and invests Jude with a more prominent role, mainly that he brings the holy cloth to Abgar himself and cures the king on his arrival in Edessa. In any case, the basic legend provides the source for the "Mandylion," the miniature of Christ seen on Jude's chest in paintings and statues that has survived until today. Considered against the background of ancient times, miniature reproductions were not unusual. Signs, symbols, and portraits of one's forebears have possessed an awesome significance at least since the days of pagan Rome, when the masks of ancestors were borne aloft as participants in funeral processions. The death mask summoned up the presence of the deceased, thereby helping to ensure his immortality. Pliny describes the ancient custom of embellishing a shield with a portrait of the dead and hanging it in a temple or other public place. In this spirit, only more powerfully, King Abgar received the holy image.

Jude was assigned to or chose Zoroastrian Persia—of all lands in the ancient world perhaps the most hostile to any other faith—as his missionary field. Here another legend takes over: the Babylonian general Varardach (Babylonia was a region of the Persian Empire) was about to wage war against India and demanded to know its outcome. The court magicians Zaroes and Arfaxat, already plotting against Jude and Simon, invoked the pagan gods and prophesied a long war and much suffering. But the apostles said that India would swiftly sue for peace, as it so proved, whereupon Varardach ordered the magicians put to death. Jude and Simon pleaded for their lives, and by such mercy earned the pagan priests' everlasting hatred. Christ's words of caution, which they no doubt remembered, resound in the Gospel of Matthew: "Behold I send you forth as sheep in the midst of wolves: be ye therefore wise as serpents, and harmless as doves."

The two saints pressed their way east and north, converting multitudes, perhaps as far as southern Russia, until after several years they at last turned back toward Edessa in eastern Mesopotamia. Within hours or days of the city gates, they said farewell, Simon heading north and Jude continuing on. But a vengeful mob, possibly incited by the magicians, waylaid Jude and hacked him to death with a battle-ax. Meanwhile, Simon, ambushed by another band, was crucified, or, some versions say, sawed in two.

Apart from the listing of Jude's name among the apostles in the Gospels, the hardest scriptural evidence we have of him is twofold: a question he poses to Jesus at the Last Supper, the only time this apostle speaks in the New Testament; and the Epistle of Jude, which, modern naysayers notwithstanding, he probably authored sometime between 62 and 65 A.D., before the destruction of Jerusalem.

As to the question, it seems clear enough, but it is the answer that stirs the imagination. Although they have been witnesses to Christ's miracles, the apostles, still plagued by doubts, question Him closely at their last Passover meal together. After they argue about the seating arrangement, they take their places—Jude on the left side of Jesus, second from the end (where tradition seems habitually to place him). The apostles question Jesus about the principles of the promised kingdom, and He replies in what are among the most immortal passages of John's Gospel. Then, suddenly, like a flash of light from a black hole, Jude boldly interjects: "Lord, how is it that thou wilt manifest Thyself to us, and not unto the world?"

Obviously Jude longed for Christ to display His dominion and majesty. Ironically, these words are spoken by a saint whose essence today is grounded in obscurity. In modern terms, we can imagine an image-maker advising his low-profile entrepreneurial client to mount a publicity campaign, hold a telethon, hire a skywriter, do anything, but just *get the word out*.

Christ's answer is profoundly enigmatic: "If a man loves me, he will keep my words: and my Father will love him, and we will come unto him, and make our abode with him."

Is He telling Jude that the best way to get the message out is to go about his work so that the efficacy of such work, *obscurely* performed though it may be, will make the world anew? This theory, of course, has the benefit of hindsight, taking into account Jude's later reputation for tackling desperate causes. On the other hand, the manner in which Jude and the other apostles will evangelize, leaving a trail of fire throughout the ancient world, could hardly be construed as reticent or obscure. The great seventeenth-century French orator Jacques Benigne Bossuet, pondering the Jude Question in his *Meditations on the Gospel,* approaches it from an altogether different angle: "St. Jude went at once to the great mystery: How is it? What have we done that makes us merit more than others? Would we have believed, if you had not given us faith? Would we have chosen you, if you had not chosen us first?"

Bossuet maintains that Jesus did not answer the question. Instead, he repeats once more the heart of his message: "Keep my commandments . . . All the rest is my Father's secret, the unfathomable secret the Sovereign reserves to Himself."

Nevertheless, Jesus seems to be saying that the world is not to be persuaded collectively by signs and wonders, that fundamental changes happen in secret within individual human hearts. It is not a matter of converting nations and bestowing victory upon chosen peoples, but of revealing God's kingdom quietly by answering each lonely cry. It was this assignment that Jude received from his Master and carried to the ends of earth and time.

The thunderous Epistle of Jude, part of the church canon, is the last Epistle in the New Testament and the next to last book in the Bible. It particularly addresses Jewish converts, cautioning them against the heresies rocking the church. Possibly written in Jerusalem and containing only one chapter of twenty-five verses, Jude's Epistle is remarkably similar to the second Epistle of St. Peter, although it is the earlier of the two. The author refers to himself in the first line as "Jude, the servant of Jesus Christ and the brother of James," possibly seeking to ensure his identification as brother to the head of the Jerusalem church. In this poetically stern letter, he ferociously denounces false teachings and heretics within the church, especially those who deny Christ's real humanity. He exhorts the faithful to avoid these "clouds without water, carried about by the winds . . . wandering stars, for whom the storm of darkness is reserved forever . . ."

Jude's authorship of the Epistle was recognized by the Roman church in 170 A.D., by the Church of Alexandria and the African church of Carthage at the end of the second century, by the primitive East Syrian church in the third century, and universally accepted by the Western church at the beginning of the fifth century. This very early and wide acceptance representing the voice of ancient tradition points to the authenticity of Jude's authorship. However, some modern scholars are in doubt, an unfortunate development that has further clouded discussion of him. They cite, among other objections, the reference ". . . be mindful of the words that have been spoken beforehand by the apostles of Our Lord Jesus Christ . . . ," arguing that it suggests the author was not an apostle and must have been writing in the second century. Refuting this claim, other scholars see no separation in time but only in "distance of place," which led Jude to avoid saying he was an apostle. Moreover, they add, none of the references made to false doctrines point to any other than apostolic times. Another objection raised to Jude's authorship is that the Greek style is too cultivated to be that of a poor fisherman or farmer from Galilee. That Jude may have dictated his words to a scribe or that an Aramaic original has been lost to us are possibilities that have largely gone undiscussed. Like so much about Jude, proof of his authorship vanishes in the fog of centuries.

In his *Ecclesiastical History,* Eusebius quotes Hegesippus as reporting that Jude had two grandsons, Zoker and James, who are arrested for bearing the name of the royal house of David, prime title of the great dispersed people of all history. Found harmless, they are acquitted and released even under the implacable emperor Domitian and go on to rule the Christian communities of Palestine. This tells us that Jude was also a husband and a father before he was called to his apostleship.

Not until the late Middle Ages was Jude remembered specifically by any prominent saints: Bernard of Clairvaux, who died in 1153, is reputed to have had a strong personal devotion to him, requesting upon his death that a relic of Jude be placed upon his breast and buried with him.

In 1548, Pope Paul III granted a plenary indulgence—the remission of all temporal punishment due for sin—to all who visited St. Jude's tomb on his feast day, an indication of an appeal alive and even thriving. From the Middle Ages to the nineteenth century, the trail dims, until books about him appear in Western Europe. Although the Second Vatican Council advised against excessive devotion to saints—sometimes a fruitful garden of unorthodoxies—in favor of more intellectual and theological discourse, the displacement of saints from modern Catholic devotion—devoutly wished by progressive liturgists in this epoch of *aggiornamento*—has never really taken hold. To the contrary, in the last decade there has been a resurgence in devotionalism. This silent but profound change in spiritual climate—"a yearning of the heart," as one priest describes it—is a reaction against what some Catholics see as an antiseptic modern church that brushes aside the mystical and dismisses devotional prayer as ethnic primitivism. "The dirty little secret is that the church doesn't like ethnics," says a white priest who works in a black and Hispanic parish. "There is a dreadful condescension on the part of very liberal people."

Others argue that many seek Jude as an intermediary because they are riddled with guilt, afraid to approach directly the throne of God. Father Joseph Chinnici, a devotional historian at the University of California's Graduate Theological Union in Berkeley, says, "We are learning that the liturgy alone cannot carry the weight of spiritual expression. After the Decree on the Liturgy formulated at Vatican II, the focus was on Scripture and the liturgy, and it coincided with a lot of thinking that disapproved of devotional practices and theology. The history of devotions—the Blessed Virgin, the saints, the lesser-known saints of the immigrant church—these were people's *personal expression of Catholicism*. Now, devotionalism has been coming back. There is a tremendous spread of icons—even of Dorothy Day and Martin Luther King."

Whatever else he is, in the modern world, Jude is huge box office. "Several hundred thousand petitions" are received every year at the national shrine in Chicago, and the mailing list for the shrine in Baltimore carries at least a half million names. "We get about five hundred letters a week," says the Brother in charge, "and many contain offerings."

There are now probably more churches dedicated to St. Jude in the United States than to any other single saint, with the obvious exception of the Virgin. While no precise figures have yet come to light, it is assumed that there are thousands of shrines and churches under his patronage worldwide, and millions who pursue Jude books and ornaments, whether in churches, religious gift shops, or from mass mailings. Nevertheless, there is a seeming paradox between the church's zeal to promote Jude and its simultaneous wariness of him, a fear that his popularity could drift into belief that is theologically suspect. Making no secret of his disdain for the devotion, a newly ordained Dominican priest in Washington, D.C., said, "Jude pays the bills and they know it."

This blunt analysis underscores the official ambivalence of promoting Jude as the church's advocate for lost causes. But one of his devout fans, a jocular priest, simply laughed: "If Peter keeps the keys to the front gate, then certainly Jude must be the keeper of the back gate."

Father John Padberg, a Jesuit, offers this considered analysis: "St. Jude's feast is liturgical, but the devotion is para-liturgical and grounded in Catholic tradition, as are rosaries, medals, the devotion to Fatima. . . . People need objects on which they can rely. It is a substratum that feels it has a stranglehold on the reality of faith, that we're all in this together, the communion of saints. And praying to St. Jude—if it means growth in piety and sanctity—then God is pleased with that."

Jude's power to endure may lie in his quiet at-homeness in the world, a simpler and better fit than the way he fits into the church, centrifugal to the center of power rather than centripetal. He doesn't *pull* people into the church, but reaches out to catch them, and somehow they respond. Minnesota Fats did. He didn't make his remarkable name by talking about religion, yet he indirectly credited Jude with his triumph over Lou Russo, a hustler from New Jersey.

"They all like to talk about me losin' all the time," he said. "That'll be the day." He paused. "I came close once. I remember about thirty years ago, I guess, I had to call on the patron saint of impossible propositions."

He weighed 275 pounds in those days, and had to admit that the floor was "creakin' and groanin'." The game, and with it big money, was riding on one last shot when Fats, silently invoking Jude's help, said flatly, "One ball, cross-side." Suddenly, just as the cue ball found its mark, the floor gave way, and the world's best and biggest pool player dropped through it like a boulder. "And that's the closest I ever came to losin'. Some guys gotta tear the house down to try and stop the Fat Man."

Perpetual pursuit of Jude is like trying to see an invisible man, running to throw a blanket over his unseen form so that an outline appears, but in the end watching the blanket collapse and failing to capture him. Even then, we are denied contact as time and time again this oblique figure evaporates in the aftermath of his proven powers. In the twilight of certainties and confident rituals, he is a spirit himself, without any of the histories and glories that glow around the cults of classic saints—the famous emblem, the great paintings, the cavernous basilicas, the moments in history: St. Stephen forgiving his persecutors under the hammering stones; St. Sebastian against a tree, impaled with arrows; St. Peter shaking the serpent into the fire; St. Elizabeth of Hungary feeding the poor with bread that turns to red roses in her cloak. Why should a saint who is almost definingly without a romance, a mighty sanctuary, or a magnetic emblem endure to tower over the din of triumphant, even tumultuous, modernizing Catholicism as it bends itself to the current age? Jude has come effortlessly upstream against the roaring cataracts of modernity like a great shadowy salmon leaping home. A most anomalous figure (if figure he can be called), he is the last person to come to the top of the roster of saints in this century, fielding all the duties of those other holy helpers presently eclipsed. Perhaps it is a question of where people go when tradition is uprooted. More important, it reflects a profound shift in an age when we seem to have run out of truths.

It is also logical that Jude and those who resort to him should erupt in this century as the church returns to plainness, turning from show in an age in which show is king. In fact, the flashy elements of religion have now become hallmarks of Protestant practice: TV ministries, cavernous churches, intense and dramatic prayer crusades. Meanwhile, Catholics, in an institution of rocklike tradition and organized illustriousness, continue to demystify and deglamorize toward a simpler church, cutting back on earthly glory. If anything, Jude seems to have anticipated the church's transition to the modern world.

He has never lost his place in post-conversion Third and Fourth World countries, especially throughout Latin America (there is a large shrine in Chile), the Philippines, and India, where he has two great shrines. Just as most classic devotions are apologetically receding into antiquarianism, we find ourselves confronted with devotion to Jude, a growth saint gaining ground over these very last thirty to forty years, that very era that has seen the steady dissolution of traditional devotions. Jude is no more visible than he ever was, but the golden chain of day-to-day miracles he spins off reaches ever further over a graying world.

"I think the impetus comes from the people rather than the church leadership," says Father Thomas Hayes, the veteran Dominican director of San Francisco's St. Jude shrine. He is plowing through his files of letters oppressed with past extremities. "I think people identify their own obscure situations with him. In their desperation or difficulties, they feel loneliness." He pauses to ponder. "There's loneliness and alienation, and so they identify with Jude, who is on the outside, one of the Twelve, but nobody knows much about him. I think they identify with that. This is for me, they say. Non-Catholics, too, are lonely and want to be part of something. We always want heroes."

Father Hayes's files are a roll call of hopeless causes reconquered by hope:

A baby drowns in Southern California—a lady applies St. Jude oil and he comes back to life.

A priest's niece is pregnant; doctors advise abortion for medical reasons—she prays to Jude and stays in bed, and now both she and the baby are healthy.

A State Farm Insurance agent prays for a big promotion in Portland, Oregon—and gets it.

A Sri Lankan steel fitter injures his back—learning of a little shrine in the mountains of his country, he hires people to carry him there, and soon he can go back to work.

Once a traditional monolith rich in ordered ceremony, the church has made its own adjustments to modernism and egalitarianism, often choosing understatement and the absence of flash to make its unique case in a world of moral relativism. But a piercing sense of Jude remains, much the way Elijah heard God's voice in the wilderness:

> "And after the earthquake a fire; but the Lord
>   was not
> in the fire
> and after the fire a *still small voice* . . ."

Jude is there when everything else is peeled away. It is his *absence* that is the point, a silent holiness so played down that the church commemorates him only by twinning his saint's day with that of a four-carat Christian celebrity, St. Simon.

While self-help is supposed to be operational, confident, and technical, Jude is saint and gatekeeper, his God the One you invoke when all else breaks. The searcher echoes that distraught father who, beseeching Jesus to cure his son possessed by evil, utters the very essence of hope as it passes into trust: "Lord, I believe. Help thou mine unbelief." Imagine a saint whose role is like that: someone who is there to say, I *know* that you don't quite believe. I *know* that you don't quite know what to hope for. But take hope instead of belief. "Jude, I hope, help thou mine hopelessness."

Amidst the clamor of relentless celebritization, the endlessly rotating fifteen minutes of fame—*People* magazine, TV programs frantic for ever more self-strippers to talk their heads off about the most embarrassing aspects of themselves—appears a figure who is utterly impersonal, but only in the sense that a résumé does not exist. The legend of Jude is that he has no legend. No Jude visions. No mytho-culture. And yet, like a thread of sunlight through a crack in the wall, he has a way of infiltrating the stressed and wrecked lives of Catholic grandmothers, Jewish producers, Anglican patricians, Hollywood movie stars, and even convicts. Prison chapels, San Quentin's for one, are often named after Jude. Those who would never dream of looking into the organized saints of core Catholicism find themselves in touch with this outsider of Christianity, this Clint Eastwood–like figure who simply does his job in a beleaguered town and moves on. They—and we—are left with the comic strip question: "Who was that masked man?"

Taking this saint to the cultural edge, hundreds of Jude home sites on the vast expanses of the Internet have beamed him into a realm of cyber reality. One can surf through Jude biographies, read the special Jude prayer alongside that of Michael the Archangel, with whom he is coupled in at least one ancient tradition, and read about the St. Jude Project Loaves and Fishes, a nondenominational group purporting to ease world hunger, or the Ecumenical Order of Charity in Vancouver, Washington, a "gay-friendly religious order." Advertisements for churches named after Jude tell you everything from how to reach the "national" shrine in Chicago to what the mass schedule is for a modern bungalow-style church in Black-wood, New Jersey.

The Power of Jude, a self-help Jude book published in Redondo Beach, California, floats through the Internet, heralding the reports of an Italian "visionary," Maria Valtorta (1897–1961), a paralyzed (except for her writing hand) Italian woman. This is Judeana at its most suspect. Relying for their primary research on a five-volume English translation of Signorina Valtorta's reveries, *The Poem of the Man-God,* the authors concede, "We set it out, not necessarily for the truth of the matters stated, but [to] make it easier for you to be more in touch with Jude."

Adding that the book was placed on the now-defunct Index of Forbidden Books under Pope John XXIII and that the Vatican newspaper branded it bad fiction, the authors of this electronic digest defend Signorina Valtorta as the possessor of an "incredible imagination," or real visions, or the ability to tune into memories of an earlier life when she actually walked with Jesus.

Plucky reincarnated soul that she was, Signorina Valtorta merely fills in the blanks of the New Testament with such exclusive findings as: Jude lived down the street from Jesus and they played together as children. Finally, in a tidal wave of dotty euphoria, the visionary reveals that Jude married a woman called Mary to whom he was long espoused and, though only a poor farmer, lost half of his income to taxes. The authors augment the Valtorta revelations with souped-up cult-speak: Jude, alias "the Great Companion" or "the Power," can only be reached by "establishing your goals," eschewing "negativism," and, ultimately, "accessing the Power."

Obviously, the Jude story is shot through with paradox; indeed, this is what ultimately defines him, for we have nothing else to go on. He functions in many respects like a pagan godling rather than a Christian saint, in effect, a saint who functions like a heathen. Nonbelievers call on him; he acts, and does not exact conversion. He is totally sealed off from the ordinary experiences of holy helpers. People are certain of him, even though they know so little. It does not seem to add up.

Peter and Paul perish in Rome and what is Rome without them? They cast their power over the central places that are enduringly Christian. Unlike them, Jude is not a routine saint, nor do his works unfold in expected ways or places. Highly individual, noninstitutional in style, his acts are not even provable. Like a hit-and-run, he is there for only the few split seconds it takes for one to realize that it is Jude who has acted. The web of Jude stretches all around, his inescapability surrounding us like a kindly spider's touch, one strand and the whole of it vibrates. Jude is entirely a saint of these obscure moments and places, not nailed into some continuous geography, some clinging historic or cultural mode. He is all people who have lost their identities as members of armies, families, churches—or just the weary shuffling crowds on every street. They are naked and their faith in Jude is almost tangible—hanging in the air— even over his own mission field, now lost to Islam.

Acting with modesty and discretion from behind the veil, he has made certain that no one will probably ever be able to establish an incontrovertible historic place for him. To pin him down is to destroy his whole mission. The telltale point is that he is always one step ahead of you, behind one pillar farther down the colonnade. He learned this technique at the foot of the Master when he asked Jesus why He had manifested Himself to a paltry band of the faithful but not to the whole world. At that moment, Jude's two-thousand-year-old secret mission was embodied. He took the hint not merely for time, but for eternity.

What Jude inhabits is the reverse of permanent: there is a "Jude Moment," not a Jude lifetime—the kind of life summary we might attach to hundreds of saints, for instance, the "Franciscan lifetime." He has not set an example, because we don't know what he's like. He is embodied strictly in action. Knowing so little about him, we cannot see him as the "role model" so obsessively sought in these times of self-improvement. All you can ask is for him to *arrange* an action. As the ultimate operator, he rushes in to fill the gap created by the erosion of faith, and, indeed, if the deepening of faith's corrosion can be found in the 1960s' repudiation of old ideals and standards, then perhaps the counterstroke, the surge back toward faith and the new emphasis on Jude, becomes clearer. The Vietnam generation held all credos and symbols of authority—perhaps more tellingly, of humane authority's indispensable companion, trust—in contempt, leaving almost no room for personal religious expression. When the idols fell, so too did the champions, and in their place the platitudes of New Age practitioners resonate like dull echoes in an empty room. Perhaps a time for heroes has come again.

"Were it not for hope, the heart would break," said Thomas Fuller—a simple explanation of Jude's universality, his fascination for non-Catholics and those who assert no faith. When all else fails, when the great sturdy world cracks beneath us, then we find Jude somehow at our side. Silent he stands, but never out of touch or hearing, requiring no ecclesiastical assent, no renunciation of former loyalty or belief. There are no strings attached. Why not take a chance? As so many of all faiths and none have done with astonishing results.

A lapsed Catholic with no plans to return to the church reflects, "I can see Jude being grafted onto any belief system. The Jude I know is a fairly amorphous presence that is universal. There is an elegant simplicity about how one approaches him. He begins as a simple prayer."

To multitudes all over the world, he is more friend than New Testament apostle, more ally than religious symbol, more secret weapon than saint, a phantom warrior in the battle for faith—and against faith's particular enemy, despair. Perhaps this is why the apostolic zeal of Jude is still felt twenty centuries after he appears in the Scriptures.

Devotion to the power embodied in Jude joins hands across all ages, all faiths, all worlds—including the realm of celebrity, where money and fame are no barriers to desperation. In fact, in the 1950s, Jude got his biggest boost in the United States when comedian Danny Thomas publicized his devotion to the saint. The oft-told story is that Thomas started out playing cheap clubs and one-night stands, and then he appealed for that one big break. He got it, and in gratitude built the Saint Jude Hospital for children in Memphis, Tennessee.

A quarterly profit-and-loss report in the business pages of the *New York Times* might seem routine enough until one sees a listing for St. Jude Medical Inc. Two years earlier, Manuel ("Manny") Villafana, chairman of Helix BioCore, a medical technology company in St. Paul, was named "Entrepreneur of the Year." He had struggled up from poverty in Spanish Harlem, where his widowed mother worked in a sweatshop, to the top of the corporate ladder in another classic American success story. The unclassical part is that Manny doesn't put it all down to hard work.

In 1971, he set out to start his own company, manufacturing longer-lasting pacemakers. Hat in hand, he sought funds. "They thought I was crazy. No one would listen to me," he recalls. At age thirty-one, Manny had no job, heavy debts, a remortgaged house, and a son in the hospital. Desperate, he visited St. John's church in New Brighton, Minnesota. His eye fell on a St. Jude prayer card in the pew in front of him. "It said two things," he remembers. "First, that Jude had been forgotten because of the similarity of his name to Judas Iscariot's, and, second, that one must promise to repay Jude by promoting his name." Manny decided to make the novena, nine days of prayer with daily mass and communion, and within weeks, found an investor.

"That's how I got started, within weeks," he says, "but I continued my prayers to Jude. My wife was pregnant at the time, so I decided to name my son Jude."

Little Jude Villafana came into this world with his own terrible extremity. "Jude had medical difficulties and needed some operations. I baptized him myself before he was a month old—in the bathroom before I drove him to the hospital." After eight operations and with Manny's continued prayers to the child's namesake, the boy recovered. In 1976, he started another business—this one to make heart valves—and named it after his holy helper: St. Jude Medical Inc., which soon was doing $250 million of nobly useful business. Manny remained in touch with the Mayo Clinic surgeon who had saved his son. One day, the Villafanas were invited to the doctor's birthday party—on October 28, feast day of St. Jude.

"I still have the prayer card in my pocket," says Manny.

Golfer Bobby Nichols won the 1964 PGA by three stunning strokes under Jack Nicklaus and Arnold Palmer and donated $3,500 of his winnings to establish a St. Jude shrine in his native Louisville, Kentucky. "I figured this was an impossible tournament to win. I'm not superstitious. There's a difference between being superstitious and having faith. I have a lot of faith."

Is this resurgence of belief, then, a genuine attempt to reaffirm faith in America? Perhaps it presages a renewal, not of religious faith alone but of belief in the very ideals of the country, which right up to the Pledge of Allegiance have been rooted in the acknowledgment of a higher power. To many, then, the prominence of the Christian right manifests not just a thirst for political power but one more symptom of a spiritual shudder throughout the land.

In the mythological tale of Pandora, she opens her precious box against dire warnings not to, and all the evils of the world fly forth to afflict mankind forever. Only one consolation remains: Hope. In fact, the sense of hope went so deep in Greek and Roman times that its personifying goddesses commanded deep reverence.

On one level, Jude is a cult object, a sacred presence who draws on those pre-Christian intuitions embodied as helper gods: a wandering light of the soul beckoning to a motley lot of believers in they're not sure what, yet drawn together by the Jude factor. He is also a startling example of supernatural intervention. Extremity is Jude's territory. And though it may not concern those who invoke this dealer in desperation, it is an ancient axiom that "Man's extremity is God's opportunity."

Over the years, millions of ordinary people have quietly testified to what they are quietly convinced are Jude's intercessions. We can only wonder at the simplicity and fervor of their whispered prayers and rapt gratitude.

Sitting by her swimming pool in Florida, Genee Bell noticed that her neighbor's nine-year-old son had a terrible scar down the side of his leg. "It looked like a zipper," she told me over the telephone. Questioning the boy's mother, Mrs. Bell learned that he had had bone cancer as a baby. Bone taken from his arm and grafted on to the leg had only deteriorated. Again, surgeons grafted, this time bone from the boy's father. Again, the procedure failed. Finally, the desperate mother consulted a faith healer devoted to St. Jude, who laid her hands on the incision as they prayed. The malignancy disappeared. "I wasn't really surprised," says Mrs. Bell. "I feel it works. Going back to my own grandmother, whenever there's a problem—I have seven children, so there is always something—we pray to St. Jude."

The Jude factor is inescapably a matter of miracles. Indeed, the one question that needs to be asked is "Does it work? Is this on the level?" A priest in a ghetto parish says, "It's certainly on the level as far as God is concerned." And even where or when it doesn't "work," so many Jude followers of all faiths attest to changes in their lives *despite* the outcome of their prayer.

Writing to a magazine that collects Jude letters and meditations, one man observes: "St. Jude seems to sort of lead the way for me either by sending someone or by hearing from someone who helps me find the answers."

The opposite pole of the debate is the certainty that the whole business of divine intervention is nothing less—or more—than manipulative priestcraft. Consider the argument of the Grand Inquisitor, the voice of organized religion as pride and power, in Dostoyevsky's *Brothers Karamazov*. Facing Christ on earth, he taunts Him with the temptation set before Him on the pinnacle of the temple, when Jesus refuses to cast Himself down to prove He is the Son of God, even though it was written that the angels would catch Him:

> "Thou didst hope that man, following Thee, would cling to God and not ask for a miracle. But Thou didst not know that when man rejects miracles he rejects God too; for man seeks not so much God as the miraculous. And as man cannot bear to be without the miraculous, he will create new miracles of his own for himself, and will worship deeds of sorcery and witchcraft though he might be a hundred times over a rebel, heretic and infidel . . . Thou woudst not enslave man by a miracle, and didst crave faith freely, not based on miracles."

Warily, the church today refrains from employing the word *miracle,* except in the most severely tested circumstances, going only so far as to say that *to these people,* what they are seeing is miraculous. This is a very real part of Jude's appeal: the heart finding its reasons independent of doctrine. But even without that endorsement, one young worker in the Baltimore shrine observes, with disarming simplicity, "There's a sense that some people—well, you can write them off as just experiencing a coincidence. But some you can't, because you can see the hand of God."

So many see the hand of God—a miracle—in events that seem to be, or to approximate, the miraculous. When people want to believe, there is little interior contradiction. Conversely, thousands seeing a potentially miraculous event unfold before their eyes are likely to reserve judgment, demanding scientific proof that nature's ordinary laws have indeed been suspended—anxious not to fall victim to some magic maker and his bags of tricks. The Roman church itself has, of necessity, raised devil's advocacy to a science. It is not a matter that plagues Jude's supporters, who know intuitively that no one great official miracle is associated with Jude, only millions of small unofficial ones.

That is why the story of Jude today is a true journey into the American heartland: Mafia lieutenant, Jewish attorney, manufacturer of artificial hearts, famous golfer, Hollywood producer, gentle mother of seven, grieving father, famous actor, former governor—and Greta Garbo: all seeking Jude. An anthology of strange happenings, a mosaic of plain belief at its most intense in a world that believed itself modern. In a larger context, Jude's story is a case history of faith, hope, and despair made flesh in countless extremities. Once more, unlikely people brought together—if they only knew it—by a quest for something beyond what they have known, something to quell the hunger of the spirit. And Jude's undiscovered territory, ancient to the church, although modern to the people, is one of the places they are searching.

Swaying on the edge of a new century, the desperate look beyond and see only an endless tunnel. Hope, in all its manifestations, both sacred and profane, sees rebirth, revelation, renewal, maybe even a miracle. The alternation of progress and disillusionment is eternal. As long as there are new frontiers of afflictions—economic recession, a surging divorce rate, AIDS, mass unemployment of people who had thought themselves secure for life, starvation, old age, and loneliness—legions of the desperate will seek Jude. Do they find miracles, peace of mind, or "just" coincidence? Do they believe he will connect them to something they have lost, or always been led to expect, something America has lost? Perhaps this reporter's quest, this pilgrimage—even if it cannot catch the gentle but determinedly withheld Jude—may yet catch his reflection in the hearts of those whom sorrow has brought into his presence.

The rain is not letting up. The bus heaves its way along the slick streets of downtown Baltimore. The men sit up from their naps, yawn, and rub their eyes. The women, who have been whispering their stories of miracles, grow tense, bright-eyed, like young girls at a country dance. They talk of "using St. Jude" as they would a psychic or a talisman.

Nina tells her story of superstition and darkness. A woman boarder in her house committed suicide. She had had a statue of Jude in her room and Nina began to have terrible dreams of the dead woman and the statue.

"I wanted the statue out of my house—and I wanted nothing to do with Jude."

One day, visiting her cousin Jerry, she saw the life-size St. Jude statue in the Pullaras's living room. Jerry began to talk about him; Nina listened, fascinated. Then, in 1990, she suddenly experienced trouble breathing. The doctor told her she had a very large tumor in her thyroid—cancer.

"I have kids and I didn't want them to see me crying. I went for many tests, radiation, and found out I was pregnant. I was so afraid that the baby would be harmed, so I prayed to St. Jude. I had a daughter and named her Judith. She was born on March 3. On the same day, thirteen years after the girl who lived in my house shot herself, I brought my baby to the shrine to say thank you. She was barefoot, which is a sign of sacrifice. You know, I even wore my St. Jude charm bracelet during surgery."

Nina looks out the window, her face more peaceful as the bus nears its solemn destination. "Today I will pray for my family, my children. I'll tell him what I want."

Across the aisle, Francesca, a Sicilian mother, also prepares to debark at the Jude shrine, which is housed in St. John the Baptist Church at the corner of Paca and Saratoga in downtown Baltimore. She remembers every detail of the day that her daughter was bitten by the family's chow dog. "Her face was disfigured horribly. Her lower lip and jaw were dangling after the attack. We prayed to St. Jude that the nerve wouldn't be damaged. Pretty soon, as it healed, the doctors said the nerve was coming back and that plastic surgery would be possible for an almost full recovery."

She is smiling as she gets off the bus, hurrying through the rain toward the steps of the Romanesque-style church.

Most of the people who visit here are faceless to the priests. On this day, a few introduce themselves and assemble for the ritual. First, novena prayers, then the mass, and a homily in which the shrine director, Father Amalio Greco, admits that facts on Jude are few and carefully adds little beyond the fact that this is a saint who gave his life for what he believed. The prayers, heartfelt and literate, are in keeping with the devotional intensity of the post–Vatican II church, and follow almost word for word Jude devotions everywhere.

"There is no real superstition involved in a novena, but it shows a lack of the real meaning of service, prayer life, and liturgy," said a priest from the now-defunct Baltimore archdiocesan liturgical commission of 1971. "For the generation coming up, the novena devotion isn't part of their experience."

Perhaps this is why the commission went out of business. Most new liturgists do not understand or like devotions such as the St. Jude novena. These bodies, almost by definition, frown on competition from saints, especially stars like Jude. Typically, the overflow crowds in Jude's shrines and churches everywhere bear unemphatic yet overwhelming testimony to this miscalculation.

As the perfume of incense lingers overhead, Nina and Francesca join the line of pilgrims praying softly and inching their way forward to kiss the Jude relic. Coffee and doughnuts are served; many visit the shrine gift shop. The throng reboards the bus: time to stop at the waterfront for lunch and head home. Nothing complicated, no colored lights or heart-wrenching music, just the workmanlike routine of those who seek Jude. Each year, a hundred busloads arrive to perform this simple but highly significant rite of passage in three solemn novenas; perpetual novenas are held every Wednesday and Sunday. Last year, the alcove that has served as Jude's shrine since 1941 was enlarged to three times its size, and the old school building was transformed into a visitors' center. The expansion of the well-stocked gift shop where people acquire tangible memories of their special saint—medals, holy cards, key chains, candles, scapulars, rosaries, pictures, booklets—is a single reminder that although Jude comes to us from ancient roots, he is burgeoning in the most modern times. The candlepower around his turquoise and gold marble statue has increased from 770 wax tapers to 1,300 electric candles, a concession to an age that has traded the flickering glow within green glass canisters for a more steady institutional glare. His blazing presence in the church's right apse transforms a side altar into the main event. The small gold statue of Christ he holds is a variant of the traditional picture of Christ, the Mandylion, which Jude usually wears on his chest. The crowds, hushed and calmed, seem reinforced by contact with him, seeing beyond the marble figure to someone who waits for their impossible plea. Many leave flowers; all light candles.

In 1887, Lithuanians organized St. John's parish in another part of the city; they moved into the Paca Street church, originally built for a Baptist congregation, in 1907. Ten years later, they moved on, to be replaced by Italian immigrants who, arriving in force, settled around the Old Lexington Market. The Fathers of the Pious Society of Missions (Pallottines) took over to establish an Italian "national" parish (indeed, the sanctuary dome reproduces the famous mosaic of the Cathedral of Cefalu, Sicily, whence most of the parishioners emigrated).

The novena began as a small prayer service during World War II, a plea for the safety of fathers, brothers, lovers, and sons fighting in Europe and the Pacific. The pastor gave out little American flags to anyone who came, word began to get around, the devotion grew. A much-read pamphlet recounted how when one person invoked Jude successfully, he would pass it on to someone else in need of a last resort.

"At the time, we only had a picture of St. Jude in the front of the church," says Mary Portera, at eighty-one the shrine office's unofficial operations brain. Officially, she takes care of the Baltimore area, while the promotion center looks after the other forty-nine states. A member of St. John's since she was nine, and a secretary in the rectory since 1957, Mary is also the institutional memory of the Jude phenomenon in Baltimore.

"We put an honor roll of the names of our boys overseas in the back of the church, and people just started to flock to us. After about three years, a woman donated a beautiful statue of St. Jude to us, and it all began to grow and grow some more."

With the end of the war the novena faded, but the shrine kept going. Spanish-speaking people moved into the neighborhood, possibly bringing their great devotion to St. Jude with them. The first pastor had come to the church as a twenty-year veteran of the Pallottine missions in Brazil, and in 1921 a second missionary with South American experience arrived. Perhaps the influence of these men laid the groundwork for Jude in Baltimore. Neighborhood patterns began to shift once more as blacks arrived and whites moved out; the church school closed and the parish had to look for members beyond downtown Baltimore, turning to the suburbs and out of town altogether. At one point, the church was in danger of being razed to make way for a new social security building, but the parishioners fought back. They knew that without St. Jude, the parish would face extinction.

When the present Italian-made statue was donated in 1968, America's own year of desperate causes, the mosaic alcove was built and the votive candles lit. A guardrail of wood and wrought iron does not deter Jude's own from reaching out to scatter bits of paper reflecting their torments at his marble feet: disease, family, sorrow, doubts—the cries never end, but neither does the hope amid hopelessness.

A woman from Chicago flew to Baltimore a few years back just to lay her daughter's bridal bouquet at the statue's feet. Others FedEx their bridal bouquets. Airline crews stop in to pray on Christmas Eve.

"We had one lady who came from New York in an ambulance; they took her to the shrine and then back to the city," says Mary Portera. "She got her wish to come to St. Jude before she died. Then there were the twins, one in perfect health, the other had a brain tumor. The parents came to pray all the time. Eventually, the child died—she was nine—but the parents felt that St. Jude took her out of her misery."

Father Greco, the burly, gravel-voiced director of the Baltimore shrine for fourteen years, sits at the kitchen table in the rectory one afternoon to explain what praying to Jude really means. Someone brings ice cream, and we sit like college students weighing the merits of a thorny philosophical point.

"Whenever we pray, we must remember two things: first, God knows best. 'Thy will be done,' as Jesus said to His Father. It's right in the Lord's Prayer, in a phrase He gives directly Himself: 'Thy will be done.' And second, that our prayers are answered—not always the way we want, but answered. Resignation is the key here, resigning yourself to the outcome, no matter what it is. It's an internal thing. I've seen so many people start out miserable and desperate, and after prayer they become happy and content. One must resign himself to the will of God. It is despair that causes suicide.

"When I was stationed in France in the service, a lieutenant's wife became paralyzed as a result of a spinal block or something and she couldn't walk and she became very desperate, didn't want to live. They finally went to Lourdes to pray for a cure. She came back and she never got cured, but all of a sudden her attitude changed. She wasn't despairing anymore.

"You hear so many things. People come up and tell me their children are on dope and then, with Jude's help, they gave it up. Some were alcoholics, and they give it up. You hear everything."

Offering the poor health of his own heart as an example of God's grace through Jude's mediated assistance, Father Greco holds up his broad hands and tells of surviving eight bypass operations in nine years.

"People prayed for me like mad. He's a powerful intercessor. You know, I've been a priest for fifty-four years, and it is this service that I've enjoyed the most. It seems that God compensated for the fact that Jude was confused with Judas Iscariot by permitting certain miracles to be performed by him. It started all over—I don't where—but it's the faith that does it."

Less than two years later, at the age of eighty, Father Greco died.

The telephone is ringing off the hook, another call for help; somehow Mary Portera appears to pacify its yearning. The diminutive presence is misleading: her toiling for Jude all these years is a study in steel.

"Would you like to hear my miracle?" Her matter-of-fact tone gives no hint of personal tragedy.

It happened sixteen years before. Her daughter, at age twenty-six, disappeared. She was gone for forty-five months, twenty-two days, and thirteen hours, at which point the missing girl called her sister. Six months later she came home. Her father did not recognize her. On the advice of a priest, Mary never asked why she had left her husband and child.

"Someone at the church asked why I wasn't in church praying. But that's unkind to say to people, because I prayed to Jude—I prayed walking down the street—you would never believe this had happened to me if you could see my family today and our relationship. I say thank you by doing things for other people."

Attendance is up again, Mary reports, and the mail has increased. "We get a lot of divorces now, people losing their jobs." She remembers a lady who arrived by bus with her son, who had AIDS. Last week, the woman called, dissolving into tears. Her husband got on the line to say that their second son had AIDS, too. They were sending a donation.

The index of Jude's multiplying devotion is measured by the letters that arrive. Some years ago, one of the priests created a mailing list by copying Irish names from a Boston telephone book. Today it contains more than a half-million entries from all over the United States, Canada, Puerto Rico, and abroad.

For those who cannot get to the shrine, the mail is their lifeline to Jude.

Every week about five hundred petitions arrive with donations enclosed: a son's cancer has been cured, a family stays together because the father did not have to move thousands of miles away, an accident insurance claim has been paid, a rare paralyzing illness disappears, open-heart surgery goes well, a house on the market for years has been sold. Excerpts from these testimonials are printed in the shrine newsletter, which provides information on how to include St. Jude in a will, the Shrine Annuity Program, and a list of twenty-eight petitions to be checked off for special prayers. They include "Happy Marriage, World Peace, and End of Gang Violence." One mailing enclosed a half-dollar–size wooden disk, the St. Jude Hope Coin, stamped with his prayer and picture.

The letters arrive from small towns in Iowa, from big cities such as Los Angeles, from non-Catholics, from those who have never believed but heard about Jude from a friend. Some people come to the shrine simply because a tragedy has already happened, like the devastated woman who showed up the Sunday after her son committed suicide. Broken, she said she did not know where else to go. Something—was it yet hope?—drove her to Jude's altar.

The world passes through the always-open doors: Danny DeVito, the actor, comes to pray and light candles while in town filming *Tin Men,* just-married couples in wedding clothes kneel at Jude's altar, old husbands dying of heart attacks ask for strength, women abandoned by their men beg for solace, Filipinos asking for special help move up the main aisle on their knees.

A satisfied silence envelops the group as our bus speeds along the interstate into the red sky of a rainless evening. If any doubt had hovered about a Jude phenomenon, my own eyes and ears have put it to rest. This can only be the first stage of a larger journey, a quest to find a man, a saint, of hidden faces. Where next to find the questions, let alone the answers? His history lies among the ruins of Mesopotamia, his institution in the cardinal red of Rome, his felt presence in the star-spangled reaches of the great world power of the twentieth century. Better to embark where all big stories break: on the street, alert to the whispers, hoping it will all fall into place.

Overtired from the day's excitements, a little boy in the seat behind me cannot sleep and welcomes my interest. Why not start here?

"What do you pray for?" I ask.

"I pray for happiness," he confides, his St. Jude medal bouncing flashes of light from the road ahead.

NEW YORK

*"In the darkness with a great bundle of grief . . .
'Where to? what next?'"*

Carl Sandburg, *The People, Yes*

NEVER HAD ANYTHING LIKE IT HAPPENED
before, never. I'd faced pressures, but never,
ever, a problem with faith."

John Cardinal O'Connor, leader of New
York's 2.5 million Catholics, sits slumped in his chair, head
bowed, the deep voice drifting down to a whisper. In 1964, as a
navy chaplain, he was serving with the marines in Southeast
Asia. His is a war story without bullets.

"It was a peculiar time, one that I rarely think about. I was
in Okinawa. We were on the way into Vietnam, and I don't
know what hit me. I hadn't been far from home before; it
was a totally different culture. I was with about six thousand
marines in a place up there called Camp Hanson. Suddenly, I

got hit with the worst attack against my faith. It consumed me. Never had anything like it happened before. We had a tin hut—a Quonset chapel—and I would go down there late at night. There was a little sanctuary lamp burning and I would go in there and kneel and look at that tabernacle, thinking, 'Are You really in there? Has this all been a dream, a myth?' I felt just an utter, utter desolation of spirit. I had my work and did it—like dragging the marines to confession and holding retreats. But for a couple of months there was this unbelievable darkness and emptiness. Among others, I prayed to Jude. And I came out of it. Certainly God was testing me. Yes, I prayed to Jude. Was he the one responsible for my recovery? I don't know—but I would have taken anybody who would help at the time."

He pauses, at a loss to explain what brought on the crisis, certainly one that most people never associate with someone who wears the red hat. At seventy-eight, this is not a man who takes his saints lightly.

"He's in the air now," the cardinal continues, blue eyes widening. "There just seems to be an emerging curiosity—is it the desperation of the circumstances, the climate in which we live, the culture of death that surrounds us, the hunger that so many people feel? An awful lot of people feel lost and desperate, so it would not be surprising that they would at least be curious about this saint. Usually the opening question is, Have you heard of St. Jude? Is it true he can work miracles? I tell them, Of course. He is one of God's instruments.

"Do I think that miracles are at work? I don't think there's any question about that. Do ordinary people get miracles? Now, of course, the question arises—and it's legitimate— What is a miracle? Technically and philosophically, it's a suspension of the laws of nature. The French novelist Georges

Bernanos says, 'Faith itself is the miracle.' Just to believe is the miracle when we live in an unbelieving world. It can seem preposterous to believe that Christ was the Son of God when He was hanging on the cross. Bernanos ends his *Diary of a Country Priest* saying, 'Grace is everywhere.' And I see it every day. I see it and—not to be dramatic—I get letters from young people and older people from all over the world, and others come to see me, and they want to talk about these things.

"There's that fascinating notion that we know him as Jude and he's the patron saint of desperate cases because he felt desperate that he was confused with Judas. For this alone, he becomes the patron saint of the outcast."

Around the corner from the cardinal's fittingly princely residence, the great Gothic spires of St. Patrick's Cathedral tower over mid-Manhattan, epicenter of the archdiocesan presence still sometimes referred to as "the Powerhouse." For the visiting millions, it forms a golden triangle with Rockefeller Center and Saks Fifth Avenue—juxtaposing the religious, economic, and cultural strains of America's largest and most vibrant city. Strangely, at first glance it fits cozily into the city's secular might.

Streams of people kneel before a life-size bronze statue of Jude in the upper left aisle of the cathedral, just as a real-estate developer from Pennsylvania knelt thirteen years ago. Disappointed with the old plaster statue of Jude, he wrote to the cardinal, offering to commission a better likeness (if the ultimate outsider *has* likenesses) of his patron saint.

"It's remarkable. I know I wouldn't be anything without him," reflects Caswell F. Holloway, Jr. Today a millionaire, he well remembers the thin soup and hot dogs of his youth during the Great Depression; his mother, a German immigrant who converted to Catholicism, nurtured in her son a fierce devotion to St. Jude. Now the grandfather of twenty-six, he had eleven children of his own and lost two—one stillborn, the other to a brain tumor at age six and a half.

"My wife and I, we pray a lot. Both of us pray to Jude. We've had so many neat things happen. You have your ups and downs, but somebody's always been there for one reason or another, and we figure he's always been there. I look at all my causes as impossible. We did pray for our little son, John, but better than his getting better, we got a saint. That's the way we look at it."

The statue, sculpted by Adlai Hardin, an Episcopalian, stands within the Holy Face altar, so named for the mosaic of Christ's face placed beside it. Although there is nothing in the cathedral's record to indicate any intended connection between Jude and this rendition of the Holy Face, their coupling reflects a theory that scholars still debate concerning ancient images of Christ believed to have been made by contact with His person: the much-contested Veronica's veil; the Mandylion, a cloth Jude bore to the king of Edessa; and the Holy Shroud of Turin. Some argue that these images are one and the same, but that is a matter for experts to settle. Jude's ministrations in the Big Apple are of a more urgent nature.

Elegantly simple, devoid of any Technicolor adornment, the figure in St. Patrick's tilts his head upward, a saint looking to his God. He is a stark image within the splendid altar of Carrera marble and Mexican onyx, for unlike most Jude statues, no bits of paper are wedged at his feet, no flowers strewn before him.

"They had to enclose the Jude statue—they even put in a door to the altar—because so many people were touching it and putting flowers there, and climbing in to get to him," recalls Mr. Holloway, whose name isn't carved anywhere on the statue or the altar—nor did he request it. Meanwhile, at age seventy-three, he's at home in Jupiter, Florida, busy raising $5 million to rebuild his local church: St. Jude's.

Grand as it is, for New Yorkers—the office workers at lunchtime mass, the Catholic power elite on Christmas Eve— the great edifice of the cathedral seems as familiar and accessible as a small chapel on a New England campus.

"We need more Jude," shouts a salesclerk to a co-worker over the display of booklets and prayer cards in the crowded cathedral gift shop. "As usual, he's always the first to go."

Why?

The clerk smiles complicitly. "He's the saint for the impossible—and it's the nineties!"

In Brooklyn, a subway ride away, the rush to Jude has its counterpart in the brisk business done by those who specialize in religious concrete statues and grottoes. Stone carvers here cite St. Jude as their best-seller, right behind the various lawn Madonnas and Holy Family tableaux. Religious article catalogues are thick with Jude paraphernalia, and churches, alert to the saint's magnetism, maintain large mailing lists to announce year-round novenas and equip their supporters with the latest trinkets, such as a Jude night-light.

A Franciscan shrine in Mt. Vernon, New York, writes, "It is St. Jude's special mission to help you when you despair. He helps you see the light that shines on in the darkness—always—and which the darkness can never overcome."

A San Diego Jude shrine encloses a flyer asking whether anyone wants to be a homeowner for "as little as 3 percent down," and announces that a free seminar sponsored by a local mortgage firm will be held at the church. The advertisement suggests that Jude may be able to "make your dreams come true."

For those trying to give up cigarettes, a Westchester County shrine periodical suggests that where therapists fail, St. Jude can succeed. The sentiment gains worthiness alongside a reminder to remember the church in your will.

Downtown in trendy SoHo, a denizen of the night tells an inquirer: "I'm wearing black 501s, white sweatsocks, Doc Martens, a sleeveless Hanes T-shirt, an L. L. Bean jacket, a little Mexican pendant number, and a St. Jude necklace." What was once considered a religious medal has established its beachhead in the counterculture.

But for most, Jude is more than a statue or a prayer card. It is his contact beyond the senses that has brought him this endless gallery of material manifestations. From those at the apex of the Roman faith to the society matron, to the blue-collar worker, to the soft-spoken Spanish woman, Jude has made his presence—or should one say his recent passage?—felt most vividly. In step with each solitary sorrow of a dynamic city, the voices of those touched by him rise from the meanest streets up to the swaying antennae that crown the highest towers.

- "I had given birth to my daughter and was so sick, and yet I crawled out of my bed to get on my knees and pray to Jude for my recovery and the health of my child," offers a patrician Episcopalian mother from Manhattan's upper East Side.

- "It's definitely an Easter miracle. I'm sure we got a lot of help from upstairs," says a New York City detective, who after praying from a St. Jude card his mother gave him, recovered a chalice stolen from a South Bronx church in time for Easter.

- Boris, a three-year-old boxer, vanishes on Christmas Eve while being shipped aboard a Delta jet from Florida to

New York. His owner was "at the point of giving up all hope." After living six weeks on the run, the frightened pet was traced to an abandoned house by a "pet psychic" who said, "We burned magic candles every day, even candles to St. Jude—and we're not even Christians."

- "Please St. Jude. Help me find a boyfriend . . . I am so desperate at twenty-five years. Help me, please, St. Jude to find a boyfriend. MHJ"

In New York, no claim to individuality, no matter how valiantly won, can outlast the city's brutally short attention span. Whether from Omaha or Canarsie, New Yorkers fight a daily war of independence, only to be squeezed back into the grueling pace and impersonality of the city itself. The dominating objective for these contestants is to pass the survival test, to overleap enormous obstacles—which is the core of a New Yorker's pride—and then to draw back into the faceless crowd, with any luck, proud of the high marks received for how you played the game. You pass an elderly man at Fifty-seventh Street and Fifth Avenue, not realizing until thirty seconds later that he was once president of Brazil, or the former captain of your college debating team, or a film star. But even instant recognition would not slow down the New Yorker straining upward to his moment in the sun. There are places to go and appointments to keep, real or imagined.

Jude more than matches the intensity of the town, striking sparks of light and life off its granite. This is not existential territory; his business is not to make philosophic doubters feel better about the world but to lift up char ladies despondent over their children's drug habits. He engages a particular danger—despair itself—not head-on but along some spiritual fencer's diagonal of which only he seems to know the secret. We gasp to swim the extra yard home, to reach his outstretched hand.

This is the Judean hope, and in this city of souls apart, it thrives, often among those pledged to another faith, or to none at all.

Larry A. can certainly relate to the wisdom of Fred Allen, who laid it down from experience that Hollywood is a great place if you're an orange. Ask any starry-eyed starlet, any struggling writer, any hungry agent, any nail-biting producer, and they will add that the orange is probably rotten. Tough town, rough game, as this transplanted New Yorker found out. Leaving a job on Wall Street, Larry went west to become one of the thousands of "independent producers" waiting for the Big One—the hit movie, the long-running TV series—that would raise him to fame and shower him with fortune.

Perhaps it is to be expected that in a culture living off myth and images, he has several times encountered St. Jude, usually in pursuit of the officially impossible. The first time was fourteen years ago, when a Greek girl at a photo lab told him that if he lit a candle to St. Jude every Tuesday before noon his prayer would be answered. "But I'm Jewish," he sputtered." As Larry tells it, "she said to go ahead anyway and I did: I lit two Yahrzeit candles—Jewish candles for the dead—to St. Jude, and one week later I got a gift. I did this for ten years, but then my mother became ill and I prayed, but she died anyway and I said, 'Forget this.'" Still, a few years later, Jude reappeared in Larry's life. His sister, plagued by guilt about not visiting their mother in her last days, told him that she had gone to a New York psychic who talked to the dead and passed her this message: "You have a brother on the coast. Tell him to light candles to St. Jude before noon. God wants it."

At one point Larry had his Los Angeles house on the market for a whole year. He drained his bank account of $15,000 per month for maintenance. "I went to St. Jude's church in Los Angeles, lit a candle, and asked the saint for help. Suddenly, outside it seemed to get very bright. I went home and told the real-estate agent to add $35,000 to the price. The agent told me I was crazy, but the next day it sold."

Easily the most obvious media presence of Jude is found in the classified sections of newspapers across the country and in English-language papers abroad. While regarded as quaint, if not silly, by Catholic "progressives," these ads create a significant part of Jude's mystique, particularly for those who have felt his touch, including, perhaps especially, non-Catholics. Petitions to Jude and "Thank You St. Jude" public notices appear regularly in New York's sophisticated big dailies, such as this one in the *New York Post:*

> "Most Holy Apostle, St. Jude Thaddeus, faithful servant and friend of Jesus, the name of the traitor who delivered your beloved master into the hands of enemies has caused you to be forgotten by many, but the church honors and invokes you universally as patron of hopeless causes and things despaired of. Pray for me who am so needy; make use, I implore you, of that particular privilege accorded to you to bring visible and speedy help where help is almost despaired. Come to my assistance in this great need that I may receive consolations and succor of heaven in all my necessities, tribulations and sufferings [here, the penitent inserts his particular petition after the word *sufferings*], that I may bless God with you and all the elect throughout eternity. I promise you O Blessed Jude to be ever mindful of this great favor, and never cease to honor you as my special and powerful patron to do all in my power to encourage devotion to you. AMEN."

This notice in the *New York Times* spoke of miracles under the heading "Don't Quit":

> "Pray to St. Jude: patron of things despaired of; intercessor of all who invoke his special patronage in time of need. St. Jude will

help you in present and urgent petition. I prayed to St. Jude; St. Jude prayed in me and a miracle took place; the same can take place for you."

According to tradition, one's gratitude must be made public if St. Jude grants a prayer. Again, an example from the *Times:*

"THANK YOU ST. JUDE for answering my prayer. MJM"

From the *San Francisco Chronicle:*

"St. Jude apostle, martyr and relative of our Lord Jesus Christ, of Mary and of Joseph, intercede for us."

"Thank you, St. Jude for prayers answered. MRA"

And in the *International Herald-Tribune:*

"St. Jude, workers of miracles, pray for us. St. Jude, helper of the hopeless, pray for us. Amen. Say this prayer nine times a day, by the ninth day, your prayer will be answered. It has never been known to fail. Publication must be promised. MG/TT"

A less traditional thanksgiving written in unrhymed verse appeared in a national magazine. The author had asked Jude's help after his mother suffered a severe auto accident, breaking several bones. Despite doctors' dire predictions, she recovered with only a slight limp.

> "This favor I should have acknowledged
> many years ago,
> Why I didn't, I don't know
> and why I am doing it now,
> I really can't say . . . ."

Opinions vary as to how the tradition of publishing one's gratitude to Jude came about. Perhaps it derives from Roman times, when promises, or vows *(vota),* made to the gods in exchange for favors not only had to be kept, but published, too. On the other hand, one might consider that the printed word itself, as a form of communication, is not inconsistent with Jude's basic story: an exchange of letters between Jesus and King Abgar leads to Jude's arrival in Edessa and the subsequent cure and conversion of Abgar when Jude presents him with the cloth on which Jesus' face is imprinted. It is this image, the Mandylion, that we see emblazoned on Jude's breast today, only reinforcing his traditional reputation as an apostolic ambassador.

The *Village Voice* runs Jude notices, too, cheek by jowl—if that is not overly appropriate—with its ads for practices of bondage and other underappreciated joys. At one point the paper ran a story saying that the Irish Republican Army was using the announcements to slip messages past the Saxon oppressor, either through the text ("They're really not so boilerplate") or by the dates of publication. In another reference to the Irish "troubles," a sympathizer, "P. M.," confesses in a letter to a magazine that "each night I pray to him [Jude] for people in prison who are innocent that they will be released. I saw the news about the five Irishmen who were set free after being convicted fifteen years ago for a bombing in England. I knew exactly who to thank for all things that I feel unlikely to happen. . . . Maybe someone who has just been freed will know who to thank—St. Jude."

Operating in a city that is a national confluence of politics, entertainment, and media, Jude often surfaces in the whirlpool of celebrity that boils at the heart of these industries. No one seems surprised at this—not in a place where results are all. One quiet afternoon, for example, the producer of the old Jack Paar TV show was visiting St. John the Evangelist Church when a woman entered. It was Greta Garbo and she was, of course, alone. He recognized her immediately, especially because he lived on her block. Presently, she approached him and said, "Would there be a statue of St. Jude?" The startled producer said he would investigate. She thanked him and left as mysteriously as she had entered. He never knew why she was seeking Jude, but he left a note with her doorman that there was indeed a statue of St. Jude at the St. Catherine of Siena Church, run by the Dominican fathers, just a few blocks away.

If the solitary Garbo ever turned up at St. Catherine, she could hardly have escaped its geographical significance on Manhattan's upper East Side, smack in the middle of Hospital Row, directly across from that institution of ominous specialty: the Memorial Sloan-Kettering Cancer Center. An all-too-steady procession files from hospital exit to church door: a middle-aged couple in tears; a brother and sister, heads bowed in grief; an old black woman bent under her troubles. I can only guess at the burden of agony that they, and those they love, are carrying to Jude.

At the alcove sheltering Jude's statue in St. Catherine, some wedge small clumps of paper written in many languages, or even money offerings, beneath the statue's feet, recalling the petitions that devout Jews press into the crevices of the Wailing Wall, or the pleas to their holy helpers hacked into the stones of the San Sebastian catacombs by Christians under Roman persecution.

Here, beneath Jude's feet, lies a catalogue of heartaches:

"Please, St. Jude, forgive my doubts. . . . Help me, I need your help. Please give me the strength to overcome my health problems—the numbness and pain, and my stomach. They are real. . . . Please help Larry and Don and Mary Ann and the sick and souls (Mom and Dad) and I will always remember and honor you. Thank you . . . P. A. B."

"I ask for the restoration of President Bertrand Aristide and the constitution in Haiti—and that there will finally be peace, order, and a good administration one day. Thank you, thank you, St. Jude, comforter to those in adversity."

"Dear St. Jude, pray for my daughter Mary Ellen who will be having a cancer operation to remove a sarcoma. She needs another miracle."

"Please help my nephew Anthony to stay drug free and get a job . . ."

"Dear St. Jude, Please help Joseph 'G' be your child. I always tell everyone. Please help him *this week*. Let him get the storeroom job, or transport. Let Mr. Lanburton help him. Let him be a little happy also. Let this week be a miracle for me and him. Maybe he can meet someone like himself, someone who he loves and loves him so he can get on with a married life . . . I promise to keep my promise to you about all my donations . . ."

"Bless my whole family. Thank you, B. G."
[Across the envelope written in a frantic scrawl, is "ST. JUDE PLEASE HELP."]

"St. Jude please perform a miracle in Dexter A.'s sickness. Please help him to get better and come out of the hospital. . . ."

"St. Jude, With all my heart I ask you to help me, to come to my aid so that in my unhappy marriage peace will return. I also ask for the forgiveness of my wife, Letizia, to give me another opportunity for reconciliation between us and her family. Blessed St. Jude, do not let my marriage be destroyed. Give us the chance for reconciliation and of forgiveness between us, and my wife. I ask and implore you St. Jude . . . Amen. S. M."

Sr. Mary Jane, the jolly nun behind the desk at the church rectory, says that people come in with hundreds of stories about "cures" and "miracles" performed by Jude involving their loved ones in the neighboring hospitals, especially Sloan-Kettering; they also buy the St. Jude oil ($1.50 a bottle) as an instrument of healing. People come from upstate to buy twenty-five bottles at a time.

Sr. Mary Jane tells of visiting a non-Catholic woman dying of cancer in Lenox Hill Hospital. The woman had an ulcer on her leg from lying helpless so long. The nun asked the nurse, who was from the Caribbean, if she would rub the oil on the patient's stomach. Nodding knowingly, the nurse began applying the oil, and the patient, unable to speak, kissed her hand. The woman died, but for a moment all three were united in a recognition of a potential beyond this world.

The most amazing case the sister remembers is that of a woman with an abdominal tumor who was going into surgery. Someone brought Jude oil, said a special prayer, and rubbed the amber liquid on her stomach. The next day when doctors took preoperative X rays, *the tumor was gone.*

Fr. Stephen Carmody, O.P., a priest from the Dominican order assigned to Sloan-Kettering, says: "You hear Jude's name often enough—usually out of the blue. They say, 'Oh, you're from St. Jude's Church.' Patients are in different stages, but if they mention Jude, usually it's because they knew about him before."

Financially, Jude is an asset to the church, especially with a mailing list of about sixty thousand friends, more than two-thirds of whom send donations. Nevertheless, despite—or perhaps because of—Jude's success here, there are those made uneasy by the emotional and theological components of the devotion, a sentiment expressed by many zealous reformers in the post–Vatican II atmosphere who look on the cult of saints as a vehicle of superstition. A newly ordained young priest from Washington temporarily assigned to St. Catherine argues that there is a "tacky side" to the devotion. "Why do they need an intermediary? Praying isn't about asking for things. Asking someone to ask someone else is the way a corporation works, like asking to see the vice president."

Theologically, his objections are no doubt very sound. But he hasn't been on parochial duty long enough to see how exhaustion, terror, diffidence, even sheer embarrassment may make an appeal to an intermediary less overwhelming than an appeal to a divine presence, or that prayer to an intermediary may indeed bring him closer to God than ever. Elizabeth Barrett Browning understood "excesses" of faith when she wrote, "And lips say, 'God be pitiful,' Who ne'er said, 'God be praised.'"

Jude chain letters and "instant novena" pamphlets left lying around churches and public places—or downloaded from the Internet—aggravate much of the uneasiness felt even among those deeply committed to him. Reeking of superstition and sometimes with unmistakably malicious overtones, these usually single-spaced blotchy missives claim to have originated with a missionary from South America. They start out by announcing that "with love all things are possible." The reader is then commanded to send twenty copies within ninety-six hours to others who "need good luck"—or else: "Joe Elliott received $40,000 and lost it because he broke the chain . . . David Fairchild received the letter and, not believing, threw the letter away. Nine days later he died." (This letter is signed "St. Jude.")

The quickie novenas scattered around pews and kneelers offend most. "Make eighty-one copies and leave nine copies in church for each of the consecutive nine days. You will receive your intention before the nine days are over. No matter how impossible it may seem." Like mushrooms, these pamphlets appear and reappear in profusion, even though they are gathered up by irate sweepers at the end of the day. This openly superstitious element is what galls priests in particular, although not all parishioners, even the well educated, agree. Ann Sheridan, a formidable Washington, D.C., wife and mother, decided to take a stand after a church carpenter warned her against leaving Jude novena papers behind because the pastor did not like it. Actually, she had found the papers in a pew, and was praying the Jude novena when interrupted.

"Keep in mind that I was not putting sand in the holy water fonts in memory of the 'Desert Experience'—and I don't mean the Gulf War—or worshiping the goddess Sophia, or claiming the right for women to be ordained, or championing sex education in the parochial schools, or waiting for an appointment to sell pita bread to the sexton for future use as communion hosts—all of which are condoned in other American Catholic churches," fumed Mrs. Sheridan.

Jude chain letters are such a staple of big-city life they have even become part of the literary frame of reference. A short story in the *New Yorker* by Jay McInerney chronicles an aimless young man who is about to lose his philandering model girlfriend when he finds a Jude chain letter in his weeks-old mail; it is almost identical to the ones lying around the Jude altar at St. Catherine. He speculates as to whether breaking the chain is the source of his troubles. "Maybe it's not too late. Maybe if he sent it out now . . ."

He then imagines what might have happened if he had sent out twenty copies: ". . . his girlfriend returned and said she loved him. . . . It seems she had been hit by a taxicab in a foreign city and suffered a case of amnesia. . . . They were married a week later and now divide their time between St. Barts and Aspen."

If McInerney's tale catches the extent to which Jude can be sadly if amusingly misconstrued, the *Cyberpunk Handbook,* from the hands or keyboards of three hip hackers—one of whom is "St. Jude"—demonstrates the long reach across cultures of a saint who probably never rode in an oxcart. We might describe him as "big status," in the words of a cyberspace citizen. This St. Jude is a bright fiftyish woman, a veteran of the counterculture who arrived early on the computer scene, long before the bourgeoisie moved in. With pierced tongue in cheek, cyberpunk disciples require a black leather jacket, "cruel" boots, mirror shades, metal earrings, a laser pointer, lots of zippers, and a furious attitude. So how did St. Jude—actually Judith Milhon, a computer programmer and cyber-magazine editor—come by her name?

"I lived through the original '6os, I know what they were like—they were completely bogus," she laughs. "But I was a Maoist with a sense of humor and I used to make fun of myself and called myself St. Jude because my name is Judith and my family and the people around me always called me Jude. So I would call myself St. Jude because he's the saint of the hapless and the homeless and the hopeless.

"When I first signed on, I tried to have my handle be 'Jude' but there was a Jude already, so, whimsically, I called myself St. Jude and it stuck . . . St. Jude's Hospital was a big deal and was always saying 'give'—remember Danny Thomas, big deal about him being patron saint of hopeless cases. So it just seemed a likely satirical point. I'm an atheist and a smart-ass, but I have a St. Jude candle on my computer monitor. That's because they gave it to me at my last book signing in Berkeley. The head of the scifi bookshop went out and got what's called a novena candle; it's like pousse-caffé with different layers of colors. It starts out green, and goes to purple and blue, and white and yellow. I thought it was funny."

The frenetic and very material world of network television news hardly lends itself to contemplation of the insubstantiality of human life, except perhaps when standing by helplessly as you miss a flight on the way to a breaking story, or when lying down on a battlefield as incoming mortars count the moments of your life. In the New York headquarters of the three major networks, about the closest anyone gets to discussing moral issues is in the reporting of stories on abortion, condoms, assisted suicide, pornography, and homosexuality, all generally regarded as "social issues." Discussion of the spiritual or religious, unless it is secularly packaged, is considered bad form. There are, of course, exceptions, like that rare day at the broadcast center when a crusty CBS News executive, uncharacteristically anxious and depressed, took me into his confidence. He was pacing the floor, gazing absently out the window, nervously smoothing the back of his head. His sweetheart of some years lived in another state. They longed to marry, but that meant she would have to find a job in the East. Why I had a St. Jude card in my wallet is still not clear to me (even as a child I never carried holy cards), but I gave it to him. It didn't matter if he was a Jew, I urged, Jude was, too.

"What the hell," he said. "I'll give it a try."

A few weeks later his fiancée made the short list for a solid job just a few miles away. It would solve all their problems. One afternoon he burst into my office.

"Hey, guess what. She's got the job!"

I shared in his delight as he talked about the marriage plans and his new life. Then, unprompted, he pulled out the Jude card.

"Hey—what do you know about this guy? It's amazing. It really, really works."

Politicians, measured by their success in divining the hearts and minds of the people, do not dismiss Jude lightly. Mario Cuomo doesn't. As Democratic governor of New York for twelve years, and a man of admirable oratorical skill, Mr. Cuomo is ever ready to expound on the thoughts of St. Thomas Aquinas. Moreover, the plight of the underdog has always been a philosophical underpinning of his politics.

"The big thing in the world today, especially here—in the richest and what should be the most hopeful part of the world, America—is, well, for example, you have a story in today's paper saying that middle-class people have gone crazy. We're talking about upper-middle-class people, not the angry white males who are being squeezed out of the economy, who are in trouble and are blaming the little black girls who are making babies. This is the so-called upper class. They talk about a woman who is a stockbroker, whose husband is a businessman sitting around snorting heroin all Saturday night and getting himself sick. What is it about this society that is more prevalent than the darkness of it, the despairing aspect of it? If ever there was a time to be talking about hope, expectation, this is it. When you talk about St. Jude, you talk about the world in despair, because *he is the last stop*.

"I remember when I was a kid, the Vincentian fathers used to hand out Jude holy cards in my school and one of the priests would say, 'Hey, look, I've seen your work, you need this guy.'

"Do I pray? Absolutely. I pray because I think it is useful to crystallize and make tangible my aspirations. I never prayed to Jude to win an election, but I remember—oh, this is horrible—I remember when my wife was about to give birth—it was our second child—and I was reading Somerset Maugham's *Of Human Bondage,* and if I'm not mistaken the opening scene is a woman dying giving birth or a child being stillborn. Whatever, it is a tragedy during delivery. I was sitting in Mary

Immaculate Hospital where Matilda was giving birth. The symbolism of it. She was inside. I was sitting in the waiting room. I went right to the chapel and prayed to St. Jude. Why? Because he was important as the patron of desperate causes and I was just scared to death. I needed at least to be able to say to myself, I've tried everything here.

"What happens with prayer is, if what you ask for occurs, you cannot say that it wasn't because you asked for it. How would you know? On the other hand, if it doesn't happen, you don't blame the prayer for that. You say, well, on this occasion, it just didn't work. God wants me to go in a different direction. Now maybe the truth is that if you failed to ask you don't get it.

"As I've grown older, I've come to understand the enormous power of emotion and the value of your controlling your emotion. So prayer fits into that. People who are praying to Jude for their own recovery—that is another way of describing their aspiration, of screwing up their own willpower. I bet a good psychiatrist, or a physician who understands the psychiatric implications, would probably tell you that the right kind of prayer to Jude can have effect because it helps bolster your own desires. You're reinforcing your desire to live."

Carolyn McCarthy, a woman pulled out of the crowd by misfortune, is one of the newest members of Congress. She went from happy housewife to grieving widow on December, 1993, when a crazed malcontent murdered her husband and five others on a Long Island Railroad commuter train. Her twenty-eight-year-old son, Kevin, was shot in the head and, after six operations, remains paralyzed down his left side and in all but two fingers of his right hand. Not only did she endure the death of her husband and the maiming of her child, but she faced the man responsible in a long and brutal trial. The wonder is how she withstood it all, and with rare grace and courage. From the day of the rampage through her son's recuperation, people were sending her pictures of the saint of last resort.

"Oh, St. Jude," she says simply. "I prayed to him the whole time."

In the Old World, Jude, the figure, passes from shrine to shrine; in the New World he is heard on the street, forever traveling by word of mouth. Highly personal, quite unseen, always paradoxical, he is in his very simplicity the essence of a modern saint. His work becomes a train of powder set afire, the flames leaping silently along its length until suddenly it erupts in the ultimate explosion of a Jude miracle.

"But he will make you work for it," cautions a veteran in Jude territory. "You will earn his help and perhaps have to wait for his answer."

In the meantime, patience must join hope. John Le Boutillier, a former Republican congressman from New York, wrestled with this for years as he fought to expedite the search and recovery of American servicemen taken prisoner during the Vietnam War. An Episcopalian, he visited a Jude shrine three times a week to light candles, with the prayer that any men left behind might not be forgotten. He has come to see Jude as a saint for all seasons and scenarios—even the worst.

Kevin Healy and his wife, who live in Queens, will always remember what it means to be pressed to the last resort. Their son, at age four, was still unable to talk. Doctors diagnosed an irreversible learning disability, and the parents placed him in a special school and started a novena to St. Jude.

"After a month of praying, my mother-in-law suggested that my son's problem might be due to allergies, since my wife and I suffer from allergies," says Mr. Healy.

They called dozens of doctors and finally found one who agreed with them. He tested the boy and, finding he had a number of allergies, plus an intestinal parasite, put him on a strict diet and gave him some medicine. Soon after, he began to talk.

"He was retested by the Board of Education, which called his recovery a 'miracle.'" Once in the first grade of a regular school, he was tested again and ranked in the top 1 percent of the country. "Thanks to St. Jude," adds Mr. Healy, with a gratitude that is all the deeper for being so matter-of-fact.

Among the Twelve Apostles—in fact among all saints—Jude has succeeded in America like none other. From the hour he set out on foot from Jerusalem to his arrival on these shores, he has walked alien territory in search of the uncommitted and the unfulfilled. Given his experience in the pagan world and the mystical nature of his work habits, he seems to have taken his place as the church's gesture toward non-Catholic America. No Vatican council made this decision; it just happened. A Pan-American saint by acclamation, he has risen to the people's will in true democratic tradition; and in a country where there is less consumption of saints than in any country in Europe, he is the charismatic being who came from behind to capture the fascination of those who tend not to believe in anything they cannot see. Against the background of New York, Jude's presence is urbanized to the point where a new aspect of his strategy is revealed. Even at the heart of this pounding, often heartless city, one senses that here is an institutional figure whose Catholicism is less significant than the fact that he is a worldwide broker of souls. As story after story is passed along, the threads of Jude unwind from a hidden spool into the lives of the people with a relentless intensity that is the harmony of the city itself.

In the late hours of the night, a voice emanates from a major radio station, vectoring the lonely staring into darkness:

"Are you feeling downhearted, lonely, spiritually dry? Don't be discouraged. You're a good person, and the Lord loves you very much. . . . If I can be of any help, please write to me. . ."

Father John Catoir's thirty-second commercial is an appeal from his St. Jude Media Ministry, which draws hundreds of letters from people in pain, some of them near suicide. Listen to the city:

"It's Christmas Eve, early in the morning. I'm feeling very depressed and alone. I don't know how I can go on. Where do I want to be? Who do I want to be with? What do I want to do? Those are questions I'm unable to answer. I feel so alienated. . ."

"I'm an alcoholic in recovery. I stayed sober for ninety-five days, and it was good. I drank a few days and then stopped again two weeks ago."

"I write just to request remembrance in prayer. I am currently a 'shut-in' [in prison for sexual abuse] for the last 2,862 days. I see no recourse but to seek a 'final solution.'"

Father Catoir, an author and syndicated columnist, is a familiar figure in the city's media circles, having served as head of the Christophers, an evangelizing communications group, for twenty years, and as a commentator on WABC-TV news for Pope John Paul II's visit to New York in 1995. His early experience at a St. Jude church in a ghetto of Paterson, New Jersey, introduced him to our common saint.

"At first, I was skeptical," Father Catoir admits. "I just knew that if it was named in honor of St. Jude, a lot of people would take notice, more than if it was named in honor of, say, St. Catherine or St. Teresa. I think people want to honor him and promote him. They believe in him. In fact, in one of the prayers, spreading devotion is something they promise.

"He's big box office only among those who have caught it, who get it. You can understand it, but can't explain it. I have a doctorate in canon law, I attend church tribunals, mingle with the brains, and I don't fit in the St. Jude novenas category. But I've worked the novenas and I've seen the faith of these people, and the perseverance, and the holiness, and the goodness."

Eloquently embodying that description are the throngs that show up regularly at St. Francis of Assisi Church on West Thirty-first Street, a busy commuter church crammed into the shadows of a packed, narrow cranny of mid-Manhattan, not the kind of place that tourists seek out. While only one church in Manhattan is actually dedicated to Jude, the Jude shrine at this Franciscan parish, actually an altar, and its setting in a densely commercial neighborhood, make it one of the city's busiest religious centers. Whether in the dimness of winter mornings or the scorching noon hours of August, thousands of commuters visit each week, many, if not most, to worship at Jude's glowing altar or to kiss his relic after novena prayers. Old men carry Jude cards, kerchiefed old women finger rosary beads, quick-footed young women swoop through draped in silk scarves, young men with three days' stubble kneel in the candlelight. In numbers and spirit, it is a Jude factory, pumping out an amazing range of comfort on business executives, firemen, laborers, actors, dancers, publishers—a full spectrum of the city's hordes.

One afternoon, shortly after the regular Wednesday Jude prayer service, a tall husky black man makes his way to the brightly lit statue in the alcove. He wears working clothes, a cap, and is carrying a lunch box. Sounds of organ music still vibrate over the throng as, suddenly, he stretches out his left hand to lay it on Jude's and, head bowed low, breaks into prayer. Moments pass. He genuflects and heads back into the clamor of rush hour.

"Yes, I'm a Catholic," he says, stopping to answer a stranger's questions. "Why am I praying?" He pauses, an engaging smile slowly breaking over his open face. "For guidance—to help me get through some problems that I've had lately, hard times, you know. He helps me with pressure in everyday life. He helps me make my values."

Leslie, thirty-six years old, is married with one child, and works nearby as a security guard. A friend, not a Catholic, got him interested in Jude about four years ago and gave him a book to read about saints.

"But I chose him on my own," he says. "I can't even explain that. It's hard to describe. He has a happy face—and I was out of work, and I kept coming to mass and then I made three or four novenas. I'm stuck on him now."

With that, he reaches into the top of his uniform shirt and pulls out a thick gold chain bearing a large Jude medal.

"I bought it in a jewelry store on Nassau Street," he says proudly. "Yeah, I'm very close to him. He brings me peace of mind. I come here every day. For me it's like getting up in the morning."

A man and his three grandchildren come to church every day for one of the Jude novenas. He says his son and daughter-in-law are addicts, so the children have been placed in foster care. "We want to adopt them, but the court keeps turning us down." At their last appearance in court, on day five of the novena, the judge reverses all decisions and awards him custody.

True to the pattern I will find over and over again, Jude's following seems to multiply of its own accord at St. Francis. Since the late 1980s, attendance at novenas has more than doubled. "The devotion always goes up, not down," reports Father Eric Carpine, in charge of Jude matters at St. Francis, a soft-spoken, pensive man who epitomizes the simplicity of the Jude phenomenon in the middle of a sophisticated city. He has been a priest for almost half of his forty-nine years, ordained "right after Nixon resigned." A champion of human rights, he has a particular fondness for Jimmy Carter, speculating that the former president "might have had some Jesuit whispering in his ear." But as a brown-robed follower of a saint who protected birds, Father Carpine is well suited for Jude territory.

"Metropolitan cities—New York especially—have a bigger share of tragedies than anywhere else. And yet I've never seen one person in the church who has been down and out broken by it—they've been scorned, abused, beaten, turned in, flogged, imprisoned—and they're not broken. Haitians, Italians, Dominicans, Russians, Irish, Germans, Bahamians, Trinidadians—all come here. Many of them come from somewhere—a village, a town—where they celebrated St. Jude. They're here because they remember a devotion to him as part of their family.

"I've come to feel that people know that this is the patron saint of the hopeless and the impossible and that is sufficient for them. And they know that in their situations they find a very best friend, and they have faith that God will help them through it. I think that [the Jude phenomenon] really does speak for the times. I don't think there has been a person in the church who hasn't known someone who has died of AIDS, a person who hasn't known one or more people who are homeless, or one or more women who were abused or abandoned, or children who have been abused one way or another. As shocking as these things seem, as newsworthy as they have been, what it comes down to is that these *are* big problems, and people are trying to deal with them as best they can, dealing through faith rather than litigation. These are very difficult times, indeed."

Far from the hustle of New York commerce, along the forlorn streets of the Inwood section of upper Manhattan, Jude has taken his place among the poor. Faded housing projects and gritty tenements loom drearily over the Hudson River, and the elevated train casts its shadow like a sleeping dragon. Even cabdrivers lose their way among the streets lined with body shops, warehouses, and *grocerias*. Once-grand houses are crumbling into the genteel decay. Like much of the city at the turn of the century, Inwood Valley was rural, a vista of rolling farmland dotted with chicken coops and cow pastures. Then the highways came, and the postwar building boom that brought middle-income public housing to hundreds of families, including those in St. Jude's church parish. Inwood provided much of Manhattan's labor force: workers in hotels, restaurants, and the garment center toiled hard and long to have a stake in the then uncontested American dream. Irish families predominated in the streets and the churches, but by the 1950s their children and grandchildren had begun migrating to the suburbs. Gradually, in the dynamic tradition of the city's ever-transforming neighborhoods, blacks began moving up from the lower West Side, then immigrants from the Caribbean, Cuba, and the Dominican Republic. Whereas in 1957 not a single nonwhite face smiled from among the graduating class in the St. Jude School yearbook, by 1974 Hispanics made up a proud majority. As the population changed, the challenges became tougher. Crime and drugs—routine scourges of the poor—blighted just one more New York neighborhood where once giving out Jude medals had been enough.

In many Hispanic neighborhoods throughout the city, Jude has run into competition with Santeria, the secret "religion of the saints" that Cuban immigrants brought to America. Nigerian slaves introduced their form of worship into the Caribbean, masking their own gods—*orishas*—with saints' names to fool their Spanish rulers. *Botanicas* ("little stores") all over the city carry small items—statues of saints and other Catholic icons, herbs, talismans, candles—that, in the minds of their customers, will drive away evil spirits or even help pick a winning lottery number. In Santeria, saints are the direct objects of worship and do not function as emissaries or intercessors. The ritual animal sacrifices that form part of the initiation rites and other feast days have enraged many opponents of that shadowy power. Catholic and Protestant leaders frown on the cult, and Pentecostal priests call it the work and worship of Satan. But the *santeros* who run the *botanicas,* and do a little healing on the side, see themselves as Christians and may even turn up at Sunday mass. Jude, of course, scores as a front-runner here, too, with the *santeros* advising their customers to buy his statue, bury it, and then dig it up. Borrowing from his established popularity among Latino Catholics, the cult was ready to introduce an alternative Jude.

Modern superheated wranglings over culture and diversity would have bewildered the early parishioners of St. Jude. Inwood's founding years lay in the era of communion breakfasts, armed-forces committees, Catholic youth organizations, and rosary societies, a pre–Vatican II time of simple faith and solidarity. In this quietly authoritarian and greatly demanding atmosphere, St. Jude's "church" actually touched down in rented space at the old Loew's Dyckman movie theater at Sherman Avenue and 207th Street. Women in flowery crepe dresses and men in hats crowded in to hear mass, while outside the marquee lights blazed "*House of Strangers* starring Susan Hayward and Edward G. Robinson." Eminently in character, Jude debuted through the back door into Manhattan during the summer of 1949, just as nuclear power and Stalinist aggression overcast hope for humanity itself with a nightmare of world annihilation.

A temporary place of worship over a drugstore succeeded the movie house, but in 1952 the school opened, housing a permanent oakwood chapel that, redolent of old incense and memories, greets today's visitors. Just across the hall stands a gigantic bust called *St. Jude, Friend of the Hopeless*. He holds to his chest a book in which a Jude relic has been placed; only one candle among many is burning, its faint light reflected on the walls covered with flowers and brass plaques commemorating donors.

Today, as you enter Iglesia San Judas, a plain brick structure on 204th Street, the rushing water of the baptismal font may be the impression that registers, a sound that became Jude's signal over this journey. One cold spring morning, about twenty people have shown up, only one man among them, for the 9 A.M. mass. An altar girl is assisting Father Elias Isla. A terrazzo floor, eight strips of stained glass, and angled pews hint at modernity, somewhat redeemed by the wilting lilies left over from Easter. An unremarkable statue of Jude stands respectfully but unobtrusively at the rear of the church. In his sermon, first in English and then in Spanish, Father Isla speaks of St. Paul's first missionary journey to preach to the Jews of Cyprus, underlining his theme that the church is for everyone, without prejudice. After mass, he reads the regular Wednesday novena prayers. The people stand, clutching their Jude booklets and murmuring, "Blessed St. Jude, with confidence we approach thee."

"We have a Spanish expression: *Primero es Dios que todos los santos,* 'First God, and then the saints,'" says Father Isla after mass. "Devotions have played a very important role in the church, and there's nothing wrong with that, theologically speaking. But sometimes people don't have a good understanding of devotions, and they become superstitions.

"I put devotion to Jude and other saints in context. Faith is the main thing, but it must be educated, based on sound theology, not sentimentality. Lots of people go for specific requests, very faithful people, and we receive testimonies from people who are really sick. Healing is so important. It is the basis of their miracles."

Are these coincidences or strange happenings?

"No," he replies, instinctively veering away from any hint of declaring miracles.

"We don't have any scientific knowledge of this, and I don't think we ever will. People need things like this—it's human. We need heroes, we need models, like Mother Teresa, who will be remembered as an educator—and for her charisma. The point is that the reason he [Jude] became so popular around the world is a good thing. He's not the patron of organized crime, the Mafia." He stops to laugh heartily at his suggestion. "St. Jude represents good things. These are good people, sound people; that he helps these people seriously is a good thing, not an evil thing."

The priest's dark eyes burn in emphasis, appearing enormous through his glasses.

"A lot of it is emotional, but for a good cause. We must look at the human psychology. I think they look with sympathy because the poor guy, he was confused with Judas Iscariot—I mean, who wants to be next to him? It's natural. The prayer says that in a way. Because of Judas Iscariot he just became nobody. Sure, maybe sometime, maybe somebody said this is unfair. Why do we know so little about Jude?"

Now he is beating his fist on the table, the austerity and pride of his native Spain apparent in every inch of his bearing. He grew up in the province of Burgos at the heart of Old

Castile, one of eight children. At twelve he entered the seminary and was ordained in 1959. Assigned to Salamanca and Rome as a member of the Piarist order, he came to the United States in the mid–1960s, graduated from Columbia University's Teachers College, and went on to serve for ten years in the poor streets of the South Bronx at a time when even Hollywood was making movies about its epic violence.

In 1985, after leaving his order, Father Isla was assigned to St. Jude's—and in a very Judean way, involving an "emergency" in the administration of the Inwood church. The parish was in shambles. "It was a big, big shock for me because I didn't belong to the archdiocese, and I had only twenty-four hours notice."

Did he know anything about St. Jude beforehand? He shrugs. "Like everybody else, very little." Twelve years later, he is looking forward to the church's renovation and the construction of an outdoor Jude shrine, which, he deeply believes, may draw even the hardest of hearts into Jude's orbit.

"The reason for Jude's importance, psychologically, is that some people want to be fair—to bring justice to Jude—because Judas Iscariot's betrayal of Christ had nothing to do with Jude. And Judas Iscariot committed suicide—and, in most cases, that happens to people who are totally hopeless. When you see no hope—within you and outside of you—what is left? It is very likely you will end your life.

"Jude, of course, is the opposite of Judas Iscariot. We need him.

"We went a little too far at one time, but the pendulum has swung. I believe today we have an opportunity to bring balance to [people's] devotions to St. Jude. Through him, we can achieve that balance. The saints must bring us to Jesus. If people feel estranged and go to saints alone, it is our fault. We have been disconnected."

Father Isla rightly warns of the danger of carrying veneration to the point of Judolatry, but the sturdy ladies who toil devoutly in the church office—from the same mighty army who have counted money and stamped envelopes (or the equivalent thereof) in church "boiler rooms" since the catacombs—seem less concerned with theological points than with the tangible results they attribute to Jude. Mildred Bird, a volunteer sorting the Jude appeals, looks up from her work to tell her own story. Her granddaughter had "a hole in her heart" at birth. Mildred prayed to St. Jude, and the child, now seven years old, is fine.

Even the St. Jude basketball team can report a Judean event. In February 1996, burglars broke into the school at night and made off with a safe containing several thousand dollars, including $1,100 earmarked for new uniforms, equipment, and a year-end awards dinner. The principal sadly warned that the future of the basketball team might be in danger. Ears to the ground, the New York newspapers and TV stations reported the burglary, and the fact that "the young people in the St. Jude's Community Basketball League were praying to their patron saint, the patron also of lost causes."

Within days, Wall Street businessmen, retirees, former teachers and staff, and even people with no connection to the school had come up with $12,000. One man, offering to replace the whole amount, simply called on his car phone.

"There are more good people in the world than bad ones," said the principal, "more good people than selfish ones."

A Judean intervention? Or a rationalization after the fact? Perhaps a "fake miracle," as cynics might declare? Or the romanticization of simple generosity? It may be one or none of these, in which case the question of "meaningful coincidences"—taking Jude in as a whole—cannot be easily dismissed. Someone who has experienced a Jude story tells it to someone else, who then passes it on and thus it goes, on and on.

The tales accumulate exponentially, defying the worldly to write off the body of Jude lore, now reaching critical mass, as religious hysteria. Nostalgia can play a role sometimes, as one reaches back into childhood for even a single incident that made the saint memorable and accessible for a lifetime.

The Judean memory of Helen S., a lady in her late fifties with an important job in a New York investment house, goes back to high school days.

"I always put one of those laminated Jude cards on my desk when I took an exam. Remember those old-fashioned desks with the place for pens and pencils? It was a French exam, and in those days at the bottom of the test paper there was a preprinted pledge, which you were expected to sign, saying that you had not given or received any information while taking it.

"In the middle of the test, the girl next to me, my best friend, turned to me and whispered that she wanted to know the answer to a particular question. In an instant, I was in a panic. I knew the answer, but here was this picture of Jude in front of me and the pledge on the exam, and my friend was asking me for help. I prayed fiercely to St. Jude at that very instant, hoping he would enlighten me, begging for guidance on what to do. My friend did not ask a second time.

"After the test period, we were walking in the halls together and she said to me, 'Hey, remember when I leaned over and asked you the answer to that question?'

"Yes," I said, dreading what was to come.

"Well," she said, "I thought perhaps you couldn't hear me, then, just as I was getting ready to ask you again, all of a sudden, the answer came to me, just like that."

In a city defined and driven by commerce, Jude's commercial appeal and potential are a perfect fit. As one candid observer of

Jude phenomena in the fast lane puts it, "The fact is, he pays the bills."

Modern churchmen are not blind to his lucrative popularity, and no matter how leery they may be of superstition replacing faith, Jude's role as a middleman between the supplicant and his God fits into a modern passion that is also an American specialty: deal-making. In the end, it means having an instinct for the right connections—in other words, choosing one's intermediary. The concept is highly marketable, especially when that intermediary, next to the Holy Family itself, is the most ubiquitous image in the army of Catholic saints. It follows, then, that certain creative members of the clergy, attuned to commercial possibilities, the theatrical themes of pop culture, and, of course, the national obsession with grieving in public, are refitting Jude's image. We live in a world where "photo ops" abound: a body is barely cold and "loved ones" weep on network television; flowers blanket every death scene; candlelit parades glide silently into close-up; yellow ribbons flutter, permanently it seems, from every telephone pole on Main Street. Once seeking dignity and reticence, grief is now up for display. Ceremony may now be a staple of the American way, but hardly that of a saint whose essence is to work in the twilight, moving obliquely among us, without fanfare.

At St. Stephen of Hungary Church in Yorkville on the upper East Side, a parish of mainly old Europeans and the well-heeled executive class, the good Franciscan fathers have decided to spruce up their image of Jude, dramatically underscoring misery. A statue representing an elderly Jude in a green cassock and a rarely depicted red cloak casts a puzzled glance upon the faithful who gather before him in an alcove at the back of the Byzantine church. Directly across from Jude, a Technicolor *HIV+/AIDS Remembrance Pietà*—a saccharine copy of a Michelangelo of rather different intent—stands as a tragic reminder of the world's deepest grief. Behind Mary and her Son, a large cross of black Velcro is mounted on an enormous red grosgrain AIDS ribbon, all this backed by a canvas wall panel of robin's egg blue, a shrewd placement overall, evincing real media savvy.

On a bleak and windy January day, votive candles blaze at the tableau's dedication. A band of rain-soaked faithful have staggered in between the worst of New York's blizzards. Fr. Neil O'Connell, the pastor ("spiritual director" in fin du siècle churchspeak) is resplendent in blood-red vestments, a surgically trimmed gray and black beard providing contrast. He is flanked at a microphone by two priests in white and gold scapulars. A lectrix in a large Irish fisherman's sweater is reading sections of the mass in a strangled voice. The choir is in full sway as a soloist leads a watery rendition of "The Lord is my light and my salvation; of whom shall I be afraid?" A priest in white tries to explain this modern-day reincarnation of the *Pietà*.

"There is no word in English for when a parent loses a child. . . . Viruses are disinterested. They don't care if it's a saint or a serial killer. . . . The devil has convinced many that this our worldly existence is all. Is it?! . . . No matter how long your time, we will enter into another world. . . . It is a contemporary plague, and we wonder why. Let us ask Our Lady of the Pietà to be with us." Wands of holy water are shaken at the statue. The priests march off. There is no mention of Jude, although within minutes his altar is once more charged by admirers.

On Wednesday, a day of devotion to Jude, a "flame of hope" is kindled on each side of the statue, flickering in green globes fastened to the wall of the shrine. For thirty dollars, a "friend of St. Jude" may have one lit for a special intention displayed beneath the flame for one week and permanently inscribed in the *Book of the Flame of Hope*.

St. Stephen's advertises as itself as "the parish of hope" and the "national shrine" of St. Jude, a claim that might invite comment from those shrines in Chicago and Washington, D.C., which also claim such exclusivity. There is a studious adherence to up-to-dateness: those seeking to become "friends of St. Jude" can call 1–800–688–JUDE; those tuned into the mania for angels (arch and guardian) are invited to an annual "Wings of Hope" devotion. No opportunity is missed to stay apace with the cultural correctness of the times. "Ever fresh diversity in unity" should be realized in Christianity, advises the parish newsletter. In worship, "creative freshness" is encouraged. In the end, all of it amounts to a deadening, if not vulgar, effort to pin down this tenuous creature called Jude through the born administrator's imperatives of bureaucracy and prettification. They miss the point: Jude is a saint of extremity, a dark hole in a dirty wall, not a creature of suburbanized domestication that seeks to surround suffering with a masking coziness.

Dickens makes the point so fine in *Pickwick Papers* when during a parliamentary election in the cheerfully rotten borough of Eatanswill, an agent briefing the candidate says with satisfaction, "There will be ten washed men at the door to shake hands with you, sir."

This may be a parish of optimism, but hope, as a theological virtue, is made of sturdier stuff.

I go off to the rectory office to wait for "Father Neil." An overwrought woman with an institutional air is handing a food bundle to a homeless young man, reminding him that he shouldn't expect to be fed on a regular basis. He seems to have come too often.

Tall and remote, Fr. O'Connell finally appears to explain that the church's connection to Jude goes back to the 1960s, when the saint may have appealed to families of those fighting in Vietnam. As for "the parish of hope," the motto emerged from a "parish image committee" formed two years ago and attended by public relations and marketing experts. Their random survey, some of it conducted by telephone, of about seventy parishioners found that the semicircular arch in the church was "very welcoming" and that they "liked blue" (the color behind the *Pietà*).

The Franciscan is sitting under a portrait of an American Indian. "Our sermons are hope-filled as opposed to fire and brimstone." he says. "We wanted to convey a sense of hope coming here—to develop the style of the ministry in a city that can be alienating.

"Jude is a very American devotion. No ethnic groups can possess it. It appeals to the diversity of racial and ethnic groups and different incomes. In all ages of the church there has been an effort to maintain the balance between theological correctness and the devotional life. We are very much in tune with Vatican II . . .

"Devotions can be manipulative. You can't underrate the effect because the answer can be different. The bottom line, however, is 'Thy will be done.'"

He then goes on to list the church's many programs, such as training homeless men for jobs. Through a "Professional Skills Development Program" at a "Coalition Professional Intern Site," the "Parish Shelter Ministry" preaches the "Good News of hope."

Tuesday evening dinners for those afflicted with AIDS are described in *The Flame of St. Jude,* the shrine's newsletter:

"The meal is home-cooked by the cook for the Rectory. Bright tablecloths, china dishware, glassware, stainless flatware, and an occasional flower decoration contribute to a homey and upbeat atmosphere. Before leaving, each guest receives a bag of nutritious groceries and two transit tokens. The guests, who become regular participants until they are too weak to attend further, become with the Parishioners a tightly knit family . . ."

Finally, in the breezy cadence of restaurant reviewing, we are told that guests give it the highest rating among such dining services in the city.

The trappings of hope certainly give St. Stephen's its style, but the grit and agony of the desperate seem smothered in the bloodless language of sociology. The impalpable presence of a saint who pushed across hard and terrible lands bearing hope to the world is incongruously evoked by entertainments, even at his own devotions. This is how the novena unfolds:

Day One: A visiting retreat master launches the nine days of prayer by playing "The Impossible Dream" on his violin. It is a swelteringly hot day. Is the Good News an impossible dream? he asks. No, nothing is impossible with God. Jude is an icon of the love of the God who appeals to the hopeless.

"Let me tell you a real-life Jude story: A man said he was paralyzed and felt the urge to go to the Jude shrine in Boston. After doing this, his M.S. went into remission. But it wasn't *zap!* It's a process . . . We are called to act on the belief that nothing is impossible with God."

Day Two: Father C. plays "Fiddler on the Roof "— He says, "To life to life, l'chaim!" He tells us that life goes beyond the boundary of death. The cross is good news; good news is always the end of the story. Resurrection surpasses the Crucifix.

Day Three: "Let Me Call You Sweetheart" is followed by applause; Father C., pudgy and smiling, says that this is what he hears St. Clare saying to Jesus: God is true. He repeats this, eyes closed.

Day Four: Onward with "images of evangelization." Holding up his violin, Father C. asks, Who'll start the bidding? then plays "Ave Maria." The church is still. "Faith is the surrender of our will to the will of God. Magic is to get God to do what I want Him to do." Some people approach Jude as though he works magic . . .

Day Five: An Irish jig on the violin, which Father C. says is a wake-up call to the gospel message—another image of evangelization. Kids scream in the back of the church.

Day Six: Before prayers start, Father C. tells me that his cousin, Joe, who was very close to him, died last night. He is sitting alone in the rear of the church, his brown robes blending into the pews. In March, he visited Joe, who lived in the South, and he was fine. The priest tells me a strange and sad Jude story about a woman from out of town visiting a friend in New York who brought her to the church. After prayers to Jude, she took Father C. aside and told him how she had been the victim of sexual abuse as a child. This was the first time she had faced it. Her miracle was recognition, the courage to meet terrible truth. Today he plays "I Have Loved You" and "Love One Another," which he describes as a '60s hymn, and then produces a hand puppet in the form of a skunk. "Some of the people Jesus loves stink," he begins. "But Jesus loves those who rejected him. Look at the person next to you." The lady on my left turns to me and says, "I love you."

Day Seven: Feast of the Assumption. "Ave Maria" again. The topic: how to use the power God gives us for good. Father C. has one hand in a black puppet and another in a white puppet. "Is God's hand empowering me to love?" the white puppet asks.

Suddenly a woman rises from her seat, her arms outstretched: "My two-and-a-half-year-old son is undergoing open-heart surgery today." We all bow our heads.

Day Eight: Father C. plays "Czardas." We can choose to spread the light, or curse the darkness. He quotes T. S. Eliot: "One thing does not change, the perpetual struggle between good and evil." There are no hopeless cases, he tells us, there is no one beyond God's love.

He tells of attending an AA meeting in New Orleans where 90 percent of the men were gay, and he heard "messages of God as the men stood up."

Today's puppet is Little Peter the Otter—I am not sure why.

Day Nine: The light that surrounds the head of St. Jude is the tongue of fire on Pentecost, the priest says. Today's "image of evangelization" is "the light." He plays "Pass It On," another '60s tune, he says, followed by "Let There Be Peace on Earth." The people shuffling slowly toward the altar wait to kiss Jude's relic.

Later, Father C. says: "I'm really a novice in doing this, but I'm finding it's a rich experience of evangelization. I was ordained in 1972 and came later to reconciliation with the saints. They weren't really on my radar screen. But in doing parish missions for three years I've learned that these people are the salt of the earth, folks finding God through devotions."

He confesses that he had had doubts, saying to himself, "I've go to do this thing with this relic!" adding, "That was my first reaction, but then I was so moved by their faith. I could taste it, smell it—and it touched my heart, and when I reached out to them, it was as though it was a way of the Lord laying His hands on them. I'm a believer in God teaching through ordinary people. I really believe that gifts described as contemplative are accessible to more people more often than we think."

One looking for Jude must be prepared to adjust some venerable old clichés of saint-watching. "Patience is a virtue," the platitude assures us, and few challenge its assumed wisdom; in fact, patience may be excruciating—literally suffering—yet it is unarguably noble. The ability to bite our lip and take it is equated with endurance, courage, and that old reliable "quiet dignity." Indeed, it appears to be a biblical axiom that patience is, in itself, a virtuous end. Consider Job suffering in his cave. But Graham Greene, who spent a lifetime pondering the moral havoc wrought by blind innocence and faith gone astray, paints a sobering picture of patience that accepts without question in his play *The Potting Shed*. He could be writing of death:

> "Have you ever seen a room from which faith has gone? . . . Like a marriage from which love has gone. All that's left are habits and pet names and sentimental objects picked up on beaches and in foreign towns that don't mean anything anymore. And patience, patience everywhere like a fog."

New Yorkers, especially the poor, are strangers to this kind of forbearance. Immune to the fundamental passivity so often found among a suffering underclass, they engage in active resistance to submission; theirs is an angry patience. They may wait, but old habits and sentimentality do not dull their cries for relief or the struggle for a lifeline.

Greene is actually describing an anti-Judean state: knowing when hope is gone, and choosing endless patience when in danger of despair. The Judean way—rejecting submission and insisting that hope need never depart—accepts that we are all desperate and invites us to call on him. Patience, that "beggar's virtue," cannot substitute for hope; it runs counter to the Judean experience. Greene's quiet heroism has its nobility, but it is an unenterprising, rather pagan nobility. The Jude-seeker rebels: "I *will not* prostrate myself before this unlimited horizon of misery: *Do something*." Instead of lying down under the wheel, he reaches out for the active intervention of someone beyond the threshold of visibility. If that isn't hope, what is? Between mainstream hope and angry patience lies Jude's answer.

If we know nothing else about this man, it is that he fought for his own truth. Perceptions of him—running the gamut from sincere to superstitious—are a salable commodity in this city of the hard sell. We are left with an amorphous figure, whose very incompleteness arouses our interest. There must be some unifying factor, an answer to why this saint of solitude and separateness appears so visible and invisible at the same time. More than ever, the impulse to follow his trail to its very beginning in the ancient world seems irresistible. Surely I can unlock the secret, find a clue, a souvenir, a document, a witness—something to put a face to this man who has none.

EDESSA

*"When apostle and king concurred the one with
the other,
What idol must not fall before them?"*

Jacob of Serug, ninth-century teacher

THURSDAY, SEPTEMBER 26, 1995

THE GENTLE CAPUCHIN LEANS INTO HIS ANCIENT book, the sleeves of his cassock brushing the yellow leaves. He has spent much of his twenty-four years in the priesthood at Ephesus weighing the possibilities that the Virgin herself lived and died there after the death of her only Son. That this belief has survived since the fifteenth century and drawn thousands to the city of St. Paul does not overrule his scholarly caution. He is even more prudent on another historical question: whether Jude's body was moved to Ephesus after his martyrdom.

Barely two hours have passed since my plane touched down in Istanbul from New York, but I am already sitting in what used to be the French consul's residence, a stately mini-palace and courtyard reminding the world of France's union of elegance with power; she was just one more of the many nations that had stumbled into the mazes of Byzantine history.

Fr. Pierre Mazoué, a man of letters who knows the East, seems intrigued, if not puzzled, by the whole idea of someone trying to track down Jude. He rubs his chin reflectively. "To prove, perhaps, the possibility of the life of Thaddeus, to prove tradition, we may say Thaddeus was here. The *possibility*"—he stresses his tentativeness—"is very important."

Bending over the stark wooden table in his private quarters, the cheerful monk presents a parallel. "You see, it is like the differences on Mary. She died in Ephesus, but the Eastern orthodox say she stayed in Jerusalem and died there." He raises his eyes to the high ceiling, the look of a man comfortable with his God. "These traditions are all over these places."

Fr. Mazoué consults his book of saints again, markers inserted in accounts of the apostles, with, of course, the exception of Jude. "I haven't really had occasion to study him," he says, half-apologetically. When we part, he bids me a safe passage to the East.

Now the jitters begin to set in, just as they did during my former life as a television correspondent: the assignment, the flight, downtime, and, with any luck, a chance to read the research on where you are going, and why, and what may have triggered the latest "development," which usually means disaster. In 1974, NBC assigned me to Turkey to cover the Turkish side of the war with Greece over Cyprus. In that case, the fighting had been implacably *there,* with living and (too often) dying people who at least showed up where you expected to find them. With Jude, the mythic Jude, I feel like the proverbial blind man trying to describe an elephant by feeling only its parts. All I have to go on this time are various and hotly disputed interpretations of an ancient legend, a broken kernel of history. That, of course, and occasional words of caution about traveling in Turkey's eastern provinces, where the Kurdish rebels continue their guerrilla war against government troops.

A few days later, I set out by car for Urfa, heading into a cloudless autumn dawn after an overnight stop at Antakya (Antioch) where the disciples of Jesus were first called Christians. It occurs to me that it must have taken iron motivation, if not downright nerve, to strike out for the heathen lands carrying a message from a humiliated, crucified carpenter's son.

Now I, too, have a sense of some guiding hand, a presence. This same hand a few days earlier had pulled me up the sharp rocks of the surreal Göreme Valley in Cappodocia, about two hundred miles southeast of Ankara, where Christians took shelter from Roman and, later, Islamic persecutions. "Fairy chimneys," soaring mushroomlike cones of lava and volcanic ash, stand like frozen giants amid the weathered cliffs and valleys, as though waiting for still one more faith on the run. Carved into the wondrous winding chain of rock formations, hundreds of cave churches harbor a treasury of still-vibrant frescoes unfolding the story of Christianity. Many years of erosion and landslides had closed the two of interest to me, and even though paths had been cleared up the hills and the structures reinforced, they were still not safe for public inspection. Nevertheless, with a characteristic willingness to please strangers, Turkish officials arranged for a guide to take me to them.

My wordless escort scales the rocks like a mountain lion. It is a bracing thousand feet up a steep trail to the entrance of the Sakli, or "hidden" church, hollowed out of the side of a sheer high-rise by early Christians and then masked by landslides at least five hundred years ago. From the age of ravaging Tamerlane, the cave was silently guarded by the fallen mountain. Then, in 1957, the year of mankind's entry into space, Sakli was rediscovered. This tiny but remarkable ancient relic shelters distinctly Mesopotamian frescoes that are a wonder to historians and archaeologists.

The cave itself is entirely invisible until you arrive, breathless, at its entrance. Inside, the small dusty space is dominated by a tenth- or eleventh-century fresco that might be a copy, or at least an imitation, of Edessa's Mandylion, the disembodied "Holy Face" looking out at a world yet to be saved—the wondrous cloth that Jude brought to King Abgar. This close-up image of Jesus, head only, wide eyes staring at the visitor—or representations deeply influenced by this ancient and haunting vision—recurs frequently in the caves that sheltered the holy refugees of this wild land. The blues and greens have dimmed, and a monochrome red predominates in the biblical scenes, but the strange authority of the forms remains to bespeak a continuum of belief. Echoes of what Edessa must have been lurk here.

The Sakli images are similar, albeit with more blacks and yellows, to those at our next stop, the Meryem Ana (Mother Mary) Church. Another rocky footpath leads to a tunnel under which one slides warily to reach the eroding chapel. The jagged beauty of the Valley of the Swords below inspires wonder at a faith so determined that its hunted followers would carve out such secret and perilous places.

At the same time, I am struck at the sight of the gouged-out eyes in so many of the holy treasures. However much this area is now part of a secular Turkish republic in which stern, passionate Islam is already reasserting itself, at moments like this we remember that it is also a lost realm of Christendom drenched in a millennium of faith, sealed off from us by a whole age of Muslim conquest, just as the boulders closed off Sakli. But the flames of religion give heat almost as often as light, and here, alas, testy sectaries—almost certainly Christian—who truly considered the eyes to be the mirror of the soul, gouged out the offending reflections in virtually every sacred representation—a reminder of the iconoclasm that tore the Byzantine world in the eighth century, only to resurface alive and well in more recent times as one of Christianity's strangest gifts to Islam.

On the drive to Urfa, it seems inevitable that the nearer I come to the ancient city, the closer I will be to penetrating the legend of Jude. The engine's numbing monotony adds to early morning drowsiness. The winding Amanos mountains, limned by early light, summon imaginings of what life must have been like in the days when Edessa stood at the crossroads of upheaved empires and remade religions.

Edessa lies just north of the Syrian frontier at the juncture of two ancient caravan routes. I approach from the west, taking the Old Silk Route unfolding east from Antioch to the Persian frontier land of Edessa (Urfa) two hundred miles away, and then continuing on horizonward across the vastnesses of Central Asia and the great mountains to the ripe and remote civilizations of India and China. A hundred generations of merchants traveled this way trading silk, muslin, gems, and spices between Europe and the East. Roman legions, too, took this route, as did Crusaders, fierce with a conviction that was all too soon tempered by the lust for riches and conquest. Another caravan road struck north and south through the city from the mountains of Armenia toward Arabia and Egypt.

This vast stretch, once Asia Minor and, more specifically, Mesopotamia—the area lying between the two great rivers, Tigris and Euphrates—is now that part of what Turkey calls the Anatolian Plateau. From the Zagras and Kurdish mountains in the east, it stretches to the Syrian Desert and extends northward from the plains above the Persian Gulf to the mountains of Armenia. From the heights of Armenia it slopes down through grassy steppes to a central alluvial plain where sand and sky meet in an endless distance. Long recognized as "the cradle of civilization," the southern portion of this immense plateau was made fertile by a network of canals that enriched the land for plentiful harvests, but also engulfed Edessa in horrendous floods.

Trucks sagging under cotton, vegetables, and pistachios hurtle toward Adana, a commercial center near the Mediterranean coast. It is a melancholy but mesmerizing ride across the great plateau. Nothing moves, very little changes. Squares of green fields occasionally interrupt the endless flat land to the horizon. This is the deculturized zone between East and West, between Europe and the Orient. Except for the trucks, it seems weighed down by the timelessness of the ancient world.

I try to picture Jude against this morose reach of rock and sand, toiling along the bleak dusty roads with his fellow-apostle Simon, bound for Iran and Babylonia. After three years of proselytizing, Simon went north to his martyrdom and Jude, proceeding westward toward Edessa, was waylaid and murdered in the desert with a battle-ax. Jacobus de Voragine, a Dominican archbishop of Genoa writing in the thirteenth century, presents an apocryphal if not fanciful account of this episode, drawing on the improbably named Pseudo-Abdias, the presumed first bishop of Babylon and author of the *Apostolic Memoir*. Writing this apocryphal account of the apostles in the sixth century, Pseudo-Abdias attributes the murders of both Simon and Jude to two priest-magicians, Zaroes and Arfaxat, whom the apostle Matthew had already driven out of Ethiopia.

According to the story, Varardach, a general to the king of Babylonia, was about to go to war against India, but could not obtain guidance from the gods. As the oracle of one temple explained, the gods would not answer while the apostles, with their greater powers, were present in the land. Varardach summoned Simon and Jude and questioned them, only to be told,

"If thou askest our race, we are Hebrews; if our condition, we confess that we are the servants of Christ; if the reason of our coming, we are come hither for your salvation."

Varardach replied that they spoke as though they were more powerful than the gods and challenged them to foretell the outcome of the war. First ask your gods, replied the apostles, and we will prove that they are liars. The general did as they said, and the gods predicted the rout of his army. Varardach was afraid, but the apostles said: "Fear not, for peace has entered in hither with us, and tomorrow at the third hour of the day, ambassadors will come from the India and bow to thy authority peaceably."

The pagan priest-magicians laughed and accused the apostles of trying to trick the general, but the very next day the ambassadors arrived. At that point Varardach wanted to burn the wicked soothsayers alive, but the apostles intervened for their lives, whereupon the general presented them to his king, saying, "These are gods, hiding in the form of men." The priest-magicians, livid in their disgrace, conjured up serpents to kill the apostles, but Simon and Jude gathered the reptiles in their mantles and threw them back among the sorcerers. Then, ignoring the wishes of king and crowd, the apostles called off the serpents and spared the lives of those who would have murdered them.

"We are sent to lead men back from death to life," said Jude, "not to hurl them from life into death." The apostles remained in Babylon for "a year and three months," during which time they converted more than sixty thousand people, including the king and the princes. But in the end, the unforgiving magicians decoyed them into a temple of the Sun. Demons appeared, talking through the mouths of the possessed, and then an angel of the Lord descended, saying, "Choose. Either these shall die, or you shall be martyred." To which replied the apostles, 'Let the mercy of God be adored, and let it lead these men to conversion, and us to the palm of martyrdom.' Then all fell silent . . .

Suddenly, the apostles called forth demons from idols in the temple, commanding them to destroy their own images, which they did.

"Seeing this, the priests rushed upon the apostles, and slew them forthwith." The grief-stricken king raised a temple over Jude's body, and his fame long endured in the land.

Legends pervade Edessa's history, especially those inextricably linked with Jesus and these early years, when the first Christians moved along the ancient roads. Such background is not required reading in Western schools. To be sure, most are surprised to hear that such an outpost survived for centuries at this extremity of the Christian world. Most don't know that pilgrims and pundits, beguiled by the tales of this magnetic city, traveled from Persia and the Far East to partake of its culture, or that this ancient capital's traditions and myths spread to Europe, luring saints, monks, and scholars to its caves; at one point some ninety thousand of them were living on water and refusing meat in the remote dry churches of the forbidding plain.

The wise men from the East who attended the birth of Christ are said to have come from Edessa. Tradition asserts that they made their way to Bethlehem because many centuries before, Zarathustra, or Zoroaster, high prophet of the fire faith, had foretold that a divine light would lead members of his priestly caste—the Magi, or Magians—to a Great One destined to rule the world. People in Aramaic-speaking countries of the "Nearer East," such as Edessa, assumed that this would be the Anointed One, King of the Jews, the Messiah, whose coming had been prophesied to salve their misery in dispersion and captivity after the fall of Jerusalem. If this is true, what the Magi saw and heard—which doubtless they passed on the whole length of their return journey—may have paved the way for reception of the gospels, and, more specifically, for the mission of Jude.

Rimmed by limestone hills open only to the south, Edessa functioned not just as a trading hub but as the cultural and social hub of Mesopotamia, a timeworn crossroads for the three great religions and a stamping ground for the mighty rival empires of Rome and Persia. Foreigners, merchants, pilgrims, learned men, and holy men created a cultural mélange that must have given Edessa a richly cosmopolitan texture, a textbook example of first-century ethnic diversity that modern social engineers would be hard-pressed to duplicate: Armenians, Arabs, Parthians, descendants of Macedonian colonists (the very name *Edessa* is derived from an old capital of Macedonia), Persians, and Jews. The paganism of the East raised temples to Babylonian and Syrian divinities such as Nabu, god of wisdom; Bel, god of the sun; Atargatis, the mother goddess and fertility symbol (believers castrated themselves in her honor); Hadad, god of the moon-worshiping Harran region; and Sin, moon god of Edessa. A host of divinized heavenly bodies mixed in with assorted divinities of the desert and a deep belief in astrology. But it was the healing power of the medicinal springs— the miraculous cures—that spread Edessa's fame far beyond her sandy borders. She could well claim her title as the "blessed city": a place of confluence where the energies of Eastern and Western culture found nourishment.

Lying within the great embrace of the Euphrates, its walls wedged against the foothills of the Anatolian massif, Edessa was the key to empire over the debatable lands. No power could claim the region unless it held Edessa. For these blessings, the city paid a terrible reciprocal price for its treasure of openness to the world, for becoming the accursed spoil of the innumerable wars that formed the bloody wake of empires fighting their way into history. Before the birth of Christ, Babylonians and Hittites were among those who occupied this region called Osrhoene—Orrhoe, Arrhoe, and Orhay—a name derived from the Syriac phrase for "beautiful flowing water." Even then, its natural springs provided the running water that played a significant role in the rituals observed in the many great temples built to honor their gods.

After the death of Alexander the Great, who swept across Asia Minor in the fourth century B.C., his empire fragmented into lesser states. One of his key marshals, Seleucus, founded Edessa and named it after the city of his childhood in Macedonia. In 137 B.C., Edessa became the capital of the newly independent kingdom of Osrohene, a dynasty that survived for 375 years. This gloomy outpost of cruel climate and squabbling chieftains walked a tightrope between conquest by the vibrant new desert empire of the Parthia and the prudent fealty it owed mighty Rome. By necessity, Edessans learned how to survive amid the jealousies of giants.

Although Rome controlled the city, the legacy of Alexander lingered to the very end of Edessa's monarchy. Even though her citizens spoke mostly Aramaic or Syriac, the city went on to become a center of Greek learning, which continued under Byzantine rule. Edessa's significance as a piece in play between the Byzantine empire and Persia inexorably declined with quarrels erupting among Christian sects and the fading of Roman power. All this paved the way for Muslim domination over Mesopotamia.

Edessa first fell to the Arabs in 640 A.D. The Crescent rose and remained for the next four centuries until the First Crusade, which ended victoriously in 1099, brought Edessa under

Christian rule. The zealous warriors of the Cross may have won their battles, but they did not bequeath a Crusader spirit, and all their triumphs only delayed the ultimate grim end to their efforts to recapture the Holy Land. In 1144, Edessa fell again to persistent Islamic forces, providing the impetus for the Second Crusade.

On December 1, 1145, Pope Eugenius III wrote King Louis VII of France warning that the end was near. He described the blessed city as one that ". . . was ruled by Christians and alone served the Lord when long ago, the whole world in the East was under the sway of pagans."

On Christmas Day, Eugenius announced that he was "taking the Cross," i.e., the vows of a Crusader knight. By Easter, exiled from Rome, Eugenius, along with Conrad, king of the Germans (the title of the heir designate of the Holy Roman Empire), and Bernard of Clairvaux, a devout admirer of Jude, began planning the Second Crusade, the last and saddest attempt to regain the city of Abgar and to save what was left of Christianity east of the Euphrates. Two years later, the expedition dissolved in a debacle of bickering and military setbacks until finally the disillusioned princes of Europe turned their backs on their doomed holy war. In Bernard's own all-too-fitting summary, the adventure had proved "an abyss so deep that I must call him blessed who is not scandalized thereby."

Five centuries after Edessa's fall, Islam owned the East. Public displays of the Cross were banned. Church bells were silenced. Edessa passed to new Islamic conquerors, the Turks, who would change its name to Urfa and fold the former jewel of the Christian church into the Ottoman Empire. After World War I, when that remarkable caravanserai of nations at last dissolved, Urfa found itself just within the boundaries of the empire's rump inheritor, the new Republic of Turkey. Virtually every trace of Christianity had been ground into the ancient dust, especially the once large Armenian population that had embraced Jude as the founder of its church. Enmity between Armenians and Turks erupted into revolt and genocide in the late nineteenth century and savagely continued into the next. What had happened to Edessa, to Şanliurfa ("Beautiful Urfa"), that so few recognize her name in the West? Edessa survives in religious pamphlets on the life of Jude and in accounts of the ill-fated Second Crusade, but Urfa really belongs to Edmund Wilson's category of "prose-interrupting blurs."

A road sign up ahead comes into dusty focus: Gaziantep. We are passing a city of grazing sheep, ocher stone buildings, Etruscan-orange soil, and countless mosques. The smell of manure—or is it the open-air toilets?—pervades the air. Half-finished modern high-rises dot the town, suspended in time like everything else. Low-lying brush trims the hills, which are abundant with fig orchards, olive trees, cotton, and wheat.

Another sign looms, this one announcing the imminent appearance of Nizip, a town perched on the western bank of the stately Euphrates. It is time to cross. At last, I have arrived at "the birthplace of civilization." The great river, curving wide like a matador's cape, drifts slowly by, its ancient currents holding who knows what mysteries of glories gained and lost.

Surely Jude would have crossed these waters. Carrying fresh, vivid memories of the presence and words of Jesus, he embarked on this assignment within weeks of the Crucifixion—an agony, say the Scriptures, that even the apostles could not bear to watch. Thomas gave Jude and Simon their marching orders: Christianize the East. Together, they fanned out across the dimly known world to proclaim a message that would turn history upside down. If dark doubts tested Jude's resolve, he may well have remembered Jesus' response to his question at their last meal together: your quiet deeds will speak for themselves, and the world will follow you.

Finally, a blue and white sign appears, just like those on any American highway. "Şanliurfa," it says, pointing east. The land goes bare, withering into rolling steppes that form a backdrop for the city nestled at their feet, creased and arid yet somehow inviting. Great Alexander and so many of his imitators slowly clanked their way toward battle on the paths to Edessa. The modern ride is hair-raising. I just miss plowing head-on into a wheat tractor. Dry hills and patches of trees provide points of reference on the horizon, alternating with telephone lines, electric substations, and occasional crops in surprisingly fertile fields. Forty kilometers from Urfa, the land is dry and desolate except for the occasional gas station. Then, without warning, two hills part in the distance, and there lies the blessed city. The reportorial mode kicks in fast: the familiar rush of adrenaline, the thrill of being on the scene of a story long coveted, the surge of curiosity that makes an imprint of every sensation. Jude Country, at last.

From afar, framed by the Tektek mountains, Urfa looks dramatically more modern than one would have imagined. Low-lying buildings crowd in tawny white groupings, blending into the sand, relieved only by the pines and pomegranates that soften the hard edge of the skyline. The two great Roman columns atop the Citadel mount, where Abgar and Jude played out their enduring drama, are unmistakable. They are the city sentinels, bearing witness to the war-scarred past. For the present, handsome young boys and girls in school uniforms spill out into school yards, cavort down streets lined with satellite dishes, and disappear into homes crowned by television antennae—a modern tableau plunked down in the middle of a city held in the grip of time and memory.

Mustapha, a well-mannered guide in his thirties, waits patiently at the shabby government tourism office. When the digging started at his village, twenty-four kilometers to the northwest, he tells me, they found many "old stones and pic-tures." In this once-forsaken plain, "digging" usually means the mammoth Southeast Anatolian Project, or Güneydoğu Anadolu Projesinin (GAP), a gigantic hydroelectric undertak-ing heralded as the answer to drought, electrical shortages, and unemployment. GAP promises to accomplish what the engineering-minded Emperor Justinian made a stab at in the sixth century: alter the course of the Euphrates and with it the topography and weather of the Harran plain. GAP's cen-terpiece, the massive Atatürk Dam, will connect to Urfa by sixteen miles of tunnels twenty-five feet wide; these tunnels will carry the water of a manmade lake expected to hold 48.5 billion cubic meters, enough to reshape southeast Anatolia forever—or at least until the next civilization. (Such reflec-tions come easy amid the Ozymandian traces of so many.)

Mustapha takes me to my quarters at the newly remodeled government guest house. The city outside my car window is a wilderness of old, new, and in-between, with flat-roofed houses bowed low and dozens of minarets pointing to an ever-present God. It is open to the sun, deprived of shadows. No subtleties of light and shade hint of mysteries and secrets. On the surface, this is hardly the classical hide-and-seek territory so favored by Jude. No matter, with very little effort, I can imagine a man of faith emerging from the harsh wilderness, perhaps resting in the courtyard of the old inns where travelers and their camels found such shelter as they could from a cli-mate of extremes—bleak in winter, sizzling for seven months of the year. Against the monochromatic background of sand, occasional colors are relief for the eye and points of reference amid the beige beauty: the intricate hues in the Oriental car-pets spread out for worshipers; the bright French-blue paint common to the Middle East that marks the latticework rails around caves, mosques, and cemeteries; the green lushness of shade trees.

We turn right onto another dirt road and pull up to the guest house. Casually indicating the building directly across the way, Mustapha says, "Oh, and there is the Jude church." I am stunned. It sits right across the narrow street from my lodgings, gleaming eerily in the thin September sunlight, a neat, perhaps newly painted mosque surrounded by the old stones of its former incarnations. St. Jude's now bears the name of Selhattin Eyyübi Camii, one of Edessa's many conquerors. As usual, the mythic Jude has just shown up, scuttling round the next corner, encountering me and not encountering me in the same moment, absent but spectacularly present. Giddy with a sense of coincidence, I silently paraphrase a strictly American legend: of all the mosques in all of Urfa in all the Turkish towns, I walk into his.

This is the western section of the city, just below the Citadel mount and its assertive Corinthian columns standing watch. Like many of Urfa's mosques, the Jude church, with its Roman arches and cathedral ceilings, was wrought from the ever-abundant stones that marked the sites of still older churches and synagogues, which, in their turn, were probably erected over pagan temples. Despite rampaging armies, fire, decay, erosion, and especially a devastating flood in 201 A.D., archaeologists and scholars have approximated some of the original sites. By the fifth century, Edessa had become a major center of Christianity, and pilgrims from throughout the world streamed into the sacred city seeking relics of Addai—Jude of Edessa—armed with an iron faith in the apostle of Christ who came to heal the king on behalf of his master. Tradition says that in order to protect relics from warring Persians, before the end of the fifth century Jude's remains had been disinterred from Abgar's ornate tomb outside the city walls and placed in a silver mausoleum in the Church of St. John the Baptist. It was the world's first shrine dedicated to St. Jude. This is the mosque I'm now staring at in disbelief, a marvel of architecture supported by thirty-two red marble columns. The Roman governor of Edessa had used the building as the provincial law court, and only later was it consecrated to Jude. During the great famine and plague of the early sixth century, the church, filled with straw beds, served as a hospice for the poor, the sick, and the dying. Even all those years ago, Jude and healing were historical handmaidens. Whether this coupling was deliberate or coincidental, we do not know, but it is reasonable to assume that Jude, who is credited with many acts of healing in Edessa, had already earned a reputation for miraculous cures.

A Syrian writer has left us a detailed and compelling description of the city and Jude's church. It is 1145, the year of the last fall of Christian Edessa. The Turkish conqueror Zangi has taken temporary lodgings in the world's first shrine to St. Jude:

> "They had rebuilt [the city's defenses] and had written upon them . . . the account of the capture and the name [Zangi]. They had razed the shrine of the Confessors . . . and built the wall with its stones. They had begun, moreover, to build a castle for the ruler beside the splendid shrine of St. John in which the ruler lodged. Over this shrine they had set guards so that nothing in it should be destroyed. . . . In it were nearly a hundred great windows. . . . The bodies of the holy Addai [Syriac form of Thaddeus] the Apostle and king Abgar were deposited in a coffin of silver, plated with gold. At the capture the coffin was carried away and the bones scattered; but the believers collected them with many fragments of [other] saints."

Within the year, the Crusaders mounted their last effort to retake the city, and when they faltered, the Turks sacked

Edessa with a vengeance, murdering and looting for months, plundering untold treasures of gold, jewels, carpets, and all manner of priceless church objects. Thousands were slaughtered, imprisoned, or fled to suffer a slow death in the desert. It was hardly a glorious postscript: a city long protected by the Creator now lay open to chaos. Many wondered if Addai— or Providence itself—had simply run out of patience. Eventually, the church of Addai became a warehouse. In 1183, a lamp ignited the wool stored there, and the shrine of St. Jude was consumed.

The Jude church stands out in triumph amid the sunburned stones, exposed telephone wiring, and forgotten mounds of rubble blending into the crumbling beauty of this old neighborhood. The dirt road, which points to the Citadel, is hardly a stop for lumbering tour buses and passengers in Gortex jogging suits worried about their comfort level. Jude's legion of followers hardly know this place exists. And if some do, will they follow Jude to where he used to be, in a church-turned-mosque in a Moslem city?

As we approach the old Jude site, the white marble mosque, engraved with gray sunbursts and gold filigree, appears luminous against a sky in three shades of blue. Entering the courtyard, we encounter an elderly mullah in a sparkling white cassock and matching beard and skullcap, who greets us with a slight bow. He offers a blue silk scarf to cover my head. In the still interior—cool, serene, empty of worshipers—we remove our shoes and pad along the rich Oriental carpets spread over an opulent green floor cover, making our way between the double rows of white marble columns that support a line of swooping arches. The staircase facing Mecca commands the focal point. I am not surprised to see it, nor does it contradict my sense of Jude's presence. He was, after all, a man of the East, and Roman cathedrals had not yet been invented.

"The old church of Addai—your Jude—was here," says Mustapha, in what seems to be an apology for the Islamic displacement of my saint.

By afternoon, we are sitting with the dedicated Professor A. Cihat Kürkçüoğlu, lecturer and one-man archaeology department at Harran University, and author of several historical guides to Urfa. The professor's gravelly voice fills his small office. The obligatory Turkish mustache accents a thin handsome face, and his frame, though slight, has the muscular hardness characteristic of men who live in rugged land.

"Yes," he says, after considering my question about the Addai church, "the building you visited was once the church of Addai, but it was a new church, not the one from Addai's time."

Whatever misfortunes had befallen the churches in time of conquest, things got relentlessly worse in this century. After the First World War, he explains, the French—in a classic example of history coming around the first time as tragedy, the second time as farce—reestablished a ghost of the Crusader realm of St. Louis in the "Mandate" of Syria and Lebanon. With Turkey flat on its back, the French absorbed a lot of non-Syrian territory as well, including Edessa. The French promised all sorts of grand things, including self-government. But Turks are hard to keep down: Kemal Atatürk and his formidable mountaineers showed their teeth. The French quit nervously after barely a year and, given what had happened to the Armenians, their poor Christian friends quit with them. In the end, one more forgotten empire had passed through Edessa, though an unusually brief one. For years, the churches stood dark and empty.

"The church of Addai was empty," continues the professor. "It was used as a power station from the 1940s right up to the end of the '60s. It was near collapse. Then, three years ago, it was restored without changing the original shape. It's only been open a year. Originally, there was an older church on that site, one of the early wonderful churches of the first century."

The Ulu, or Great Mosque, was a church, too, the professor reminds me, referring to one of Urfa's oldest temples, a synagogue taken over by Christians in the fifth century and known as the Red Church for its many red marble columns, several of which remain. The courtyard walls have weathered the years, too, and the octagonal bell tower is now a minaret. "There are shafts beneath that mosque," he says. "The well of Addai was there, the one in which the Mandylion was thrown."

But the professor then offers a second version of the story, leading me to refer to the "two-wells theory"—one well at the Great Mosque, and the other near the cave of the prophet Job. The latter version was recounted by a Syriac clergyman to the Islamic conqueror Zangi:

> "A visitor to Edessa stole Jesus' handkerchief and put it in his pocket. That night in the Cosmas monastery the handkerchief in the visitor's pocket began to give off light and radiance. Afraid of being burnt, the thief threw the kerchief into the well of Job, out of which then began to pour a light like that of the sun. Thus, the kerchief was found and restored to its proper place in the monastery."

I am still reeling from the professor's first mention of the Mandylion, which had struck me with the force of a blow. The legend is yet alive in Urfa, and I am hearing of it from a scholarly Muslim who tells the tale with the equanimity of simple faith. He believes there was a Mandylion in Edessa, that Addai brought it here, and that Addai was one of the Twelve, the one sent here on behalf of Jesus. It occurs to me that the kindly professor knows more about St. Jude than the average Catholic—that is, up to the point where he becomes master of lost causes, a Western belief that is foreign here, even though Jude is said to have healed King Abgar's incurable leprosy.

"As all Moslems, we believe that Jesus was sent by God and we believe everything about Jesus, and the book of Jesus," the professor goes on, his brown eyes excited with possibilities. "But our prophet, Muhammad, was later than Jesus, and Jesus' time was finished."

I smile to signal understanding of his conclusion and to salute his remarkable tolerance. He reaches into a folder and takes out a color photograph of a mosaic depicting a bearded man wearing a floppy hat and a multicolored cape over a caftan. His right hand is extended, and the first three fingers appear to be indicating something or making a point. Edessa was long famous for its mosaics. Time passed and conquerors came who thought representations of the human form a sorcerous impiety. A handful of those glorious mosaics have survived, and judging from this photograph, one of the masterpieces has retained its beauty.

"Abgar," announces the professor, pointing to an inscription on the right side of the picture. "This is King Abgar, son of Manu."

Caught off guard, I feel as if the old toparch—the ruler himself—has come striding into the dusty little office.

"May I see the original?" I ask, fully expecting it to be in the Urfa museum, high on my list of sites to check, even though every modern account I have read reports that almost no Christian objects exist there either.

"Unfortunately, no," he replies, a trace of unease in his voice. "It is covered, to protect it."

"Well, can't you lift the cover for just a few minutes?" I insist, my anticipation edging toward impatience.

"No, it is buried."

"Buried? Where?"

"Behind the museum."

I faced many such moments in my television reporting years, almost always achieving my objective through healthy debate or compromise. Exhuming an artwork owned and protected by the Turkish state had never come up.

The professor, vague about who had actually unearthed the mosaic and where, describes how he was present at its discovery in 1982. Since then, he adds, there has never been money or expertise sufficient to prepare it for display, so it was reburied. From what I've seen so far in Urfa, it seems the government has turned its attention and capital toward the powerful future to the exclusion of the abased past. Abgar has been put on hold. He has waited this long, no matter.

"History says this is the right Abgar," the professor continues, which tempers my disappointment at running into yet another invisible man. But the picture itself is stunning news. The discovery of the Abgar mosaic, like the hide-and-seek nature of the Judean experience itself, adds up to one more clue in an old mystery. Jude is beckoning; I am sure of it.

"The Jesus letter, can you show me the Greek text of it that is inscribed in stone, in the Kirk Mağara (Forty Caves) section of the city?" I ask urgently. "Mr. Segal's book has a picture of the inscription from the cave." (The professor, like most educated Edessans, is well aware of the solid scholarship of J. B. Segal's remarkable book, *Edessa: The Blessed City.*)

"I've tried to find the inscription many times," he answers sadly, "but I couldn't. The pictures you refer to are from the years 1952–55. It was the only Christian inscription in the city, but I cannot find it anymore. There has been no effort to preserve it.

"In fact, the last time Mr. Segal visited Urfa, in 1980, he stood on the Citadel, and looking down at the changing city, he wept. You see, people don't apply for permission to live in the outlying area. They just build houses, illegally. And it is often over a piece of antiquity.

"There are only two gates left, the eastern one and the toll-gate, with a few inscriptions still visible. The old west gate [through which the Mandylion entered the city] is gone. Because of the GAP project we are removing valuable archaeological objects and taking them to the museum before the area is flooded."

His words echo what I had learned weeks earlier in a telephone conversation with an American archaeologist working in Urfa: teams of them were racing the implacable clock of GAP. In short, their dig for artifacts of a chain of civilizations stretching over a hundred centuries can hardly compete with a dig into the economic future of the country. Urfa is looking forward; once more, she is reinventing herself, probing the ground with drills and jackhammers, harnessing the power of the water—always the water. The past must be reburied in order to have a future, but perhaps not completely. In a video-tape the Turks made for their city, a narrator predicts that Urfa is "on its way to becoming a metropolis" and "preparing for the twenty-first century." He also observes that "water will heal once more."

Running water has always defined the integral rhythm of the city: the exotic pools of sacred carp, the fountains in pagan temples, the river Daisan running through the old town, the holy wells within and outside the walls, countless drinking fountains, and the inevitable pool in the center of a traditional Edessa house. At least one hotel conserves the precious liquid by offering "waterless rooms." Today, the life-giving sound of running water may be more difficult to hear above the din of drilling, but persistent streams from the underground labyrinth burble to the surface, befouling the modern machinery and reminding some of Edessa's glorious past.

For this is not the first time that engineers with great plans have tried to reshape the city's capricious water supply to match a grand design. Emperor Justinian built a dam northwest of the city to divert the Daisan and prevent the disastrous floods that had scoured Edessa throughout her history. But by the thirteenth century, an anonymous chronicler concluded that it was Addai himself who originally built the dam: "The Apostle was zealous and with the zeal and help and care of King Abgar a great dam was made of mighty stones . . ." No more was the city torn apart by cascading water. But this is simply historical and archaeological nonsense embodying the amiable habit of ascribing the credit for all significant achievements to the most legendary citizens of a neighborhood.

We stop for lunch in the one restaurant in town where, I am told, women are accepted in this strict Islamic society. After sampling the kebabs and stuffed meatballs for which the city is famous, we drive to two lakes southwest of the city and stroll around the ancient carp pools. The sound of hammering is not far off. All manner of machines—cranes, jackhammers, bulldozers—have gathered to gash the earth, and where water spouts freely, men sweat over shovels and stack cinder blocks. Earthmovers plow up the rich red soil of "the fertile crescent," a sobering contrast to the surface of gray clay that envelops Urfa. The blessed city is about to be blessed with boutique-style shops and hotels.

The city is a blur of noise and traffic—roaring motor scooters, glossy new cars, rickety buses, supply trucks huffing and puffing, old men and women scurrying in terror to get out of the way; it is a classic Third World show of sound and light. Meanwhile, the trees are alive with small birds lost in song. Old men toss chickpeas into the serene aquamarine water of the carp pools where sunlight has turned the fish to silver. Thick schools of them follow potential benefactors with flat shiny eyes, leaping at the sight of an outstretched hand. A large network of underground springs has fed these pools, replenishing the lifeblood of the city. Age-old artifacts have endured: an old theological school on the banks of the pools, a water fountain fashioned from a slice of Roman column, a Corinthian capital now a public bench.

Just a hundred yards east of the pools, the place of Abraham's birth is thronged with Iranian pilgrims veiled in black and squatting at prayer in the stifling underground cave. Their black eyes telegraph fierce disapproval as I gingerly take a place among them. I can't help wondering if they are going to erupt into cries of "Magbar Amerika!" (Death to America!), a replay of the madness I witnessed outside the American embassy in Teheran during the hostage crisis of 1979.

Historically, this is Edessa's ground zero: the two sacred lakes or pools; Abraham's cave in the courtyard of the Mevlid-i Halil mosque; and a healing well named for him in the Halilür Rahman mosque, just yards away. The well itself is simple   a thick piece of chain hangs from a square piece of old marble, passes through a silver bucket, and disappears into a hole in the floor, around which is set more marble. Closer inspection reveals a very modern pipe running parallel to the chain. This focal point of the city encompasses the legendary basis of Edessa's pre-Christian founding and is part of a tapestry of traditions threaded with the names of prophets and patriarchs, twenty-one of whom are counted as having lived in the "City of Prophets." Most notable among them is Abraham (Ibrahim), said to have been born in the pre-Seleucid, pre-Edessan region or, some say, in Harran, twenty-five miles to the south. One tradition, very much alive today, says that the father of all prophets was actually born in the cave where I saw the crowds of Iranian pilgrims, the cave of Abraham that Muslims regard as their Lourdes. The original Ottoman mosque proved too small to accommodate the tides of modern pilgrims, so in 1986 another went up next to it. Together they shelter the hordes praying at the cramped quarters where Abraham is believed to have remained until he was seven.

Unfortunately, Abraham incurred the wrath of Nimrod, who is credited with building the city. A popular version of the tale says the fierce king, determined to annihilate the patriarch's denial of all gods but one, bound Abraham between the two great pillars on the Citadel (the "throne of Nimrod") and slung him into the valley. Abraham miraculously escaped harm, and on the spot where he landed, a fish pool formed—Birket Ibrahim, the Pool of Abraham. It is a crime to disturb the sacred fish of Abraham, and as late as the nineteenth century it was believed that anyone who ate them would be struck blind. (The Spanish pilgrim Egeria seems to have challenged this belief in the fourth century, reporting that the famous fish "tasted so good.")

Job, exemplifying patience, is revered in Urfa, and the place just outside the city where it is believed he found a cure for his torments is known as Bir Eyüp (the Well of Job), the very well into which the professor has said the Mandylion was thrown, or so one rendition of the story goes. Also here, the cave infested with worms where Job endured his great sufferings. A flood of Muslim pilgrims surrounds the cave and well, many of them purchasing plastic bottles to scoop up the healing water as they chant their prayers. Even the conqueror Zangi, who retook Edessa from the Crusaders in the twelfth century, cured his gout with this water. In that time, a nearby hospice, an infirmary, and a leprosarium drew the sick and dying from afar. Shrines rose here, too, dedicated to Sts. Cosmas and Damian, physician-martyrs. In fact, Edessa's association with healing was widely known throughout Mesopotamia, its doctors and medical centers as numerous as the holy men within its borders, also associated with the power to cure. It is tempting to conclude that Jude's association with healing, a breeding ground for impossible causes, grew out of Edessa's widely known tradition for attracting the ailing and those who could cure them. But there is no evidence for this conclusion, only a logical assumption that at the very least, the old city's reputation for healing connected Jude with having this special power from the moment he arrived. As for prophet graves, Job's tomb is honored in a village just a few miles from Urfa; Elijah, said to have died en route to visit his fellow prophet, lies entombed fifty miles east.

Fascinating tales, but they hardly shed light on Jude, except, perhaps, to underscore that so far all I have to go on are a missing inscription, a buried mosaic, and a hunch that the root of the story lies here. Scholars deploy skepticism, the clergy advise caution, and yet Jude lingers here, a historical figure, unchanged—a Jewish Christian, intensely Oriental, with no Roman trappings or connections. Geographically, this is as close as I will ever get to him, following the shadowy trail he left for ancient chroniclers to wrestle with and ultimately ignore.

Apart from the few mentions of Jude (Thaddeus) in Scripture, what is known of his pilgrimage begins after the Ascension. King Abgar Ukkama ("the Black"), toparch of Osrhoene who ruled from 13 to 50 A.D., was then twenty-eight years old. Jude, by most accounts—and they are all sketchy—set out from Jerusalem, some six hundred miles distant from Edessa as the crow flies. He stopped at Galilee—where it is thought he had a family before Christ summoned him—went next to Capharnaum, and continued northeastward. On his way, he may have stopped in Damascus and Beirut, where he is still venerated. The traditional route continues through Aleppo in northern Syria, a key point on the major caravan route, and from there to Edessa. Leaving this base, Jude is believed to have taken his mission north into the small states of Bithynia, Pontus, and then into the mountains of Armenia on the Black Sea, now a southern area of modern Russia.

Some scholars suggest that Jude ventured as far as the Transcaucus and preached in Tiflis (Tbilisi), the capital of Georgia, about 150 miles north of Mount Ararat, the city where Stalin later studied theology and was expelled from the seminary. Tradition also strongly suggests that he preached about three hundred miles farther east in Baku on the Caspian sea, now the oil-rich capital of Azerbaijan. It is particularly intriguing that just south of Mount Ararat, in northern Iran, a St. Thaddeus monastery is still functioning amidst the crumbled remnants of what used to be a wall.

To trace Jude in the records, we must begin with the distinguished church historian Eusebius. Even though Eusebius was writing in the early fourth century, almost three hundred years after Jude's time, he had access to many now-perished documents and long-silent traditions, as well as his own clearly sound judgment. His work provides the core of what we know of Jude's activities. He begins his account of Thaddeus by recording the vast number of people who had heard of Christ's miracles and journeyed to Judea in search of the carpenter's son who healed the sick and gave life to the dead:

"Thus . . . when King Abgar, the brilliantly successful monarch of Mesopotamia . . . dying from a terrible physical disorder which no human power could heal, heard continual mention of . . . Jesus and . . . His miracles, he sent a humble request to Him by a lettercarrier, begging for relief from his disease. Jesus . . . honored him with a personal letter, promising to send one of His disciples to cure his disease, and at the same time to bring salvation to him and all his kin . . . After His resurrection and ascent into heaven, Thomas, one of the twelve apostles, was moved . . . to send Thaddeus, himself in the list of Christ's seventy disciples, to Edessa . . . Through him every word of our Saviour's promise was fulfilled . . . "

Eusebius explains that he has taken the correspondence between Jesus and Abgar from the "Record Office at Edessa." First he quotes a copy of the toparch's appeal delivered to Jesus at Jerusalem by the royal courier, Ananias:

"Abgar Uchama [Ukkama] the Toparch to Jesus, who has appeared as a gracious saviour in the region of Jerusalem—greeting. I have heard about you and about the cures you perform without drugs or herbs. If report is true, you make the blind see again and the lame walk about; you cleanse lepers, expel unclean spirits and demons, cure those suffering from chronic and painful diseases, raise the dead. When I heard all this about you, I concluded that one of two things must be true—either you are God and came down from heaven to do these things, or you are God's Son doing them. Accordingly I am writing to beg you to come to me, whatever the inconvenience, and cure the disorder from which I suffer. I may add that I understand the Jews are treating you with contempt and desire to injure you: my city is very small, but highly esteemed, adequate for both of us."

And, says Eusebius, Ananias brought back the following reply:

"Happy are you who believed in me without having seen me. For it is written of me that those who have seen me will not believe in me, and that those who have not seen will believe and live. As to your request that I should come to you, I must complete all that I was sent to do here, and on completing it must at once be taken up to the One who sent me. When I have been taken up I will send you one of my disciples to cure your disorder and bring life to you and those with you."

It should be noted that the reply attributed to Jesus is often deemed an oral response put into writing by the messenger Ananias. In any case, the consequence of this exchange is the seed of the original Jude legend told throughout the Greco-Judean East and even as far as Europe, to explain the very early Christianization of Edessa.

Eusebius continues, describing events after the Ascension of Jesus:

"Thomas . . . sent to him as an apostle Thaddaeus [Thaddeus] . . . When his arrival was announced, and he had been made conspicuous by the wonders he performed, Abgar was told: 'An apostle has come here from Jesus, as He promised you in His letter.' Then Thaddaeus began in the power of God to cure every disease and weakness, to the astonishment of everyone. When Abgar heard of the magnificent and astonishing things that he was doing, and especially his cures, he began to suspect that this was the one to whom Jesus referred when he wrote in His letter: 'When I have been taken up I will send you one of my disciples who will cure your disorder.' So summoning Tobias, with whom Thaddaeus was staying, he said: 'I understand that a man with unusual powers has arrived and is staying in your house and is working many cures in the name of Jesus . . . Bring him to me.'

"So Tobias went to Thaddaeus and said to him: 'The toparch Abgar has summoned me and told me to bring you to him'. . . . Thaddaeus answered: 'I will present myself since the power of God has sent me to him'. . . As he presented himself, with the king's grandees standing there, at the moment of his entry a wonderful vision appeared to Abgar on the face of Thaddaeus. On seeing it Abgar bowed low before the apostle, and astonishment seized all the bystanders; for they had not seen the vision, which appeared to Abgar alone.

"Are you really a disciple of Jesus the Son of God, who said to me, 'I will send you one of my disciples who will cure you and give you life'?

"'You wholeheartedly believed in the One who sent me, and for that reason I was sent to you. *And again, if you believe in Him, in proportion to your belief shall the prayers of your heart be granted'* [emphasis added].

"'I believed in Him so strongly that I wanted to take any army and destroy the Jews who crucified Him, if I had not been prevented by the imperial power of Rome from doing so.'

"'Our Lord has fulfilled the will of His Father: after fulfilling it He was taken up to the Father.'

"'I too have believed in Him and in His Father.'

"'For that reason I lay my hand on you in His name.'

"When he did this, Abgar was instantly cured. . . . It surprised Abgar that the very thing he had heard about Jesus had actually happened to him through His disciple Thaddaeus . . .

"After this, Abgar said: 'It is by the power of God that you, Thaddaeus, do these things; and we ourselves were amazed. But . . . explain to me about the coming of Jesus . . . by what power did He do the things I have heard about?'

"Thaddaeus replied: 'For the time being I shall say nothing; but as I was sent to reach the world, be good enough to assemble all your citizens tomorrow, and I will preach to them and sow in them the word of life—about the coming of Jesus. . . . His mission and the purpose for which his Father sent him; about His power and His deeds, and the mysteries He spoke in the world, and the power by which He did these things; about His new preaching; about His lowliness and humility, and how He humbled Himself and put aside and made light of His divinity, was crucified and descended into Hades, and rent asunder the partition which had never been rent since time began, and raised the dead; how He descended alone, but ascended with a great multitude to His Father; and how He is seated on the right hand of God the Father with glory in the heavens; and how He will come again with power to judge living and dead.'

"So Abgar instructed his citizens to assemble at daybreak and hear the preaching of Thaddaeus . . . he ordered gold and silver to be given to him. But Thaddaeus refused them and asked, 'If we have left our own property behind, how can we accept other people's?'

"All this happened in the year 340."

This date is reckoned to be 340 of the Seleucid era, or 30 A.D. of the Christian epoch, most likely the year of Christ's Ascension.

Even if scholars call the story of King Abgar's miraculous conversion a fabrication concocted by the later Christians of Edessa, the great, indeed, repetitive, weight given it by early Christian historians points to the distinct probability that this "legend" most likely contains a kernel of truth about Jude and the advent of Christianity in Mesopotamia. Certainly no one has already succeeded in proving that there were no Christians in first-century Edessa, or that St. Jude never set foot there. Nor has it been conclusively demonstrated that the documents apparently ascribed or addressed to King Abgar V, the ones Eusebius saw in the archives, were simply forgeries. Quite the contrary. By the end of the fourth century, Syriac writers in both the East and West accepted Addai as the founder of their church. It does not seem far-fetched to accept that Jude undertook such a mission in the first century, for it was during his lifetime that the Christian community in Jerusalem was dispersing—largely eastward—under persecution. Further, the early Christians possessed a markedly Jewish rather than Hellenistic character; and Addai, a Jew born in Galilee at Caesarea Philippi (Paneas), knew the Jewish traditions and, according to reports of the time, found his earliest converts among them.

Two pertinent points must be made about Jude's answer to Abgar in the Eusebius account. First, Jude reveals that God's answers to prayers will be granted "in proportion to your belief." One could argue that with this stipulation Jude was declaring his role as a broker of lost causes to the entire world, announcing that hope without doubt will succeed. Second, many commentators have noted that Jude's words on Christ's descent into hell and ascension into heaven are almost a verbatim foreshadowing of the Apostles' Creed, which, it is believed, the apostles composed as a statement of their doctrine before leaving to preach the gospel over the earth. The Creed was handed down orally from the first century—when Jude spoke to Abgar—and not written down until much later, but the continuity survived.

As late as the middle of the nineteenth century, prominent English and European scholars attested to the authenticity of the Edessa archival tradition. The British Museum acquired priceless and sizable caches of manuscripts from the Nitrian monastery in the deserts of Lower Egypt between 1841 and 1847, many of them believed to be the same Syriac manuscripts that Eusebius had consulted. Although Dr. W. Cureton, the British scholar who studied the Syriac documents for years, died shortly before their publication, a colleague wrote in the preface: "He [Cureton] was himself firmly persuaded of the genuineness of the Epistles attributed to Abgar, King of Edessa, and our Lord."

Eusebius himself says that he is drawing from an account of early Christianity that had been translated into Greek from the Aramaic "archives of Edessa which was at that time ruled by its own kings." Indeed, the detailed *Doctrine of Addai* (400 A.D.)—a document written in Syriac, a late dialect of Aramaic, and tracing the origins of Christianity in Edessa—was taken from her archives and still survives. It concludes that the story of Abgar's conversion is probably true, or at least plausible in its essentials, despite admittedly nonhistorical embellishments made by imaginative later writers.

Although it does not appear in Eusebius, an additional sentence, believed to have been either copied from the archives or added later as an embellishment—is cited by several fifth-century writers, including St. Augustine, and also appears in the *Doctrine of Addai.* It asserts that the letter conferred immunity on Edessa: "The town in which ye shall be blessed, and the enemy shall not prevail against it forever." So, whenever the Persians tried to storm the wall, the letter of Jesus was held aloft to work its miraculous powers and repulse the enemy.

While some modern scholars have cast doubt on the various sources of Jude lore, it is significant that the learned J. B. Segal gives credence to the reliability of the city's archives, even though he has reservations about the legend of Jude, "the apostle Addai" as he is often known in ancient texts. He doubts the Jesus letter's authenticity, especially given Eusebius's distance from the event, and he points out that among scholars a common rebuttal to the tradition is that Abgar V ("the Black") of the Jude legend—who reigned in the early first century—is the wrong Abgar. Instead, they contend, it is Abgar VIII ("the Great"), ruling from 177–212 A.D.—long after Jude's death—who favored Christianity, and, if only for reasons of state, would have been more likely to adopt Christianity. This observation hints at the possibility that Addai was a man who may have lived much later than the apostle Jude. Any historical certainty is precluded by the confusion of names—Addai, Thaddeus, Judas, Thomas—the profusion of languages and dialects, and the differences of belief between the Roman Catholic and Eastern Orthodox traditions.

Segal concludes: "When this has been said, an explanation is still required for the choice of Edessa as the scene of the Christian acts of healing which are a central feature of the Abgar-Addai story."

Over the centuries, even Catholic scholars have challenged the Jesus letter's claims to authenticity, prompting a decree issued by Pope Gelasius in 494 A.D. This "Gelasian Decree" sought to establish which writings were inspired Scripture. Without denouncing belief in the Jesus letter as heretical, the pope omitted it from the canon, along with many far more obviously absurd texts—including one in which Jesus saves Joseph's reputation as a carpenter by miraculously stretching to adequate size a piece of furniture made too small. Over the years, the credibility of the Jesus letter suffered from association with such examples of pious moonshine. Nevertheless the popularity of the letter went undiminished, and in fact spread farther. Amid the countless additions and lacunae, infuriating inconsistencies, and paradoxes, there is an astonishing persistence to the Abgar story: something extraordinary happened here in the first century.

THURSDAY, OCTOBER 5, 1995

"I believe in miracles," says the pensive Turk. "If there are no miracles, such great legends would not last for two thousand years."

Nasi Ipek is looking out at the world through the open door of his bookshop. His angular face, wavy salt-and-pepper hair, and neat mustache contrast elegantly with a bold blue-and-white-striped shirt under a very Western navy blazer. An Anatolian Oleg Cassini. He was born in Urfa sixty-five years ago, "but my heart is twenty-eight."

A journalist and newspaper publisher, Mr. Ipek is a man of books. Miracles and legends are his specialty. He is living proof that the legend still bewitches Muslims. To him, King Abgar indeed put the Mandylion in the well of the Great Mosque, once known as the Red Church. He exudes the confidence of a man who has read the countless well-worn books lining the walls and floors of his shop.

"Even today," he says, "people believe that the water in the Red Church well will cure their blindness. Maybe they don't know about Jude, but they know about the Mandylion and Christ.

"When I was in elementary school, glaucoma and blindness were common, so students were brought to the well to wash their faces—and it worked. A cure did not come in two days, but eventually they could see.

"Many in the Syriac-Christian community in Mardin came here to heal their illnesses. There was a group of people, Turkish Muslims from around Mount Ararat, asking about the Mandylion. [Jude is believed to have preached there.]

"I am opposed to false legends, and if my people—the people of Urfa—believed this legend for two thousand years, then it is believable. We know Jude came to Urfa."

He pauses to sip the dark tea steaming from a dainty glass. Fingering his well-worn worry beads, he speaks of his belief in the prophets and in the miracles described in the Bible, in the Koran, especially those in "the crowded history of Urfa." He says he accepts and respects the stories of the twelve apostles and of Moses leaving Egypt and parting the Red Sea, adding that the prophet Aaron, who gave Moses the staff he used to part the sea, lived near Urfa.

He then tells a story told to him by an Muslim friend: "In 1948 or '49 there were articles in Italian newspapers about how the apostles brought the bones of Christ to Edessa after his death. It is they who built the church that is now the Grand Mosque. Underground there is a mausoleum. There were efforts to research it, to get money for excavation, but the pope stopped it, because if they found the bones of Christ in Urfa, it would be a bad thing for the Christian world. Urfa would be more important than Rome. That man who told me the story said that he believed in a relationship between Muslims and Christians, so he appealed to Ankara and wrote letters to parliament. The response simply said that the matter was closed. Anyway, now a road has been built over the site."

Even for veteran legend-seekers, this one strains credulity beyond the breaking point, but it is just tantalizing enough to imagine, if only for a second, the colossal implications of such a story, and the bold ingenuity of one who would initiate it. A sip of tea may get us back on Jude.

As though reading my mind, Mr. Ipek turns his attention to the Jews of Urfa—after all, Jude was a Jew. The last Jews, he says, relatives in fact of the great Israeli general Moshe Dayan, left in 1944. He recalls that one of his school friends came from a family that converted to Islam, but not for long. Their throats were cut—by whom he didn't say. His anecdotes only reinforce the continuity of the Jewish thread that winds through Edessa's history. A synagogue stood in the city's center, and another in front of the old cathedral. To the east, in Adiabene, the ruling family adopted Judaism in the first century A.D. Nisibis had the largest Jewish population in the region. Most important, it was to here in northern Mesopotamia that Jews fled in times of persecution. Like so many of his brethren, Addai-Jude may have sought refuge to the northeast, crossing the Jordan at Pella, just below the Sea of Galilee, and then making his way along the caravan route to Damascus and, beyond that, Edessa. All three religions were linked by the Old Silk Road. Christianity, however, advanced fastest in the places where Jews were firmly established, for Christians and Jews were alike in two respects: they formed a united front against the dominant pagans, and they possessed a deep knowledge of the Old Testament—the only testament in that springtime of Christianity.

Accordingly, Jude employed a practical strategy in his mission, not only targeting the nobles and royal family of Edessa, the pagan religious leaders, and just plain common folk, but especially Jews "skilled in the law and prophets, who traded in silks," as described in the *Doctrine of Addai*. As a Jew in Edessa, Jude's God was the God of Abraham and Isaac, not the God of imperial Rome and the still unformulated Hellenistic-Christian tradition.

The Jewishness of this Christian saint, a Hebrew family man of his time, is dramatically recorded by Eusebius in an anecdote referred to earlier that centers on two of Jude's grandsons, Zoker and James, who were hauled before the Emperor Domitian because of their connection to the House of David. It is a rare, if not unique, allusion to descendants of any of the apostles. The strong affinity to one's family is paramount with Jude, epitomizing a sense of tradition unending, of personal devotion, and, in this story, of continuous persecution.

Eusebius tells us that during the despotic reign of the emperor Domitian, from 81 to 96 A.D., an order went out to put to death all who were of David's line. Jude's grandsons were singled out for interrogation and possible execution. A group of "heretics," Eusebius writes, let it be known that Jude's descendants were not only of David's line, but kin to Christ Himself. He then quotes Hegesippus:

"These were informed against as being of David's line, and brought by the evocatus before Domitian Caesar, who was as afraid of the advent of Christ as Herod had been. Domitian asked them whether they were descended from David, and they admitted it. Then he asked them what property they owned and what funds they had at their disposal. They replied that they had only £1,500 [9,000 denarii] between them, half belonging to each; this, they said, was not available in cash, but was the estimated value of only twenty-five acres of land, from which they raised the money to pay their taxes and the wherewithal to support themselves by their own toil."

Eusebius picks up the story, relating how Jude's grandsons showed their callused hands to the emperor as proof of the hard labor they long endured. When asked about Christ's kingdom, they replied that it was not of this world. Domitian, writes Eusebius, finding no fault, let the men go.

The story rings with the kind of spiritual courage that marked the crossroads of ancient Judaism and Christianity. Curiously, and perhaps shrewdly, under the Edessan monarchy the conversion to Christianity did not cast down all the idols of the pagan past. People still worshiped the planets, drawings of which appeared on the walls of tombs and in literature. A crescent moon is depicted on Abgar's crown, in mosaics, and on Edessa's coins. A great pagan altar stood below the Citadel mount, the only one to survive the zeal of the converted chief priests who, as a sign of their joyful submission to the Word newly brought by Addai, cast down the other altars on which they had sacrificed to their gods. Yet even the pagans who partook of the region's amazingly complex cults possessed some sense of the primacy of one dominant god that made itself felt among the shifting pantheons. Indeed, the idea of a single god, a monotheistic system of belief, had already made inroads into northern Mesopotamia during the early centuries of Christianity.

After taking leave of the courtly Mr. Ipek, Mustapha and I weigh what we have heard. Allowing for small variances, it is

clear that Jude set off a string of indelible events with the introduction of the Mandylion. The overriding point is that many of
Jude's descendants risked all to preserve a piece of cloth, the
talisman—the palladium at the epicenter of the legend that has
baffled even the most skeptical since Jude first appeared in the
desert of Mesopotamia: a portrait of Christ with miraculous
powers.

The tale of this portrait is more widespread in the United
States than that of the correspondence between Jesus and
Abgar, probably because it is more easily reproduced. Jude is
conventionally depicted in American Catholic iconography
with an oval image of Christ on his chest, or held in one hand,
no doubt an echo of the Mandylion, or handkerchief, that
found its way to Edessa. How it traveled so far varies with the
authors and tellers of the legend.

The *Doctrine of Addai* says that Abgar's messenger, Ananias,
carried the king's letter to Jerusalem and painted a portrait of
Jesus, which he gave to Abgar on his return to Edessa. The
king installed it in his palace, and Jude arrived well after the
king had done this.

Later versions of the *Acts of Thaddeus*—the earliest account
(third century) in which an image of Christ in the possession of
Abgar is attributed to a miraculous origin—claim that, like the
letter, the painting had protective powers. Some even believed
that Jesus painted the picture Himself, or that the Master
wiped His face on a handkerchief and gave it to Abgar's messenger. Most modern accounts say that after the Ascension,
Jude himself brought the holy cloth to Edessa, and that it was
by this gift that the king was cured of his leprosy.

After Abgar V's death, his son, Manu V, reverted to paganism and launched a reign of terror against Christians. According to the tenth-century *Story of the Image of Edessa,* this
persecution forced the Christians to hide the sacred cloth—and

perhaps a copy of it that Abgar had mounted on the Kappe gate in the west—in a space where some believe it remained until the sixth century. Such a concealment in a high six-foot-thick wall encompassing the city would have protected it from the terrible floods. So important was the portrait to Edessan life, some traditions say, there were three "true" copies of it *and* the letter within the city. It may well be that the mysterious portrait of Jesus had replaced His letter as Edessa's unique symbol.

In the years after Abgar's reception of the Mandylion, accounts of its location and ultimate destiny vary greatly. However, in 544 A.D., a Persian king's abortive siege of Edessa—wherein the attackers tried to scale the Citadel mount by night—was believed to have been repulsed by the power of the sacred portrait. Writing fifty-two years later, the chronicler Evagrius reports that when all seemed lost, the bishop of Edessa had a vision in which he was instructed to find the portrait hidden between some tiles in the city wall. He did, and when the Edessans sprinkled water on the portrait and cast the water toward the enemy, his siege works were consumed by fire. Even today a sense of the protective power of holy objects pervades the city, manifesting itself in the citizens' practice of mounting tiles above their doorways to proclaim their Islamic faith and the date of their last Haj, a pilgrimage to Mecca.

For many, the miraculous portrait "not made by human hands"—a phrase that first appeared in 569 A.D.—often passed as a substitute for the letter. Indeed, some modern writers have suggested that the cloth of Edessa was really the larger shroud of Turin folded up, or "doubled in four," so that only Jesus' head was visible.

The Mandylion and its protective powers lured the faithful and the desperate to Edessa for four centuries, over which time it played a central role in the seemingly endless epoch of frontier war. Armies at the gates threatened to invade unless Edessa surrendered the famous relic. But the Edessans—Christian and Muslim alike—held on. "If you take the portrait they will sell their children and themselves rather than allow it to be removed," a disloyal Edessan advised the tax collector.

In the early ninth century, in a letter to Emperor Theophilus, three Melchite (Eastern 'Christian) patriarchs made a list of the icons "not made with human hands" that had brought forth miracles, and the Mandylion topped the list. A century later, Edessa's walls trembled again amidst the maelstrom of war. Menaced by crusading hosts seeking the Mandylion and a Muslim sovereign in Baghdad anxious to swap a mere Christian holy object for the liberty of True Believers in captivity, the Edessans traded the object whose safekeeping had set their city apart from all others.

In exchange for many Muslims in Byzantine hands and a mass of earthly treasure—twelve thousand pieces of silver—the city yielded the object closest to its soul. As the Christian warriors bore the Savior's face reverently back to Constantinople, a great storm shook Edessa: God Himself, whispered the terrified citizenry, was manifesting His anger at their breach of trust. After that moment of surrender, the guilty Edessans did not have to wait long for retribution: Byzantine invasions, marauding Muslim warlords, and cruel famine struck their city, each successive blow following fast upon the breaking of faith. Edessa had begun its slow decline from one of the famed and glorious cities of three great faiths into the dusty backwater that it remains—from which fate, no doubt, GAP will save it.

Meanwhile, the Eastern relics, including the Mandylion, reached Constantinople on August 15, 944 A.D., and were installed in the Church of St. Sophia "for the glory of the faithful, for the safety of the Emperors, for the preservation of the entire city and of the way of life of the Christian empire."

An interesting detail emerges in "The Story of the Image of Edessa," a special feast-day sermon commissioned by Emperor Constantine VII and delivered before the Byzantine court in the Church of the Holy Wisdom (today the Great Mosque) to mark the first anniversary of the Mandylion's arrival. This sermon records the basic outlines of the main legend, but with tantalizing additions:

> "When he [Jude] was about to appear before him [Abgar], he placed the portrait on his own forehead like a sign and so entered. Abgar saw him coming in from a distance, and thought he saw a light shining from his face which no eye could stand. . . . Abgar was dumbfounded by the unbearable glow . . . and as though forgetting the ailment he had and the long paralysis of his legs, he at once got up from his bed and compelled himself to run."

Is it coincidence, or too eager embellishment, that led Eusebius seven hundred years earlier to describe a brilliant "vision" emanating from the face of Thaddeus? Was the light that dazzled Abgar really a tongue of fire, the gift that Jude and the eleven other apostles received in the upper room after the Ascension of Christ, the gift of tongues that gave them the power to speak and understand all the languages of the world?

The last historical trace of the Mandylion—one that finds some agreement among scholars—is its residence in Constantinople. Presumably, the sacred cloth remained there until the sacking of the Byzantine capital in 1204. Drained and shrunken, the Holy Eastern Empire fell to the contemptuous West, a foretaste of its extinction at the hands of Islam two and a half centuries later, its treasures scattered, smuggled, and plundered. Here, the Mandylion disappears from history.

Probably the only Christian artifacts left in the city are on display at Urfa's archaeological museum. The half-dozen or so statues of saints (Jude is not among them) dating from the 1700s were found in an old church in the eastern part of the city in the 1960s. The museum's front porch is laid with an extraordinary array of mosaics, amazingly preserved images—a lion, a bull, a ram, a veiled women—of pre-Christian life in Edessa.

Adnan Misir, director general of the museum, explains some of Urfa's traditions over the deafening and discouraging roar of digging and drilling nearby. The Abgar mosaic, he says, dates from the third century A.D. Workmen building a new museum over an ancient cemetery behind the old one found it at the bottom of a burial cave. It was reburied where they had unearthed it, in an unmarked patch of sloping dust. Only one man in Turkey knows how to raise it, says Mr. Misir, and he has been working for two years on a special device to do so.

The noise of drilling borders on unbearable, and Mr. Misir, a bull of a man with a raw face, tolerates my questions, although the noise clearly irritates him, too. "We walked all around the old caves in 1978 and never saw the cave with the Jesus letter inscription," he says. "It's gone. We have tried to excavate everything underneath without losing the historical shape of the city. There are irrigation channels, the houses of the Harran culture, all kinds of historical ruins underneath the city. But when we go and ask permission to excavate, they say we cannot do it. It's all political. We are losing the old city."

Later, I ask Mustapha about Mr. Misir's frustration.

"Mr. Misir is tired," he replies. It is clear that the disappointed museum director fought long to preserve the Urfa of uncountable centuries—but now even he must acknowledge defeat.

As though to hammer home the point, literally and figuratively, the grinding and pounding grow louder as the day wanes, turning the swirling dust to red in the angled sunlight. Dust, dust, dust, invading eyes, nose, mouth, shoes. Tired and thirsty, I feel at one with the many who each century braved the dust of the desert to allay their thirst in Edessa, to dress their wounds, to find the something or someone driving them to this forgotten place.

Back in my room at the guest house, I tune in Channel 2 television. Although I cannot make out the Turkish words, there is no mistaking the omnipresent station logo: TNT-GAP. Reading it as the mythic trademark of a new age, archaeologists still unborn may one day proclaim it an inscription of highest simple faith, like IHS or JHVH. The faith is intense enough right now. We shall see how long it endures.

A mild autumn wind rises from the direction of the Jude church, brushes the shutters outside my window and, muted, like soft laughter, ripples into the night and vanishes.

FRIDAY, OCTOBER 6, 1995

This is the Muslim Holy Day of the week. By noon all have rushed to pray at the mosques. Shops close. Traffic is nonexistent and traffic lights (the few there are) operate only during the evening rush hour, sporadically the rest of the time. The covered bazaar is closed, too, usually a serpentine parade of swarthy men smoking pungent cigarettes as they offer handmade saddlebags, woven silk, and polished brass. A thorough search for any souvenir of a Christian past has turned up nothing.

Professor Kürkçüoğlu arrives in his bush jacket and climbing shoes, ready to escort me on a tour of historical sites. At the Red Church he explains that most of the old columns have been stored underground to protect them. Ignoring the roar of motor scooters threatening to drown him out, he continues, "Addai's bones are believed to be underground. During an excavation in 1979 they found catacombs, graves, and other ruins, but they were covered again. No one could prove the bones belonged to Addai because they couldn't look inside the catacombs. To go further would have meant destroying the mosque."

His words assuage my lingering anxiety about Mr. Ipek's friend who contended that the pope had intervened so that Urfa wouldn't get credit as the greatest of Christian shrines. It is difficult to imagine that churches—perhaps as many as three hundred—once gave Edessa its architectural character and made it a literary and intellectual center of Syriac culture, with its own theological school. At the former site of the Armenian Church of the Twelve Apostles, the professor explains that every community and religion constructed an altar or church, synagogue, or mosque on the place he wished to worship.

"There is room on the planet for all," says the professor, warming to the range of God's possibilities.

Huge rocks and boulders left over from the city's old walls cover the ground, and the once-revered west gate through which the Mandylion entered Edessa and the small twelfth-century guard house beside it—the one Segal saw some thirty years ago—are no longer discernible in these piles of stone left behind by force of man or raging river. As we scramble around caves, mosques, wells, a dank old prison, and what is left of the city gates, I can't help but think of the inimitable Egeria, the chatty pilgrim-nun who pithily recorded the wonders of Edessa in her diary. Named after a goddess associated with water, Egeria proved an inquisitive and loquacious tourist, enthusiastic in her observations, energetic in setting down her impressions of Edessa in 380 A.D.

She undertook this arduous journey in order to visit the shrine of St. Thomas, the apostle who sent Jude on his mission and is at times confused with Jude. Without mentioning Jude by name, she writes of seeing documents regarding the King Abgar episode—probably the same ones Eusebius had consulted sixty years earlier.

Egeria's escort, the bishop of Edessa, like my guide Professor Kürkçüoğlu, proved a gracious and learned soul as he guided her around the principal holy places. "My daughter, I can see what a long journey this is on which your faith has brought you—right from the other end of the earth," she reports him as saying. "So now, please let us show you all the places Christians should visit here."

Like so many tourists, Egeria decided there was so much to see that she planned "a three-day stop" in Edessa, not only visiting churches, monasteries, and martyrs' shrines, but monks in their cave cells outside the city. She saw the pools of fish, too, which she described as "a great river of silver," and Abgar's palace with its elegant statues of the king.

> "[The bishop] showed me the large statue which, as they said, was a very close likeness, made of marble of such lustre that it might have been of pearl. From the features of king Abgar it was truly seen that this man was greatly wise and dignified."

Other vestiges of Abgar and Jude's time still survived in Egeria's day, supposedly near the west gate of the city. The cemeteries lay outside the clay walls, but, she observes, no corpse was ever taken out through the gate by which the letter of Jesus had arrived. The bishop talked with her about the correspondence between Abgar and Jesus, adding that not long after the arrival of the letter a Persian force had been turned away from the city as King Abgar brandished the letter in its face. Then—in one more example of Edessa's critical dependence on water—the Persians diverted a mountain stream from the city into their camp. But immediately, the springs we know today miraculously burst forth, and the diverted channel dried up. In fear and thirst, the Persians fell back.

A fanciful tale, perhaps, but a margin of error should be allowed for the fact that Egeria spoke Latin and probably had a guide who spoke Syriac and Greek. The important point, however, is that the Edessans believed that these things had happened, and their faith in these long-told tales—in which Jude played a key role—spread from east to west and is alive today. Consider that when the bishop offered Egeria copies of the Jesus-Abgar correspondence as a souvenir of her trip, Egeria was able to tell him that she already had a copy back in Spain!

> "Although I had copies of them at home, I was clearly very pleased to accept them from him in case the copy which had reached us at home happened to be incomplete; for the copy I received was certainly more extensive. If Jesus Christ Our Lord wills it and I return home, you, ladies dear to me, will read them."

When the time comes to bid the professor farewell, he realizes that I had not been prepared for the total absence of anything Christian still standing in Urfa. With great delicacy he asks how I feel about the churches being reworked into mosques.

"It is practical," I assure him. "History is dynamic and we must recognize its ebb and flow."

Smiling, perhaps with relief, he agrees.

It the few hours left before dark, as we stand atop the great fortress of the Citadel, it is easy to imagine the ferocity of the battles waged to conquer Edessa. A moat carved from the gray rock surrounds three sides of the castle, while the north—the fabled spot from which Nimrod cast Abraham into the fire—is a steep rock face. Though a massive ruin, a repository of tales the world has long forgot, this forbidding pile still commands the city in all its weathered majesty. Feeling the smooth stone of the two Roman pillars, I am sadly aware that this worn marble and the hill are all that visibly remain of Edessa's old glory. A Syriac inscription on the eastern pillar reads:

> "I am Ethusa, son of the sun;
> I have erected these columns and the
> statue in the name of Queen Shalmath,
> the daughter of King Mano."

King Abgar, through his descendants, still speaks to us from the center of his ancient kingdom. He built his winter palace here on the Citadel, and the nobles erected their great houses and tombs on the high ground to the east. But most intriguing, this is where Abgar himself instructed his subjects to assemble—in Beth Tabara ("the wide space of the house of 'Awida son of 'Abednahad'")—to hear "the Apostle Addai"—Jude—preach a new doctrine.

From this high view where the city turns to amber in the fading afternoon sun, I am tempted to picture him not as a martyr savaged by the blows of Persians in some nameless desert, but as a man who died here peacefully. The *Doctrine of Addai* said it first: that after ten or eleven years of preaching, converting, and even building a church, "Addaeus" was stricken by disease and died in Edessa on Thursday, May 14, of an unspecified year. The whole city was in great mourning, especially King Abgar:

> "And in the sadness of his soul he despised and laid aside the magnificence of his kingly state on that day, and with tears mingled with moans he bewailed him with all men. . . . And with great and surpassing pomp he bore him, and buried him like one

of the princes when he dies; and he laid him in a grand sepulchre adorned with sculpture wrought by the fingers—and that in which were laid those of the house of Ariu, the ancestors of Abgar the king: there he laid him sorrowfully, with sadness and great distress. . . . And all the people of the church . . . celebrated the commemoration of his death from year to year."

SATURDAY, OCTOBER 7

Before departing at 3 A.M. the next day, I stop under a full yellow moon to pick up old stones—for remembrance, and perhaps some kind of protection—at Jude's Church. Taking one last look at the street his steps may well have worn two weary millennia ago, I realize that he has proven to be a figure out of the ancient pagan world, still geographically present in this city, yet never revealing his individuality, veiling his face as he maintains intimacy of contact. When confronting the Jude paradox, the scholar and the pilgrim must doubt every resemblance, for he is remembered in a place where Christianity has been annihilated, but not his personal religious presence. As an embodiment of the discreet power we call luck, he is a figure of force so indirect as to seem unreal until it acts. As usual, Jude has done his work here through intermediaries—a doctor, a friend, a professor, a journalist. Someone or something else is always the agent. There are no apparitions, no flourishes to announce him. After all, he just walked in on Abgar.

St. Jerome said long ago that on pilgrimages, it isn't *where* one goes that counts, it is the frame of mind in which one goes. Driving to Adana, past the Asurus mountains and Crusader castles, I suspect that Jude himself drew me here from the beginning, that the journey is more summons than pilgrimage.

Truly, the weight of history supports Edessa's claim to blessedness, and broadly hints at history's riches beneath Urfa now being lost so rapidly and irreversibly to the ages. But Jude, outside of time, present in his material absence remains, as constant and renewing as the city's precious water. His legacy took root not in an airless monastery, a splendid cathedral, or the fancies of the superstitious, but here, written in the minutes following the cure of Abgar. Having destroyed the statue of a Greek god in front of the city gates, the king replaced it with a likeness of Jesus Christ and ordered these prophetic and lasting words to be inscribed in gold:

"Christ the God, he who hopes in Thee is never disappointed."

Long after the statue was smashed and the gold looted, the message on Jude's calling card endures for all time: Hope.

ROME

". . . And, behold, you were within me,
and I out of myself, and there I searched for you."

St. Augustine, *Confessions*

ROMANS AND ARABS ALIKE LOVE THE SOUND OF rushing water; it is so here, just as in Edessa. That cadence, so inescapable to any lasting sense of a city that calls itself eternal, echoes along the cool, shaded streets jumbled between the Forum and Via del Tritone. The sound lures me through a maze of dim alleys that opens abruptly into a mellow world of sunlight and tumbling streams. As my eyes adjust to the brightness, I am pleasantly jolted by the sight of the Trevi fountain, that baroque staple of the tourist industry, rising up like a quaint but well-worn memory, cloudy with coins. It is an unplanned detour on the long journey toward Jude, but not the first time this apostle of the church has been sidelined by pagan gods, marbled though these may be.

Japanese tourists swarm over the ancient square, their Nikons busily immortalizing sullen Italian young men swathed in black leather. A Benetton store has taken the place of the square's welcoming old cafe; a motorcycle roars down to the water's edge. The anti-uniform of a new world disorder—baseball hats, baggy shorts, and T-shirts—has thoroughly displaced any formal acknowledgment of the world's most celebrated tailor. Just as the GAP hydroelectric project is reconfiguring ancient Edessa, the homogenized mass culture of the global village chips away at Rome's weathered face. It is, once more, a changed city, but perhaps more profoundly so by intense commerce than by its many conquerors. Still spontaneous and unpredictable, but as a mass marketer of her innumerable pasts, Rome continues to crumble under her very power to lure the world to her door.

Jude's material remains exist here, but in the ten days of my visit, finding any revealing traces of him has proved as daunting a task as it was in Edessa. The weight of church bureaucracy, so utterly Roman with its presiding canon lawyers, theologians, layers of prelates, and acolytes of every stripe, is centralized and anchored. Yet Jude Thaddeus, the non-Roman anti-institutionalist, is ever-expanding, continuing to assert himself *out there*—on the edge, pushing that envelope toward new horizons way beyond that of the city where his "official" presence rests.

His bones lie only a walk away, and yet, like Rome itself, the martyred holy man has been profoundly affected by foreign influence. Caught in the vortex of nations held together by the microchips of instant communication, Jude has ceased being just a Catholic devotion. As the classical outrider, he has overleaped the walls of Catholicism, while Rome, its institutional center, relies on a bedrock of ecclesiastical tradition to prove its case in a world leery of most traditions. Surely a Polish pope did not emerge at random as the world's disorder beat at the Vatican's well-sealed doors. Not a moment too soon does John Paul II arrive with his Master's—and Jude's—message of hope: "It is very important to cross the threshold of hope, not to stop before it, but to let oneself be led." Here—I thought on my arrival—surely stands the gateway to Jude's territory.

This famously obscure saint and the Roman Church are changing parts of the modern age. Jude gains as the guerrilla saint of the unfolding age, while Rome struggles to hold the line. As the ultimate solo operator, he seems an unusual foil to the proclamation that once rang round the world: *"Roma locuta est. Causa finita est."* (Rome has spoken. The case is closed.) Those voices have fallen silent now, and more personal solutions are required. Smiling behind the curtain that has been his garment since gospel days, Jude awaits his next opportunity.

Tracking him here, where I have always felt a strong ancestral connection, has brought me one small step closer to the elusive saint. As a tourist or reporter on assignment, I never lost the feeling of having access to an ancient secret in this great city. This time, I thought, the quarry will have to reveal himself sooner or later. Or so it seemed. The yellow autumn sky is turning darker now, on this the eve of my departure. St. Jerome has proved right about pilgrimages: it is not the destination that counts but the frame of mind in which one goes. That's how it began just ten days ago.

THURSDAY, OCTOBER 26, 1995

The Franciscan convent—a *pensione,* really, with space for pilgrims—was once an orphanage. During World War II a bomb smashed through into the cellar, but fortunately—or miraculously—it did not explode. The building stands at the peak of Via Monte del Gallo, its ochre walls and white marble steps imparting the look of a fine villa. From the top of the stairs to the front entrance, you can see the majestic dome of St. Peter's reaching into a clear French-blue sky. The sight reminds me of my last trip to Rome, to cover an unshaven wacko, backed by the Bulgarians, who shot down the pope in the shadow of the basilica.

Sister Mary Grace answers the door; she is warm, soft-spoken, totally without self-preoccupation.

"Ah, welcome," she says. There is an air of distraction about her, as though I am interrupting some interior conversation.

She sees me first, my eyes having focused well above her diminutive height. She is chubby, with dimples and a disconcerting angelic presence. Tufts of gray hair peek out from beneath a white-trimmed black veil falling over her traditional brown Franciscan habit. A simple silver crucifix hangs from a long chain. She wears the look of one accustomed to accommodating others in the service of God.

"You must be tired. Come, I'll show you how the keys work. One for your room, the other for the front door. We lock it at eleven every night."

Then, perhaps anticipating a compliment on her smooth and Americanized English, she adds, "I lived in the states for awhile. I liked it."

Soon, another tiny Franciscan, Sister Placida, appears. Dark and a bit snaggle-toothed, she makes a perfect foil to Sister Mary Grace's northern composure and fair skin.

"Nice to meet you," she says, making two syllables of "nice." She wears that expression of perpetual wonder, so common to the rare and truly holy. No taller than Sister Mary Grace and, like her, more or less in her sixties, she limps badly but silently from years of unrelenting work. Retiring she is not. Her Sicilian verve and large black eyes hooded by fierce eyebrows could knock Lucifer himself back to his sulfurous pit. One day a young male guest threw open the door with a bang. Sister Placida was on her feet in a flash, "You break-a my door, I break-a your face."

On my arrival, she is padding around the church, which is attached to the convent through a long dark hallway A young priest celebrates mass, his blue jeans and sneakers barely hidden under ornate green vestments. A quick inspection after the service turns up no Jude statues, but as I climb the stairs to my room, Sr. Grace appears to say that the butcher's wife is very much devoted to St. Jude and prays for her son to find a job and her husband to stay in good health. It's a start.

The small terrace fronting my room glows full of light. I step out, inhale the swaying pines below, and watch the sun setting beyond a skyline of pink layers. No matter how many times you have passed through its gates, the city is pure theater, a fabulous complex built to impress. But real dramas took place here long before they inspired dramatic performances: Caesar died in the Senate house, on real knives, a mile away, before he died for Shakespeare's purposes; and Peter's body took the Roman nails before—indeed, so that—his successors could parade around surrounded by dour Swiss mercenaries in Michelangelo uniforms. The drama created the stage set, not the stage set the drama. Meanwhile, on this evening, I imagine Jude, behind the scenes, almost vulgarly tugging at my elbow to follow an unseen course. The Roman sky darkens, and I fall into a deep sleep.

FRIDAY, OCTOBER 27

The autumn morning is chill, but languid summer air returns as the sun gains. The sound of bells courses through the neighborhood, from convents, churches, and, of course, St. Peter's. This is Rome's background music, marking the ages, touching a deep yearning in the hearts of all, believers and atheists, those who hope and those who despair. Though Rome lies on the bottom of a river valley, like Washington, D.C., it is a city of hills. Except for Via della Concilazione, Mussolini's showy parade route, you are always in a corner here, always going up or down, with a view that is behind you and sealed off. It is, finally, a city of mystery in a way logical Manhattan and wide-open Washington are not. All roads may lead to Rome, but they disappear into nooks and crannies, the kind where Jude flourishes. Secrets, assignations, and indiscretions have found a welcome niche in this city, seeping into its very foundation, providing cover for those who wish to remain obscure.

Vatican Square is only a twenty-minute walk down the slopes of Monte del Gallo to a little grotto of the Virgin, around the railroad station, through two of the 284 columns raised by Bernini to form the right arm of the square's embrace, and into the enormous piazza. The twelve apostles form a straight stone line across the facade. Which one is Jude? A priest at the information table just inside the entrance tells me, with the faintest trace of annoyance, that "Jude's at the end of the line, the far right." I run out to check, and there he is, off by himself, on the edge as usual, a giant ornate clock separating him from his eleven brethren.

I enter the cavernous basilica, which, like Jude himself, has been remodeled and reformed by layers of history's glorious and inglorious chapters. Since Constantine the Great undertook its construction in the fourth century, the great church has been subject to a series of marbled, gilded, and bronzed overhauls. The most complete renovation, begun in 1605, superimposed a Roman cross over the original Greek cross. Suddenly it strikes me that in all the times I've been to St. Peter's, only once before have I thought of Jude, on a winter evening years ago. Having just fired off a story for the *CBS Evening News* on still one more Roman strike, I taxied to the Vatican and found myself praying to, or at least thinking about, Jude. Why at that particular time I sought Jude I cannot remember; and, equally strange, it did not occur to me that his last earthly traces lay beneath the worn Roman stone within a few feet of where I knelt in a center pew.

Looking at Jude in the historical record, especially in the liturgy, we find that from time to time devotion to him seems to vanish for long stretches, and then inexplicably reappears. His mysterious death in the first century is the last we hear of him until he surfaces in church liturgy more than a half-dozen centuries later. The earliest extant text of the Roman canon (Eucharistic Prayer) that includes St. Jude, or "Thaddeus," in the commemoration of saints, began to appear in the various later editions of the *Gregorian Sacramentary* and the *Gelasian Sacramentary* from 800 A.D. through the ninth century. These prayers were prepared for use in the Carolingian liturgies of France and Germany. At about the same time, mass prayers for the Feasts of Sts. Simon and Jude on October 28 turned up in a liturgical book of the distinctive Ambrosian Rite of Milan (the *Sacramentary of Biasca*), which is known to have been influenced by the Carolingian liturgy of the Holy Roman Empire under the Emperor Charlemagne. If there is any one event around 800 A.D. that could explain the introduction of the new celebrations in honor of these two apostles, it would have to be the transferral—or "translation"—of some of the Jude relics (and those of other apostles) from Rome to Toulouse by the emperor, who received them as gifts from Pope Leo III after his coronation on Christmas Day. Considering the influence that Charlemagne and the liturgists who worked under him had on the subsequent history of the Western liturgy, it is reasonable to infer that this particular relic transfer at the outset of the emperor's reign may have acted as a catalyst for the composition of special mass prayers in honor of Sts. Simon and Jude. With an annual mass in their honor becoming the norm across medieval Europe, there was increased opportunity for these apostles to play a prominent role in the devotional life of the faithful.

Benedict the Canon, writing between 1140 and 1143, when the popularity of saints' cults was running high, reports the presence of Jude relics in Rome. In the *Roman Ordo XI,* a book on the liturgy, the learned theologian offers his eyewitness account of ceremonial Rome and provides what appears to be the earliest testimony to the presence of Simon and Jude relics in Rome, and *within* the old St. Peter's basilica. Benedict tells us that these altars were incensed during solemn night vigils:

> "And now the Pontiff incenses first the altar of Saint Leo; then with a procession advancing through the pontifical portico to Saint Gregory, he incenses first his altar, and the altar of Saint Sebastian, and the altar of Saint Tiburtius; then the two altars in the middle toward the crucifix, where from ancient fathers we have heard rest the Apostles Simon and Jude."

The endless procession of relics, true and otherwise, from east to west had been long and tortuous—looted by Crusaders, hidden by catechumens, traded for gold, burned out of hatred, proffered to kings, smuggled in lard, buried out of faith. Relics, in fact, have always possessed an innate magnetism for the faithful. St. Bernard of Clairvaux, a holy man of the twelfth century, was so devoted to Jude that he had a relic of the apostle brought to him from Jerusalem and buried with him upon his death. An early biography recounts:

> "In the very tomb a small box is placed upon his breast, in which the relics of blessed Thaddeus the Apostle are contained, sent to him the same year from Jerusalem. He had ordered them to be placed upon his body. . . ."

In that same century, Pope Innocent III related an unusual story in a letter to Octavian, bishop of Ostia, discussing the consecration of altars. A certain priest—"devout, as he is believed"—came to him to describe a vision he'd had of the Apostle Peter directing him to tell the pope that many altars "in my church," including Jude's, remained unconsecrated and must be consecrated by the Holy Father. When after two visions the priest did nothing, the displeased apostle struck him deaf.

Bitterly lamenting, the stricken priest begged forgiveness and fled to Pope Innocent. Although speculating that the tale could be a trick—that "in such a matter might not an angel of Satan have transformed himself into an angel of light?"—the Holy Father nevertheless concluded that it is better to believe than to doubt and ordered the consecration of six altars, including that of Simon and Jude. Apparently Jude had slipped enough minds so that even his own altar was once forgotten.

Indeed, much has been made of how "forgotten" Jude was, particularly before the eighteenth century, but a patchwork of far-flung historical references make it clear that devotion to him really never ceased. He did not evolve into a great institutional saint with an ordinary cultus, and he never acquired the kind of official and organized following that a saint of his weight, ancientry, and distinction would ordinarily require. However, the endless fragmentary and scattered historical references to him indicate a devotion so intense that at no time was he universally forgotten.

With all the rebuilding and reshuffling of the saintly hierarchy, the number of altars in St. Peter's basilica varied from one century to another. Jude's significance is underlined in the earliest records we have that delineate the tradition of visiting seven "privileged altars" in St. Peter's. These documents, dating from 1130 and preserved in the basilica's archives, list the altar of Sts. Simon and Jude as among those most revered. *Stations of Rome,* a fourteenth-century English commentary, poetically observes:

> "In that Munster [the church], men may find
> An hundred Altars, before and behind . . .
> Among the Altars, seven there be,
> More of grace and dignity . . ."

Among the hundred altars, Jude managed to make most of the top seven lists, sometimes ranking as high as number three, a solid indication of the impression he created among the hierarchy and the masses. He was never completely out of everyone's mind. Vivid accounts of these legions of the hopeful are respectfully recorded in *Ye Solace of Pilgrimes,* by John Capgrave, a book that pilgrims must have carried in their knapsacks as modern jet-setters do the latest Clancy novel. Writing in Middle English in 1450, Capgrave presents a picture of a Rome jammed with pilgrims obsessed with collecting indulgences and seeking the most important and interesting relics to be had. A head is better than a finger seems to have been the well-meaning but vulgar rule. This account, taken with many others, lists Jude's tomb in both the old and new basilicas as one of the "seven privileged altars." These altars changed from era to era, but were usually dedicated to the top heavenly hitters: for example, the Virgin and Sts. Gregory, Andrew, and Leo. Of course, the more relics available, the bigger the attraction for the crowds. Capgrave, an Augustinian monk, observed:

> "Seven altars be there of principal authority . . .
> Also in the Church of Saint Peter are Simon
> and Judas [Jude] lying above in the wall . . ."

He also took careful note of indulgences—the remission of temporal punishment due for sin. Anyone who visited any of eighty-eight particular altars on the saint's dedicated feast day, or during the octave (eight days) thereof, was granted an indulgence of twenty-eight years. And at the seven altars, a seven-year indulgence came with each visit.

Indulgences for those who came to Rome began in 1300, the first jubilee or holy year. During the jubilee of 1450, plenary remission of all sins was granted for penitents who stayed in Rome for at least fifteen days and visited every day the four churches of Sts. Peter, Paul, John Lateran, and Mary Major, or Mary the Greater. It came down to a brisk calculus: the more altars you visited, the less time you spent making up for your sins in the afterlife. It was not a worthless pursuit, especially in an age when public penance was often imposed.

A combination of hospitality and good marketing adjusted indulgences from time to time. For example, on the rare occasions when church authorities exhibited the Vernacle, or Veronica's Veil, the indulgences were meted out quite democratically: three thousand years for Romans, nine thousand for "other people," twelve thousand to those who crossed the sea to fulfill their holy purpose.

Tiberius Alpharanus, who indexed the basilica's relics in 1582, contributed a macabre, if possibly accurate, touch to the record by claiming that Jude's arms were no longer under his altar!

> "They are not present in the basilica now. And thus under the already said altar of Saints Simon and Jude the whole bodies of them were not preserved, if in fact the arms of them will have been inserted in other altars and from that place thereafter lost completely."

The seventeenth-century archivist Jacob Grimaldi writes that on October 1, 1605, the reliquary of the comradely saints was opened and their remains carried in procession and entombed after the singing of Vespers in the rebuilt basilica. Paul V granted indulgences to all those present.

I try to locate the original altar-chapel of Sts. Simon and Jude on a sketch of the old basilica: center aisle on the left, directly across from their fellow apostles Philip and James the Less. Not a trace. Just the portrait of a smiling Innocent VIII, the only holdover from the old basilica. I recheck my notes. Tiberius Alpharanus, who clucked about the dismantling of the saints' bodies in 1582, describes the old tomb in detail:

> "Toward the doors of the Basilica, between the seventeenth and eighteenth column thus far there still exists a most ancient altar of the holy Apostles Simon and Jude, in which their bodies rest; at which altar was erected a most elegant, very flowery chapel of most precious twisted columns, and enclosed in bronze columns and marble stones, stucco, adorned with pictures and emblems, and very many great lights graced with indulgences for honorably watching and keeping safe the Most Holy Sacrament of the Eucharist in that place."

Is this further testimony that Jude was drawing the crowds even then? In 1548, when Pope Paul III reconsecrated the altar, he granted a plenary indulgence to those who during the feasts of Corpus Christi and Sts. Simon and Jude, and their respective octaves, visited the Blessed Sacrament at their altars. This added inducement, plus the altar's central location, could only mean that Simon and Jude were still a main attraction in the Rome of the Renaissance popes.

I head southward and to the left, carefully studying an armful of guidebooks and historical notes. Without exception, all them state that the reliquary holding Jude's remains lies beneath a rather solemn picture of St. Peter being taken down from the cross and very near the actual spot where the prince of the apostles was crucified upside down. The basilica was, after all, created to mark the site of Peter's martyrdom, and the proximity of Jude's altar to Peter's was in itself a mark of profound regard.

The Altar of the Crucifixion of Peter is "so-named," declares one modern account, "because the mosaic reproduction of Guido Reni's painting *The Crucifixion of St. Peter* above it is dedicated to the martyred Apostles, Sts. Simon and Jude, whose relics are under the altar."

There is the picture of Peter, but again no trace of Jude. This is obviously not the right altar. I walk briskly around to the other side, and then the other, and then to another altar, and then down another aisle, until I realize that I am running amuck in the seat of Christendom—a whirling dervish, not unlike the troupe I had witnessed just a few weeks earlier in a country where Jude had made a quietly enduring impression two thousand years ago.

I am not a superstitious person, nor even one of great faith, but I cannot shake the feeling that an unseen hand is choreographing this quest. I am a pilgrim on a pilgrimage, but I am also a reporter on a story. If someone keeps dodging you, then he must have something to hide. Finding Jude—at least corporeally—is becoming a matter of professional pride.

I circle again and end up back in the left transept. Suddenly, there it is:

SS.
SIMON ET THADDEUS
APOSTOLI

The letters, shining in gold against a dark bronze plaque, are set in a series of three large concentric circles of gold, which form a grill. Behind the grill, the relics of St. Jude Thaddeus lie in an ancient sarcophagus brought out of the Constantinian mausoleum of St. Agnes. My mind flashes back to the cautionary words of an uncommonly spiritual Franciscan monk in New York. "Ah, Crusader naiveté," he'd sighed, when I told him of my determination to see the relics. "We know so little of St. Jude." Such intellectual distance from one so devout put me on guard. He was warning me that relics are not always reliable, especially in the case of someone as untrackable as Jude. Still, now that I have finally stumbled on the tomb, it is difficult to contain my excitement. I am about to learn just one of the many troubled and circuitous histories attached to the Vatican's incomparable treasury of art. For the picture, or mosaic—since almost all pictures in the basilica are mosaics even when they appear to be oils—above the reliquary does not depict St. Peter, as advertised. Instead, there, in the center of Jude's altar, staring into unfathomable space, is a likeness of St. Joseph, a work by Achille Funi, which, as I will later discover, usurped St. Peter's picture in 1963. In these years the broom of Vatican II swept out more than the church intended, and even the art collections did not survive intact the campaign for change. The well-loved John XXIII, a perfect personality for the flower-power decade, had declared Joseph to be "patron of the universal church." In some scholarly accounts, even in tourist guidebooks, that is exactly what the altar is called—and not the altar of Simon and Jude.

An oval mosaic of Jude, arresting though worked in muted tones, hangs to the left of the St. Joseph picture, while a similar mosaic of Simon hangs to the right. A democratic artistic arrangement for a shared altar, yet a possible disappointment to Jude's American followers, who so readily recognize his superior popularity. I look hard at him. A dark-haired, bearded man, broad-shouldered and virile, in a reddish-gold cloak, perhaps in his late thirties or early forties, holds a massive book in his right hand (this is generally interpreted as a copy of the gospels he preached in Palestine and Mesopotamia). He is so unlike the traditional American renderings, all those holy cards and plastic statues of an elderly man radiating stark concern, dressed in a white robe and green cloak and gripping a long ax or halberd, the instrument of his martyrdom. The Jude figure before me is not playing to his audience. I stare at the face. The light of three candles plays eerily upward over his features.

He is gazing over his right shoulder in an attitude of arrested anticipation, intense eyes trying to comprehend, as though he had perhaps caught the sound of his approaching murderers. The tomb itself is a mosaic wreath of flowers and vines tied with a red ribbon. White marble balustrades support the marble rails for those who kneel to pray. But only a few people are here, although carloads of tourists continue to unload in the square. In fact, the sole sign of festivity on this, the eve of Jude's feast, is a modest spray of potted white orchids sitting on the altar rail. It seems strange that a saint so well-attended in America should seem so, well, obscure in Rome. On the other hand, given his exalted company at the seat of Peter, the judgment may be premature. So many of my assumptions about this apostle of last hopes are being shaken up, the usual prelude to discovering the real story. I am seeing through my own eyes now, not those lent to me by biographers, scholars, and institutions. When suspicion whispers your name, it usually means you are hot on the trail.

Now I notice the rows of confessionals lining the transept, each one marked with the language it receives. I walk over to the "English" box and soon see that the priest, obviously between penitents, has turned on his reading light and opened the small front door that shields him from the outside.

"Excuse me, Father. Is there anything you can tell me about St. Jude?" I am very nervous: even after a lifetime of reporting, I still dislike approaching strangers. But in this case, talking to him seems better than dealing with bureaucrats. Father Roger, or Ruggero Cahilleri, is a native of Malta, a fireplug, short and sturdy with great kindness in his brown eyes. His robes are brown, too, the familiar robes of the Franciscans who specialize in staffing holy sites around the world. The St. Jude altar is his territory. How fitting. I am about to question a man wearing the mantle of St. Francis of Assisi—the supreme beatnik saint—about an apostle equally unconventional. Franciscans seemed to be turning up all over the place as I follow the shadowy path to Jude. I explained the trouble I had in finding the altar as directed by the guidebooks. "It happens all the time," he laughs. "They just don't get it right."

"What kind of people come here?"

"Only the Americans are here all the time. They come from all over the world, but only the Americans all the time."

"Before St. Joseph, was there a different picture in the center?"

"Oh yes," he replies, glancing over at the altar. "Once, there was a magnificent oil on canvas of Sts. Simon and Jude—six and a half by ten feet—painted by Agostino Ciampelli."

Underscoring how tenuous Jude's status had been, Fr. Roger describes how church officials in the late eighteenth century wanted to clear out the Ciampelli painting. "It had hung over the shrine for two hundred years, but they removed it in 1822. It was a picture of the two saints rebuffing poisonous serpents set upon them by evil Persian magicians and turning the serpents toward their oppressors instead. But the Ciampelli, which I have seen only in photographs, was taken away to make a place for a St. Peter mosaic. Then, the St. Peter was replaced by St. Joseph after a hundred and fifty years."

In the Vatican scale of time, I think to myself, a hundred and fifty years is like a long weekend.

"At one point, they commissioned Antonio Cavalucci to make a mosaic copy of the original painting of the Simon and

Jude martyrdom. Cavalucci's picture, however, apparently didn't meet Vatican standards. Because of what they called 'particular circumstances,' or, to be exact, 'in truth of modest quality,' the church sent the finished work to the collections of the Accademia di San Luca.

"And just as the Ciampelli came down in 1822, the two mosaic ovals you see there set in black, gray, and rose-colored marble were mounted above the Jude relics, St. Simon on the right side of the altar, St. Jude on the left. The records say that three days after they were hung, the artist—he was Vincenzo Camuccini—received a final payment."

"Hmmm," I mumble, privately noting that precise accounting is the Vatican's time-honored way of keeping track of its treasure.

"I'll look up some more sources. Meanwhile, I suggest that you go to the Fabbrica." He launches into giving me directions. The Fabbrica is the nerve center of St. Peter's, in charge of all matters pertaining to the basilica's operations.

"Will you be here tomorrow?" he asks.

"Oh, yes, it's Jude's feast day, I'll be here for the early masses."

"See you here tomorrow then."

Someone enters his box. He pulls the door closed, and I can hear the slide open, followed by the soft murmur of contrition.

The Fabbrica lies to the left of the great stairway leading to the basilica's entrance. The relentlessly pink-cheeked Swiss guard told me to seek out "Padre Andrea." I note that he, too, carries a halberd—lethal in Jude's time, but no match for terrorists bent on murdering a moving pope.

Once into Vatican City itself, I am directed to another office and given a pass and directions to still another and then given another pass. Father Andrea proves to be a harried wisp of a young man in a black clerical gown. He says he is running late to an appointment. I say I can wait. With an indulgent air, he hands me a saccharine St. Jude holy card and disappears in a swirl of efficiency, no doubt hoping that I will be gone by the time he returns.

I sit down. Half an hour passes, at which point I tell myself that two thousand people serve the world's 990 million Catholics from a sovereign state of 108 acres. Now a total of forty-five minutes has passed. I place the holy card on the good father's desk and leave, reminded once more of Jude's contrarian attributes: unbureaucratic, unharnassed, unofficial. If anything, he is slightly suspect in the eyes of the establishment, as has just been demonstrated.

Walking slowly across the square, I wonder once again if it is Jude's absence that is the point, not his presence. Not even tomorrow is exclusively his own. Jude's commemoration exists only by hanging his feast day on Simon's. This is not really Jude's natural milieu, except when, as a shadow, he can slide behind the pillars of St. Peter's, avoiding the light and the pageantry.

I walk to the souvenir shops in the crowded square, and then to the Scala Regia, a tiny street incongruously leading out from the extreme end of the portico and running alongside the basilica. Here, the clamor of tourists echoes off the weathered stones. Nuns staff the crowded shops, their patience strained by the human armies giddy with the prospect of taking home from headquarters a sign of their faith. Rainbows of rosaries, mountains of books and saint cards, armories of wallets, medals, and medallions, crosses of pearl, wood, zircon, and even pure gold. Loitering near the well-presented Jude memorabilia with studied disinterest, I ask how well Jude mementos are selling.

"Oh, the Americans," a tiny Filipino Franciscan sister speaks up. "They always want St. Jude, especially the statues." She smiles beatifically, and I am persuaded to join the rapture, springing for a Technicolor gold-plated medal and a plastic statue. They seem more good-luck charms, or ex voto offerings, than expressions of ordinary piety.

Hours later I stagger back up the hill to the convent. Sister Mary Grace is mopping the convent floors while Sister Placida madly cooks up huge pots of pasta in the kitchen. Hunks of delicious bread and personal wine bottles dressed in linen napkins sit on the green-checkered plastic tablecloths. My companions include a Belgian couple and a fellow New Yorker, John W., thirtyish and Catholic. He displays a keen knowledge of theology and an inordinate zest for packing churches into each daily itinerary.

"I thought you would all like one another," beams Sister Mary Grace. She is surrounded by a regiment of Austrian "pilgrims" who rise with the sun each morning and tramp the hushed corridors in grim precision. Sr. Placida pushes her serving cart through the plain beige dining room, scolding those who dare to leave a morsel on their plate. A cross, a ship's barometer, and a few religious pictures dot the walls, in sharp contrast to the large parlor off the foyer.

Like so many artifacts in Rome, the parlor sits empty and somewhat foreboding, a large ancient room that whispers of old triumphs. The overstuffed chairs are draped in delicate antimacassars, and faithfully polished old silver is laid out neatly in glass cases. Pictures of long-dead prelates hang in rows on the red brocade walls. An ungainly television set topped with a crooked antenna adds a Dali-esque touch to this Victorian tableau.

Tomorrow is the critical day. First to the basilica to take in the festivities and meet with Father Roger by his box; later, on to visit the only church left in Rome still dedicated to Jude. In it, I have already learned, hangs a reproduction of the Edessa legend—Jude curing King Abgar by delivering the

Mandylion, that sacred cloth upon which the face of Christ was imprinted.

Disappearing pictures, old bones, a kindly Franciscan, seven ancient altars, and a magic cloth. Perhaps tomorrow will yield an answer.

SATURDAY, OCTOBER 28: FEAST OF ST. JUDE

When I arrive at the square, shortly after dawn, the wooden barricades have been arranged so that visitors on their way to St. Peter's must hug the walls. Workmen are setting up an army's worth of chairs—but not for Jude's big day. The red carpet is being rolled out (literally) for three Swiss nuns who will be beatified at the pope's mass the next day, Sunday. Security men fan out within the basilica.

Over in Jude's area, a thin stream of people begins to arrive for the three morning masses to be said in his honor. No crowds, no extra flowers. It must be too early. Columns of light spill through the ancient stained glass, but at his grave the shadows linger over those kneeling before it. Their murmured prayers rise with a stirring intensity and a terrible concentration, ascending like burnt offerings into the vastness. No one looks at anyone else, just as in a New York subway, where no two people lock eyes and everyone seems distracted by some unseen presence. These worshipers are too neatly dressed to be Americans—and, indeed, they aren't. Several men lean on canes or walkers that bespeak severe disabilities. An elderly couple in matching white jogging suits strolls by, possibly American, but without a clue as to whose feast day it might be.

"Any Americans here today?" I ask a security guard, immaculate in his blue uniform blazer.

"No," he replies. "St. Jude is the protector of the Americans isn't he?"

I smile and nod.

The his-and-her-jogging-suit couple saunters by once more.

"They have no idea Jude is here," says the security guard, shrugging, palms up. "This happens all the time with the Americans."

Suddenly it hits why my countrymen have not shown up. Jude may be a very American saint, but few of his admirers actually know that he is buried in Rome. Facts about him remain as dim as the proliferating suppositions and legends are vivid. And, of course, it makes sense. Jude is an everywhere saint working Everyname Street. He requires no baroque extravaganza, no ceremonies to prove his power. Like the Roman statesman, he would much rather be asked why he had no statue than why he has one. Even among nations, he emerges early as a figure at the back of beyond—Armenia—where he remains a most revered saint in the Eastern church. Spiritually and geographically, he always operates on the edge, bringing about a national conversion in the far bleak mountains, and then embarking on the long invisible march that shows no sign of reaching a final destination. It is a quest for those who, scarcely more visible than he, lie huddled by the roadside, hidden in its dust—those at the very end of hope.

On the practical side, why would a church that tiptoes around the question of devotion to saints encourage bus tours? The organizing principles of the church have not been applied to this Third World, preliterate figure. Lourdes, Fatima, the Holy Land, yes; Jude—with no luminous miracles to recommend him, no string of certified anecdotes to precede him— no. Even the one Epistle attributed to him in the New Testament has come under revisionist attack by biblical scholars who doubt his authorship.

The bells sound, their emphatic rhythm shuddering through the stones. They seem to reverberate from every corner of the basilica. At Jude's altar, mass is about to begin. People here seem lost in the reverence etched in their faces, in the serenely deep genuflections, the slow signs of the cross. Some finger their rosaries, others kneel on the cold marble, heads bowed low. "You would not seek Me, if you had not already found Me," God says to Pascal. And perhaps this explains the journey itself.

The smoke from burning incense reshapes itself as it rises into the shafts of sunlight. At Jude's altar, the dozen rows of seats are filled now. One woman, smartly done up in an emerald green silk suit with matching shoes, offers her own elegant salute to Jude and his traditional color, green, by which the church symbolizes hope. One man, arms outstretched, bows toward the altar, mouthing his prayers. Another, standing in the back, engages in endless conversational prayer with himself. A young man in black kneels next to one of the two giant gold candelabra. A thin blonde girl falls to her knees, her face buried in her hands. An elderly man staggers forward on his crutches. The priest arrives, genuflects, and, turning toward the people, crosses himself and begins the mass. It sounds better in Italian. And so does the interpretation of the gospel in his sermon.

> "We have heard that before making the solemn and important decision to create the college of the Twelve Apostles, Jesus passed the night in prayer. . . . We see Jesus addressing the apostles, so that they can be the transmitters of His word, those who after having been given everything necessary for their mission, go out into the world to spread the light . . .
>
> "Thus we today, as we look at these two glorious apostles, Simon Cannoneo [the Canaanean] and Jude Thaddeus the Zealot,

we think about how the apostles continue their work today through their successors, the bishops, the college of bishops—they who guide our church. Thus we are truly called, always, to see the work of the apostles—and thus to be ever ready to accept their own message, even when it contrasts with our own vision . . ."

Jude's place sounds fossilized in a vague history, as it so often does in public appraisals of him, whether in Rome or at home. To the cautious, he is still the figure who disappeared two thousand years ago, the apostle at the Last Supper who posed a puzzling question—certainly not the great extraordinary who keeps popping up for seventy generations to deal with the impossible. Taking into account the assembly line of special masses falling on every day of the liturgical year, I shouldn't have expected revelations, or even a new angle, from this commemoration of Jude; still, the letdown of Rome's modest salute to him does suggest the worst of all reportorial scenarios, a dead end.

Mass is over. The candles are still burning as the priest and altar boys depart.

Just then, Father Roger pulls open the slide on his confessional and beckons me over.

"How did you do over at the Fabbrica?" he whispers.

"Not very well," I answer, sparing him the details.

His round face deepens into a single expression of his own long experience with bureaucracy. "Ah" is all he needs to say.

"Meet me again tomorrow at noon. Over there, by the pillar on the right." Father Roger, the charging Franciscan, suddenly seems to be part of his own Assisi underground

Thanking him, I head toward the bronze doors.

By mid-afternoon, the Rome air has turned sultry, heavy with moisture from the yellow waters of the Tiber and its marshes. I strike out far from the normal tourist routes, northeastward to, as far as I know, Jude's only remaining church in Rome. Built in 1924, it commands the top of a steep hill. Crosses and globes adorn the bell tower, its graceful arches triggering memories of Byzantium and Jude's old church in Şanliurfa. It is a small, stately Italian Renaissance structure, surrounded by a tall iron fence interspersed with marble pedestals. Shading hawthorns lean into the facade, their sharp points a reminder since medieval times of Christ's crown of thorns.

Neither Roman emperor nor papal architect has realized his grand dreams in the quaint streets where Via Gradisca and Via Rovereto intersect. Jude has held on in this snug neighborhood, probably because, like him, the little church is so obscure. What a relief to leave the celestial dimensions of St. Peter's for the human-scale spaces of "S. GIUDA TADDEO," as the sign reads over the main entrance. My main mission here is to see the painting over the altar. I walk to the side of the church at 16 Via Gradisca, where a white marble plaque is mounted on the iron fence.

> Istituto
> Suore Carmelitane
> Di S. Teresa di Firenze
> Piccolo Casa
> S. Guida Taddeo

After ringing the bell, I am buzzed into a small courtyard. *"Buona Sera,"* says the vivacious lady who lets me into a vestibule crowded with Italian women, chattering and gesturing as they pore over two long tables covered with Jude memorabilia. Here, unlike the Vatican souvenirs, copies of the painting in the church adorn much of the merchandise,

Mandylions (or, classically, "Mandylia") in every size and in brilliant color. The women welcome me effusively, impressed that an American would come this way; indeed, they embrace me when I tell them my mission. Out comes a copy of their newsletter, *La Voca Di San Guida Taddeo Apostolo* ("The Voice of the Apostle, St. Jude Thaddeus"). Some form of written word to tell the story, to spread the news, seems the earmark of Jude's followers everywhere. One of the fascinating paradoxes about this invisible man is how he inspires people to announce his latest interventions.

A section of "Historical Notes on the Little House of St. Jude Thaddeus" tells of the church's early years, when "straitened financial circumstances came again." The nuns and children turned to St. Jude for help, and help arrived by a characteristically indirect route:

> "Having returned from America where she had gone with Her Excellency L'Onorevole and her husband and daughter, Her Excellency Donna Ida Orlando brought back nothing less than fifty thousand lire. Before her departure, the incomparable benefactress had promised to think of the Institute and indeed obtained this sum from a very rich Argentine lady. She received another one thousand lire from a young lady she met on the steamship, Miss Sara Pinasco di Rosario di Santa Fe, who is greatly devoted to St. Jude Thaddeus.
>
> "You can imagine with what festive gratitude she was welcomed to the Little House. As though that were not enough, she inquired what the children needed, and made a gift of fifty metres of beige wool to make winter cloaks for all of them . . .
>
> "Donna Ida Orlando had another piece of good news to share. Through her efforts several people pledged nine thousand lire for landscaping so that the garden could properly encircle the House that the Sacred Heart of Jesus through the intercession of Most

Blessed Mary and St. Jude Thaddeus had given to the Word. Imagine the delight and enthusiasm of the Sisters who were already going to the nearby convents in search of a few shrubs.

"Now the chapel would no longer lack flowers, and their perfume, mixed with the prayers of the blessed children in grateful homage, would arise every day to 'that God who raises up and tears down, who tries and consoles.'"

The sheer sweetness and childlike faith of the story brings me back from the overarching majesty of official Rome to the humble and piercing belief and everyday obedience of the silently faithful. No cynicism laughs off these words. No Jesuitical logic. They are as real to the people of this little church as they were fifty years ago. Innocence, faith, charity—they have retained their essential meaning in this corner of the Western world.

On the cover of the church bulletin there is a copy of the painting hanging over the church's main altar that I am eager to see. Another picture inside depicts Jude, eyes heavenward, with his book open and a scapular of Christ's face hanging from a cord around his neck. In the background, dusty and sunbaked, stand the yellow-domed buildings of ancient Edessa.

The vestibule is now jammed with Jude feast day celebrants. One of them, Mrs. Vittoria Ansini, is a soft-spoken woman who looks thirty years younger than her age of eighty-four. She says she has a story—*un racconto*—about St. Jude. We, and several of the other women, adjourn to a quiet visiting room, an old-fashioned parlor of soft chairs and lace curtains. Matter-of-factly, as though offering a legal deposition, Mrs. Ansini explains that she became a two-year-old orphan when her mother died in 1911. She went to live in an orphanage and, later, came to the Carmelites at St. Jude's. Now, she is a mother of five and lives near the church.

"Jude," she says, "is for the *casi disparati,* the desperate causes."

Smoothing her flowered dress, she begins: "I had my own miracle on September 17, 1980. It was about 5:30, early in the morning. I was on my way to work, and not far from my house I crossed a familiar street. From out of nowhere, it seemed, a big bus struck me. The left side of my body was crushed and my head was severely injured. I was lying in the street—for about two hours, I think—right near my home, but my family was asleep.

"Other people came to help me and called a doctor. I woke up in the hospital. But later—when I regained consciousness—many people who had been at the scene told me something remarkable: as I lay in the street, passing cars did not run over me. Why? Because there was a strange white light surrounding my body. I have always been devoted to St. Jude, before and after the accident, and so I knew it all happened—the white light—because of his help. I always say, 'St. Jude, help me.'

"After the accident I put a picture of St. Jude around my neck, and I have never taken it off. He always helps people, but not just in desperate cases. I pray for peace in my family, particularly for a problem involving jealousy and my grandson.

"Six years ago my son-in-law had a tumor in his goiter. He had a seven-hour operation, but the doctors said he had no chance. He is well now, and now even his wife prays to St. Jude."

Valerie Diotallevi arrives and sits down with us. She is a woman of great charm, vulnerable, but joyful.

"I came to this church four years ago because a friend of mine was suffering from uterine cancer," she says. "I prayed to St. Jude. She had an operation and soon recovered, so my friend Concetta and I came to the church to say thank you. Then the time came when she needed a second operation. The doctor said she would probably die. Again, she recovered and, again, we both came here to say thank you to St. Jude."

The parlor is filling up with people arriving for the 6:30 P.M. mass.

"Is St. Jude popular in America?" asks one lady.

I assure her that he is, to the astonishment of all seated in the little parlor. It is beyond my linguistic capabilities to explain how completely different Jude's place is in America.

Soon the Mother Superior, known as Sister Gilberta, arrives. A presence. Again, I saw the dark intense eyes of the zealous, the true believer. She seems sorry for the world. Years of prayer and obedience had prepared her well for her responsibilities. Born in Lucca, she joined the Carmelites at sixteen.

With her was fourteen-year-old Ruth Mahari, a thin mulatto girl from the Cape Verde islands off the West African coast. She is one of twenty immigrant children taken in by the Carmelite sisters. Ruth isn't a full orphan, but she has no father, and her mother works. This was not the traditional Hollywood orphanage of playful youngsters in plaid bows and starched dresses curtsying to a visitor. Ruth wears jeans, a sweatshirt decorated with a picture of Snoopy and Linus, and bright lipstick on a pouting mouth. She seems the embodiment of a new kind of orphan, a cultural hybrid in a strange land who shows little outward interest in strangers, or even in Mother Superior herself. Waving her slender fingers, showing off black nail polish, she sulks through the ordeal of facilitating translation. The nun and the teenager are a study in the sacred and profane. But Sister Gilberta seems to take it all in stride— just one more test that God has sent her.

"People who ask that we pray for them—people who are sick, who are in trouble—donate money," she says. "If there is something that is not good, prayer can help." She is an angelic eagle, with large tinted glasses magnifying her keen black eyes and thick eyebrows. A white border trims the veil and neck of her traditional black habit.

"Many young people come to the church to pray, too," she adds.

"I don't think young people go to Jude," chimes in Ruth, swaying her long silver earrings.

Sister Gilberta contradicts her softly. I get the feeling it is a difference of opinion that will be sorted out later.

"I'm sure he works in my life. I pray to him every day," says Sister Gilberta, her voice keyed to the tone of perpetual prayer.

It is time for mass. The church is full, many are standing. The congregation has spilled beyond the vestibule, down three steps, and into the leaf-strewn street. I wedge myself in between a radiator and a pew.

Then I see the painting. Large and luminous, it glows in a wide golden frame. The entire church seems to gather itself as a backdrop to this magnificent work, as though the saint himself chose this repository of his legend. He is wearing a white gown and a red cloak. A long pole rests at his side; a rolled-up scroll, perhaps a letter, is half visible under his garments. A tongue of fire hovers over his head as he proffers with both hands the sacred Face to the awed king leaning toward it from his throne, face-to-face with the Nazarene he has sought so long.

The Carmelites commissioned a certain Professor Ballerini, who found enough inspiration in the story to paint the picture. He finished it in 1940, just as the Wehrmacht rolled across Europe and Italy invaded Egypt. As Mother Superior had predicted, many young people were seeking Jude here, along with some 350 other worshipers, at least half of them men. Stories of a still-pagan Rome would be put hard to the test on this night. Only Christmas and Easter draws crowds like this in America.

A nun conducts a choir of girls with tinkling voices, most of them from African countries. Some people sit with their eyes shut in prayer. Others dangle rosaries. But it is the sermon that finally connects Jude with tradition, as the priest expounds the story of Edessa. When the time comes to kiss the Jude relic encased in gold, an avalanche surges toward the main altar.

Fifteen hundred miles away from eastern Turkey, the promise of healing still beckons pilgrims, and the man behind the curtain continues to extend an almost seen, certainly felt hand. I can almost hear that father of a boy possessed, begging Christ for a miracle, "Lord, I believe. Help Thou mine unbelief."

The night feels cool, a relief from the humidity and emotional weight of a long day. It is late. I hop a bus for Monte del Gallo. Sister Placida sits waiting for me at the convent's front desk, drumming her fingers on the dark wood.

"No supper!" she thunders as soon as I set foot in the foyer. Ignoring my apologies, she waves a crooked finger at the clock and continues the upbraiding—all the way to the dining room where she has kept my supper warm.

SUNDAY, OCTOBER 29

Sunday morning mass brings the beatification of the three Swiss nuns, their pictures hung on great banners over the portals of St. Peter's. Jude, distinctly un-Swiss, has been upstaged all week by these blessed, but not yet sainted, women.

Early morning light streams through the arched windows, writing patterns on the marble floor. As Pope John Paul II begins his slow walk down the center aisle, imperially red-robed cardinals in his train, a tidal wave of applause sweeps the throngs—beginning in the sections near the entrance, rolling across the midsections, then, as he reaches the great Bernini altar, bursting in the front pews until the church booms with adulation.

Frazzled nuns dart around at the edge of frenzy. A mild hysteria, albeit religious, seizes the crowds as the pope ascends the altar. Some are in tears. Others, standing on tiptoe to see him, cry out *Viva Il Papa* as the pope, stooped, yet curiously radiating strength, moves forward to officiate. A paradisiacal choir chants the music of Gregory the Great.

In the left transept, the chairs set for Jude's followers have been turned around to face the main altar. I have stumbled on a Solemn High Pontifical mass, a pilgrim's dream—but my business lay elsewhere.

At noon sharp, Father Roger emerges from his box, walks over to our designated meeting place—a column on the right—and slips me some written material that he has turned into English from various languages. At his suggestion, I head for the Piazza dei Santi Apostoli, just across the Tiber, to search the sixth-century Church of the Holy Apostles. It sounds promising, but the visit yields little. Jude is not to be found amidst the long-forgotten tombs of Roman noblemen.

"He is not here," says a priest, with an air of detachment. Sorry, no paintings, mosaics, statues. . . . He suggests I check the statues of the apostles over the entrance.

"And which of them is Jude?" I ask.

He shrugs. By now I am used to the "Jude shrug."

Back at the convent in late afternoon, Sister Placida is intensely watching the pope's mass rebroadcast on the ungainly old television set in the front room that is frozen in amber. She barely looks up.

MONDAY, OCTOBER 30

The humidity seeps into every corner. Rome's Indian summer is dying hard. I arrive for another assignation with Father Roger. A storm has darkened the glittering sanctuary. Earsplitting thunder reverberates on the stones as rain heaves against the mighty roof. The moment freezes—and turns itself back in time: the moment of Jude's martyrdom as he and Simon face the villainous Persian priests. A Dominican archbishop of the Middle Ages, Jacobus de Voragine, describes it:

> "Seeing this, the priests rushed upon the apostles, and slew them forthwith. And in that very hour, although the skies were exceedingly serene, such immense lightnings leapt forth that the temple was riven in three parts, and the two sorcerers were burnt to coals. But the king [of Babylon] transported the bodies of the apostles to his city, and built a church of wondrous size in their honour."

Father Roger's slide is open, but his eyes are closed in meditation, his lips moving slightly. Confessions have been heavy all morning, but he has been jotting down more Jude notes between absolutions.

"Come, I want to show you something." We start walking.

"How long have you been here at the Jude altar, Father?" I inquire.

"I've been in that box for fifteen years," he replies. No trace of regret colors his tone.

We cross a small cobblestone campus on our way to the Franciscan house within Vatican City. There, Fr. Roger presents me with his handwritten scholarly jottings on Jude, and an article in the June 1994 edition of the official St. Peter's basilica newsletter. With delicate understatement, the good authors confess that the Ciampelli painting of Simon and Jude repulsing the Persian magicians and venomous serpents, "like other works of art in the Vatican basilica, had a somewhat troubled history."

After the Tuscan master's huge oil on canvas was taken down, it was moved to a lesser room in the recesses of the Vatican, where it remained for many years. "Long forgotten in the Sacristy and in other warehouses of the building, the painting of Agostino Ciampelli in 1925 was carried to the Museo Petriano and exhibited in Hall 'L' where it remained for more than twenty years." More recently, the work was restored in preparation for display in one of the basilica's halls. Poor Ciampelli, he went into and out of obscurity much the same way his subject has.

How fortunate it is that we met, I tell Fr. Roger, and that my information has come from the Jude underground, if only by happy accident.

"Providence again," he observes with a grin. "Remember what God said, 'Seek and ye shall find.'"

I have never heard reporting described quite that way.

"Well," I say, in parting, "so the church is not doing so bad after all?"

He smiles broadly, "The Spirit is always there." And then he adds, "God Bless," raising his hand in benediction and farewell.

The smell of rich, wet earth permeates the city. Walking uphill to the convent, I see clearly that Father Roger falls into the unplanned plan of all things Jude. Unfolding the Jude newsletter that the Carmelites had given me, I see that it features a section on "Unexpected Encounters." These are, of course, Jude stories, striking in their universality.

The September-October issue has a letter from Aldo Rispoli, who describes "a congenial old man" he knows:

> "Poor thing, suffers from serious ailments in various parts of his body while submitting to intensive therapies. Hearing him say, almost weeping, that he 'no longer knew where to put his head,' I

recommended that he turn to Saint Jude and invoke him with faith every day.

"For an instant he looked at me, astonished, then he said: 'How is it, have they now made a saint of the one who caused Jesus Christ to be crucified? I can't believe such a thing; it isn't possible! You're making fun of me!'

"And I, smiling: 'But no, I'm not making fun of you. Look, it's not a matter of Judas Iscariot, but of the apostle Jude Thaddeus, a relative of Jesus and a powerful faith-healer. As soon as you can, go to via Rovereto where a beautiful, trim little church rises up, where they venerate the great saint of whom I am speaking.'

"I saw the old man again a few days ago. He was radiant! He embraced me, saying: 'Thank you for having introduced me to St. Jude Thaddeus. Do you know that I never get tired of invoking him? He gives me so much, so much serenity. I still suffer, but I accept my cross, conscious that the one carried by Jesus was a good deal heavier.'"

Aldo Rispoli

The story yields not just one more example of the serene yet practical acceptance of Jude's presence but of the confusion between the two apostles that persists to this day. The enduring theme of coincidences, unimaginable encounters, and bewildering outcomes are the unifying themes of the Jude experience. As we consider the events, usually much later, the sense of a larger pattern forces itself upon our consciousness. Having looked at a beautiful painting close-up, one sees only a blur. One must back up twenty feet to have the whole picture burst on the vision in all its richness and harmony.

C. G. Jung, the Swiss psychiatrist and founder of analytic psychology, wrote at length in the 1920s about his theory of synchronicity, or "meaningful coincidences." It was Albert

Einstein, he said, who first led him to ponder it, who set him thinking about a possible relativity of time as well as space, "and their psychic conditionality":

> "Meaningful coincidences are thinkable as pure chance. But the more they multiply and the greater and more exact the correspondence is, the more their probability sinks and their unthinkability increases, until they can no longer be regarded as pure chance, but for lack of a causal explanation, have to be thought of as meaningful arrangements."

Jung is speaking the language of experience. One might say the language of bewilderment that follows sustained inquiry. He does not conclude that there are miracles, nor does he resort to the vocabulary of miracles. He leaves the question open, only suggesting that we cannot shrug off a sense of pattern, rather than coincidence, at work: a harmony exists. This is, after all, the crux of all faiths; and for those without faith, he has left us a scientific conclusion to ponder.

"Meaningful coincidences"—whether it be Father Roger, or the recovery of a loved one—are the heart of the Jude experience.

By the time I arrive at my room, Jungian thoughts have dissolved into far less lofty meditations about the role of chance in my own life. Memories rise slowly out of the past, of the times that death shuddered close by and then, implausibly, moved on. Was I alive because my mother honored him? And why had I not thought of this until now? If he kept me alive, then for what? I am *listening*—just as John Paul advised as he recalled St. Paul's bracing words in his Epistle to the Romans.

> "The Spirit too comes to the aid of our weakness; for we do not know how to pray as we ought, but the Spirit himself intercedes with inexpressible groanings."

That evening, my table companion from New York—John—announces to my surprise that the pizza in a nearby trattoria rivals the best that America can offer. So off we go to the "Quatro Gatti," where no cats were in evidence but a kindly host, a double for Rosanno Brazzi.

Gradually, the lush Chianti nudges us into telling our life stories, one of the unsung pleasures of traveling. John is a curious fellow. Extremely bright, he has a mostly bald head that only adds to his scholarly manner, and an air about him that says he is afraid of not being on time, or perhaps of wasting time. Each morning, after daily mass, he is the first out the door to relish the riches of Rome, but his interest seems to center on matters Catholic. It crosses my mind that he might be homosexual, but only as an observation, not a judgment. He is obviously not married. When he tells me his sister is a Carmelite nun, I see an opening.

"Have you ever wanted to become a priest?" I ask.

He shifts a little nervously and looks down at his glass.

"Well, that's a long story. But I can't."

Taking the cue, I decide not to press the case. But he continues to talk about the churches he has visited, and wants to know how a television correspondent has wound up a pilgrim in Rome. Another carafe or two, and we return to his theological interests; I have the feeling he is trying to tell me something, to reveal what is driving him.

Finally, it comes out: "I have AIDS."

It is not the first time someone has confided that piece of news to me, but the word itself always comes as a blow. Here, indeed, is the dark hall in which hope dies.

"I made the whole scene in the 1960s, screwing everything in sight. And then, just recently, my lover, a person I had known and loved for some years, died of AIDS."

Trying to make light of what had become a somber conversation, he swallows some wine, shakes his head in disbelief, and adds, "And six weeks later, my cat died, too." He laughs, but what may seem to some a ludicrous connection of events had pained him deeply.

By dessert, a creamy floating confection that he specially recommends, John is talking easily about his past and uncertainly of his future. He has a very good job in the city with people who will be understanding. Although a vocation to the priesthood still gnaws at him, he does not want to saddle any religious order with the expectation of large medical bills.

Anticipating my queries, he says he is not praying to St. Jude in particular, but that he has returned to the church after a nineteen-year separation. He recalls, however, that after his return, the first time he went to confession he encountered a statue of the saint as he departed.

"Naturally," he'd muttered, "the patron of lost causes."

WEDNESDAY, NOVEMBER 1

It is All Saints Day, a holy day obliging Catholics to attend mass. Most of Rome will be closed. While families picnic on the beach at Ostia, foreign visitors prowl the ancient paths now called streets, cross the bridges built before Christ, and search in vain for a shop that is not *chiuso*.

It is easy to be alone in Rome. Sight lines fight for your attention: great wrought stones, massy marble monuments vaulting in sovereign confidence, walls upon leaning walls. Moods are august here rather than romantic, overpowering instead of insinuating. "Look at me" commands the city as it pulls you into its inexhaustible layers of power and memory. If Rome is grand opera, then Jude is strictly street theater. At the center of a series of worlds, the city wakes you to the historic jolt of the centuries. Jude, however, just taps you on the shoulder, coming from behind, but still one step ahead of you. While Holy Mother Church gathers inward like the spokes of a lobster pot to hook its souls, Jude operates in reverse. He reaches outward, extending into all other faiths and doctrines. As in eastern Anatolia, there is a corner of the human heart that is his territory. Searchers must look for the perpetually hiding spirit, a touch of the sense of heaven, a perdu—one lying in ambush—out on the fringe. This powerful anonym is on the ground with me now—or I with him—to be found, only briefly, just on the other side of the door, not amid a crowd of stars.

He is, after all, the crucible of hope, the one human emotion, the one virtue, that keeps mankind afloat—diverting tragedy, healing the sick, comforting the desperate, deciding with some certainty that there *is* a way out. Hope—the boundless expectation of good—is the most profoundly persistent theme in the prophecies of the Old and New Testaments. St. Paul describes Abraham, the father of Judaism, as one who "hoping against hope believed." The great prophet knew that God would fulfill His own purposes, even against finite human expectation.

At the end of the first century, the infant church had to make its painful, resolute way against the persecutions of emperors, the hostility of pagandom, and the bitterness of stricken Jewry driven from Jerusalem and confronting the success of the faith that had sprung from it. Heresy, vice, false expectations, and disappointments (where was the Second Coming?) only further roiled the dark currents. Exiled to the island of Patmos by the emperor Domitian, St. John, last of the living apostles, wrote his revelations, or Apocalypse, about 96 A.D. It is at once radiant with otherworldly hope and terrifying in its anticipation for this world.

Decrying the heretics and charlatans who spread false teaching, he warned: "These men, like irrational animals created by nature for capture and destruction, abuse what they do not understand, and will perish in their own corruption."

Against the backdrop of St. John's apocalyptic prophecies, Christians prepared themselves to leave the apostolic age and await the dawn of a new century, the new millennium—just as the world does now. Some believe we are already living John's dark prophecy, and that Jude's reemergence may be more strategic than accidental.

Shortly before noon, pilgrims huddle for the usual Sunday papal blessing in St. Peter's Square. Puffs of white clouds hang low, and the sky has turned a postcard shade of blue. As usual, most of the anxious have cast their eyes on the wrong window. As the bells chime out twelve o'clock, the curtains move slightly, and then he appears, arms raised in blessing. At that exact instant, a large flock of pigeons lifts off with precision, cutting across the window at an angle into the brilliant azure sky—ecclesiastical timing at its best. A clutch of cheering nuns standing next to me wave wildly, their fervor electrified by the papal presence.

I feel very short on zeal, especially as a pilgrim. I would never live up to the standard set by St. Bridget of Sweden in the fourteenth century. Bridget—the Swede, Birgitta—ranks among the most famous of pilgrims. A noblewoman, married for twenty-eight years and the mother of eight children, she founded the Order of the Most Holy Savior, the Bridgettines, after her husband's death. Birgitta's extensive *Revelations*—accounts of her visions—attracted a wide readership during the Middle Ages. Tradition tells us she was devoted to St. Jude Thaddeus, and is believed to have invoked him for impossible causes, of which she undoubtedly had vast experience. Tradition also says it was revealed to her that "Jude would be a powerful protector of those in desperate straits." Or, supposedly in her own words: "In accord with his surname, 'Thaddeus,' he will show himself most willing to give help."

This is the version handed down by well-meaning but inaccurate commentators, usually reprinted in the treacly accounts written before Vatican II and still in widespread use.

However, in answer to my queries, Dr. Birger Bergh, professor of classics at Lund University in Sweden and an authority on St. Birgitta, points out that she mentions Jude only twice. The first reference, he writes, appears in the *Revelaciones Extravagantes* ("Extraordinary Revelations") as part of a description of the different altars she was commanded by Christ to place in her monastery church: "The fifth altar should be consecrated to Thaddeus, who manfully fought the devil by the purity of his heart."

The second reference, continues Dr. Bergh, turns up in the Regula Salvatoris, her monastery rule, and sets forth proscriptions for the fasting of nuns: whenever two apostles are celebrated on the same feast—such as Simon and Jude—one day of fasting is sufficient for both of them.

This excellent scholarship sorely challenges Birgitta's reputed devotion to Jude as reported by popular church pamphlets. And, in keeping with so much of Jude's story, once more raises the question of where tradition ends and documented history begins.

According to her *Revelations,* St. Birgitta received her travel orders—which included Rome, Sicily, Cyprus, Jerusalem, Bethlehem, and Jordan—during visions of Christ and the Virgin Mary. In one of them, Christ commanded her to set out on the daunting journey from Finsta Gaard in Sweden to Rome, as a pilgrim for the Jubilee year 1350.

"Go to Rome," he urges, "where the streets are paved with gold and reddened with the blood of saints and where there is a compendium [a shorter way] to heaven because of the indulgences that the holy pontiffs have merited by their prayers."

On the way, her tutor, Master Peter, is said to have made her proficient in Latin. Her specific object was to venerate the many relics of the saints and, especially, to pray at the tombs of the apostles. Although we have no evidence that she was there, one of the main routes for Scandinavian pilgrims could have taken her through the city of Goslar, in Germany, where Henry III had dedicated a church to Sts. Simon and Jude three centuries earlier.

An account prepared by her two confessors soon after her death in 1373 places her among the thousands of praying and singing pilgrims who followed the old Via Ostiense along the winding Tiber into Rome. At a bend in the river, they had their first view of San Paolo, first of the seven pilgrim churches of Rome. Soon they came to the city, on through the dingy alleyways, past the shops and taverns, and finally to Piazza San Pietro and the medieval basilica of St. Peter's.

Birgitta and her company of pilgrims climbed the steep stairway leading to three portals and then a courtyard where the faithful washed their hands in a fountain. Once inside, she crossed the cold mosaic floor to kneel at St. Peter's grave. One can only assume, and rightly, that she did the same at the altar of St. Jude, then a most popular altar—one of the main seven—among pilgrims. Sanctity, however, could not blot out the rest of her surroundings. The filth, grazing cattle, overgrown grass, knife fights, and painted women caused Birgitta to exclaim to her tutor: "Alas, Master Petrus—is this Rome?"

When not laboring for the return of the pope from Avignon, Birgitta probably worried about family matters. Her daughter married a man Birgitta called "the Brigand," and her favorite son, whose wife was living in Sweden, became the lover of Queen Joanna I, whose third husband was living in Spain. Indeed, her life and many torments have the ring of so many cases submitted to Jude today.

Peeling back the layers of this city uncovers the unexpected. In this sense, Jude is very Roman. Consider that just across from the Vatican, where the Tiber half loops around, a church once dedicated to him and Simon lay crumbling until recently, when it was converted into apartments. The apse is still visible in the former church of Sts. "Simone e Giuda" at No. 9 Vicolo del Montaccio, a dead-end on a steep hill in the neighborhood of Piazza Navona. Here, the noble old Orsini family built an immense fortress leading down to the river and controlled the palace and grounds from the early thirteenth to the seventeenth centuries. Dante, a pilgrim himself during the first Jubilee year of 1300, in which he sets his comedy, made a point of mentioning the Orsini castle:

> "Just so the Romans, because of the great throng
> in the year of the Jubilee, divide the bridge
> in order that the crowds may pass along,
> so that all face the castle as they go
> on one side towards St. Peter's, while on the other
> all move along facing towards Monte Giordano."

The *Acta Sanctorum,* in its October 1867 commentary, reported that Jude's old parish church was "suppressed" on November 1, 1824, in an Apostolic Letter by Leo XII. Whatever the mysterious reason for its suppression, possibly because of financial problems, it was allowed to continue as "a sacred shrine" in the care of the aristocratic Gabriellis, who had taken the compound over from the Orsinis two hundred years earlier. But by 1888, they, too, became just one more memory of the noble Italian families fading from Rome's crowded rosters. The Jude church, however, endured, at least for awhile.

Cardinal Ildefonso Schuster mentions this "small church ... near Monte Giordano, close to the Orsini palace" in his 1925 sacramentary, or commentary, on the Roman missal. He also cites the post-communion prayer for Jude's feast day in one of the rare "official" comments about Jude's special powers:

> "We who have received thy sacraments, O Lord, humbly pray that through the intercession of thy blessed apostles Simon and Jude what we do in honour of their martyrdom may avail us for a healing remedy."

THURSDAY, NOVEMBER 2

The bells seem to be ringing everywhere, counting down my last hours in Rome. The cats in the old Largo Argentina are getting ready for lunch. I lean against the railing above the open square, a pit really, where temples from the republic that Caesar once knew now stand in ruins. Among the most aged to be found, even in Rome, these remains—four holy precincts and eighteen Corinthian columns—date back to the sixth and fifth century B.C. As is so often the case in Rome, they surfaced during demolition work in the 1920s. The labyrinth of broken marble is a haven for cats, dozens of smudge-faced orphans with street smarts borrowed from Cleopatra, whom some imaginative Romans credit with delivering the first cats to their country. The legendary woman who tends them appears with a bucket of pasta, and they ambush her from every ancient crevice. Lunch over, they pad out of the midday sun into their cool and mysterious warrens.

How Jude-like. Like the cat, he rarely appears when expected, usually takes the long way round, and always arrives obliquely and in silence. The great naturalist Henry Beston could have been writing about the saint of lost causes when he described the cat as one "gifted with extensions of the senses we have lost or never attained, living by voices we shall never hear."

The day begins sultry, Mediterranean. The city has not quite exhausted its repertoire of moods and spells. Toward nightfall, on the slopes of Monte del Gallo, a riot of thunder and lightning rumbles overhead. Jagged traces of lightning dance around the dome of St. Peter's, each flash throwing it into an intermittent silhouette against the black sky. The French doors shiver as rain cascades over the terrace, bending the tentative geraniums, washing away the last traces of summer. Centuries ago, fearful citizens would have heard in these great claps the raging Jupiter Tonans scourging his worshipers. For a thousand years he held the fate of this great city in his godly hand, only to be overthrown by an enigmatic preacher and a few fishermen.

The sisters fuss over my departure. My tablemates, fellow pilgrims passing through, say their good-byes.

New York gathers me up again. Somehow I felt lighter, refreshed. And yet that sense of quest—that thirst—although slaked, remains. Who was this man Jude? Rome has never called him, and yet he lurks in every street, in every pew, in every rustle of wind or silk that filters through the drafty churches and ruined reminders of fallen empire. I have found only a *sense* of him, a notion, a mood, a confidence. Something new is in the air. Is it, after all, Hope?

MESOPOTAMIA
TO AMERICA

". . . their voice goes out through all the earth,
and their words to the end of the world."

Psalm 19:4

T HAT CLEAR COLD EVENING IN LATE MARCH 1996 stands out as a precious winter souvenir. In retrospect, it emerges as the night a chain of Judean events began to unfold . . .

My friend and I are sitting in her elegant apartment high above Central Park, aware of but accustomed to the pinpoints of light filtering through the trees and the muffled bursts of animated conversation bouncing off old snow. I am trading industry gossip and thoughts on the dubious pleasures of "maturing" with my hostess, Pia Lindstrom, a well-known New York television broadcaster with whom I had worked at NBC News—the usual girl talk, much the same as it sounds in Bangor or Butte. Conversation turns to books and films and I raise the subject of an old movie I had seen just a few days earlier, *Come to the Stable,* a sentimental postwar tale often shown at Christmastime.

What follows bears a remarkable similarity to Abbot and Costello's unforgettable "Who's on First."

"I saw this wonderful old movie," I begin. "It's about two nuns, played by Loretta Young and Celeste Holm, who arrive in America from France after the Second World War. It's called *Come to the Stable,* made in the late 1940s, and it has a Jude angle. The nuns build a hospital and a convent because he protected them during the Occupation."

"I never heard of it," replies Pia, a respected movie critic for many years.

"Really? Are you sure? It's the kind of film your mother might have starred in," I answer (Pia's mother, the lustrous Ingrid Bergman, had played a nun and even Joan of Arc). "Well, anyhow, the nuns settle in a town called Bethlehem and . . ."

"Oh, I know that place," she breaks in. "It's in Connecticut."

"No, it's in a movie," I rattle on.

"But I didn't see the movie. I went to the place."

"The place?"

"Yes, the Abbey of Regina Laudis. I went there and visited Dolores Hart, the actress, who's a nun there. She's not in any movie about a convent. She's *in* the convent."

"You mean it's a real place?"

"Yes, I went there with Maria Cooper," she says, referring to Gary's daughter, a friend since childhood and now married to pianist Byron Janis (who often wears a St. Jude medal inside his jacket while playing concerts). By this time I am slightly woozy from the Hollywood-as-reality crossover.

"Did any of the nuns mention St. Jude?"

"No."

"You didn't hear anything about two nuns burying a St. Jude medal where the foundation was to be laid?"

She shook her head. "But look, we can go to Regina Laudis to find out. And in the meantime you can ask Celeste Holm. She lives in this building."

Once again, I had the unavoidable feeling of sequence, of "meaningful coincidences" coming into play.

To follow Jude, one must be prepared to make—or to follow—enormous leaps. From the leafy serenity of Connecticut to the wilds of Armenia certainly qualifies as one. You cannot cross these mysterious gulfs alone, but always something, or someone, enables you to bridge the forbidding chasm. To put it another way, the pattern appears only after your hand is moved to join the dots on the invisible path. In this case, however, the connected events—a trip to the Abbey of Regina Laudis and another, largely overlooked, occurrence in modern-day Armenia—fell barely two years apart.

In April 1994, Pope John Paul II sent Cardinal Achille Silvestrini, the prefect of the Congregation of Eastern Churches, to Etchmiadzin in Armenia, now emancipated from the Soviet Union, with a gift of the highest importance: relics of Sts. Jude and Bartholomew, the First Illuminators of Armenia, the original founders of its church. As the bells of the fourth-century cathedral tolled, Cardinal Silvestrini presented the saints' long-wandering relics to the Catholicos of the Armenian Apostolic Church amidst resonant "statements of mutual recognition of the apostolic origins of both churches." These words added great weight to the already manifest significance of this "translation"—a term applying to holy relics as well as languages—and foreshadowed, it was devoutly prayed for, the eventual reunion of the churches. Such a development would of course be a mighty event in the apostolic history of Jude, especially since the Armenians claim theirs to be the oldest Christian church.

Msgr. Robert L. Stern, writing in *Catholic Near East,* says of that day:

"It wasn't a very elegant entrance into the holy city of Etchmiadzin. We had all piled into a jeep that morning in the Armenian mountain town of Ashotzk. The papal nuncio was driving, Cardinal Silvestrini was in the front seat . . .

"We thought we had an 11 A.M. appointment with Catholicos Vasken I, Supreme Patriarch of All the Armenians, and we were running a little late . . . Well, we did have an appointment, but not as we thought . . .

"As we pulled into the precincts of the Catholicosate . . . the great bells of the cathedral began to peal in celebration. We hastily got out of our jeep and arranged our robes for what clearly was a major liturgical reception. A procession of Armenian Apostolic clerics met our quickly improvised entrance procession bearing the reliquaries of the two apostles. Reverently accepting the relics from our hands . . . they led us into the cathedral.

"The Catholicos awaited us at the throne with all the bishops of Armenia grouped around him. Bishops, priests, and deacons were solemnly vested. A magnificent choir chanted while the relics were placed on the altar amid candles and flowers.

"We were shown to places of honor to either side of the Catholicos. His firm words belying his frail appearance, Vasken I welcomed us bearers of these holy relics with great emotion.

"'Just as the Church of Rome is founded on Saints Peter and Paul,' he said, 'so the Church of Armenia traces its faith to Saints Thaddeus and Bartholomew. Just as the Apostles were brothers in Christ, so must be the churches founded by them.'

"In the American Armenian church, there is no particular tradition devoted to Thaddeus as a patron of lost causes or refuge of hope, as there is in the Catholic church, but his role as founder of Christian Armenia is unassailable. It is against this backdrop that the presentation of the relics took place."

In this context we see that the importance of the pope's gift lay in its implicit recognition of the Armenian church's claims to apostolic origins. Not so subtly, it also recognized the indelible impression that Jude had made in America almost two thousand years after he blazed an indelible, however terrestrially ephemeral, path from the dust of ancient kingdoms to the hard chrome axis of American business and technology.

From the pitiless peaks of the Caucuses and the burning sands of far Arabia, the desperate dreams of Hollywood were still a long way off. First, Jude had to follow a resolute and steady course as his reputation spread across the vastness of Asia Minor, Armenia, Russia, Syria, Lebanon, Eastern and Western Europe, India, Latin America, and, finally, the United States. No passports or manifests document his passage, but the ever-increasing number of those who had seen his wonders passed them down the line. If he galvanized multitudes while he lived, his everlasting celebrity only came after his martyrdom. Where he perished remains unestablished, although there are quite telling claims for the wilderness of Mesopotamia—even the ancient urbanity of Edessa—as well as corners of Syria, Persia, and Lebanon.

In Armenia, where strong historical tradition and many legends attest to his journeyings, Jude's life expands beyond Edessa to a place where from a reportorial, if not scholarly, perspective, an unworthy kinsman of Abgar had him stoned to death. Such is the basic Armenian legend of Jude set down in the thirteenth-century manuscript *Le Synaxarion Armenien de*

Ter Israel, which is preserved in the fourteenth-century *Patrologia Orientalis,* a martyrology of the Armenian church. Despite its forbidding ecclesiological sound, it is a colorful and reverent summary of the basic oral tradition surrounding Jude that emerged from the colorless landscape of that harsh hill country. Interestingly, even though he is Thaddeus, "one of the disciples," in some of the stories, and Jude, "one of the Twelve," in others, the Armenian tradition does at times specifically identify the two as one and the same.

Worth noting is that the term *legend* (from the Latin *legenda,* meaning "something to be read aloud") passed into church usage in order to describe the lesson or reading of selected portions of the lives and passions of martyrs or confessors. Only by extension did it come to be applied to those accounts of saints' acts collected for monthly readings in "legendaries." Thus, the original significance of the word had no implication of the fictitious. However much the term *legend* conjures up fantasy and fiction today, this is not a fair assumption about these historic texts.

According to the *Synaxaire,* after winning the favor of King Abgar with his miracles in Edessa, the apostle Thaddeus pressed eastward to Armenia and the court of King Sanatrouk, son of Abgar's sister, whom Abgar had made king.

"The apostle arrived at the king's court to preach the good news of the kingdom of heaven, and there performed miracles and marvels and cured all kinds of infirmities and sicknesses. Many believe his words and were baptized.

"The charming daughter of the king, whose name was Sandoukht, also went and, after having seen the apostle's miracles, she believed, was baptized, and from then on never separated herself from him. Upon learning this, the king grew wrathful and sent the greatest of his princes, heir to his kingdom, to murder the apostle and Sandoukht.

"So the prince went unto the apostle and beheld a light all around him, and he and the people with him believed in Christ. A woman of the royal family, Zarmandoukht, went to find the apostle and, witnessing the miracles, also believed. King Sanatrouk, angered, ordered the execution of the prince and Zarmandoukht and many others. They were put to death immediately. Above them, a column of light appeared, and Sandoukht secretly buried their bodies.

"By the king's command, the apostle and Sandoukht were cast into prison where Christ appeared and lifted up their hearts. The following day, the virgin saint Sandoukht was taken before the king, who said: 'Come close to me.' But she did not move. The king, in his wrath, ordered her to be put to the sword. The executioners, seeking to follow his command, struck at one another's throats, but one, a young man, drove his sword into the virgin's bosom, and immediately she surrendered her soul. A bright light appeared over her, and the apostle buried her body . . .

"After the martyrdom of Sandoukht, Christ appeared to Thaddeus and said: 'Take courage, for today you will come to Me.' When the apostle was parted from the disciples, they broke into tears.

"At the king's bidding, two princes bound the apostle and brought him before the king who said: 'Why did you lead my daughter astray that I must have her slain?' But Thaddeus replied: 'Your daughter has gone to her Betrothed and has been crowned with immortal crowns.'

"The king ordered that the apostle be thrown to two lions to be devoured, but the wild beasts knelt down and licked his feet. Then he was cast into a furnace, but he did not burn. A great violent wind arose and bore the flames toward the onlookers, some of whom were consumed. And that day four hundred people believed in Christ.

"The king, fleeing, commanded that the apostle be put to the sword, whereupon the executioners seized him and took him down into a small valley somewhat below the town of Chavarchan; there, they forced him to climb to a ledge raised in the midst of the rocks. Stretching out his arms in prayer, Thaddeus cried: 'My Savior Jesus Christ, do not abandon my diocese, do not leave the people in the errors of idolatry, but illuminate them at the fitting moment in the knowledge of your faith.' Then, they murdered him with a sword and buried him in the midst of an overturned rock.

"A sweet odor filled the air and a bright light shined, and that day many believed in God. Much later, the miracles of Sandoukht the virgin saint and the apostle Thaddeus were manifested in their remains, and a church was raised over their graves . . . The feast of St. Thaddeus and of those who died as martyrs with him took place on December 22nd."

Another version of this story in the same text asserts that Jude went to upper, or northern, Armenia and met the apostle Bartholomew "on the hill of Artasat" (or Artashat), where they prayed together and then planted a cross. Some scholars believe the "hill" was Mount Ararat, which lies in eastern Turkey, just over the Russian and Iranian borders. Other traditions claim that Mount Ararat, actually a combination of two mountains, was the final resting place of Noah's ark after the flood.

At least five hundred years earlier, the *Georgian Lectionary,* a collection of church ceremonies observed in Jerusalem during the Middle Ages, offered the oldest-known assignment of a particular liturgical text—two verses of Psalm 19 known as the

"Psalm of the Apostles"—to commemorate Jude/Thaddeus on December 20, off by only two days from the Armenian legend.

Tradition can be very exact. "We rely so much on the written word that we don't give enough credence to the oral traditions," says an expert on the churches of the East.

We cannot casually dismiss tradition, or those powerful voices assigning Jude's slaying and burial to the otherwise obscure village of Ormi in southeast Armenia. Frontiers and names, if not the bones of the land, change: Ormi now lies in the Maku region of Iran, no longer styled the Artaz (Ardaz) province of Armenia, but still the site of a monastery dedicated to St. Jude. Remote, barren, and rocky, it is virtually cut off from the pace of modern civilization. Some years ago, a reporting assignment took me as far as Tabriz in northern Iran, about 145 miles to the southeast; the memory of that bitter cold remains in my bones. During a dire overnight ride through frozen mountain passes that vanished under falling snow, it had crossed my mind that here, hope might be in unusually short supply.

Jude labored to bring the gospel to Armenia for roughly twenty-three years, by some accounts from 46 A.D. to 66 A.D., although the kingdom was not officially converted until 314. In the fifth century, P'awstos Buzand, the first Armenian chronicler to mention Jude, referred three times to the See of Armenia as "'the throne of the Apostle Thaddeus" and recounts the tale of Jude's death:

> "'Others have testified to these events long before us,' wrote Moses of Khorene in the eighth century, recalling Jude's death in 'the canton of Chavarchan, now called Ardaz, and the stone opening to receive the body of the apostle, and the removal from the stone of this body by his disciples . . . his burial in the plain.'"

Dates of his martyrdom vary. *The Menology of Basil,* a Byzantine martyrology, commemorated St. Jude Thaddeus on June 19, saying: "This man made strong by Christ Himself . . . finally headed for Arat, and there he was driven against a cross and stabbed with spears until he died."

So popular was Jude that the Frankish liturgist Alcuin eulogized his mission to King Abgar of Edessa in a poem, probably set to song, proclaiming that Jude was "put to sleep in death in Armenia."

Another tradition holds that Jude was buried on the Lebanese coastal island of Arados, not far north of Beirut; still others set the grave in Beirut itself. In fact, the *Acts of Thaddeus,* an important Syriac source of Jude's tradition, quite specifically establishes Jude's death in "Berytus, a city of Phoenicia by the sea; and there, having taught and enlightened many, he fell asleep on the twenty-first of the month of August. And the disciples having come together, buried him with great honour; and many sick were healed."

At a very early period, probably the second century, legends of the apostles and disciples sprang up in languages of both East and West; some probably arriving first in Hebrew and Syriac, then later translated into Greek, Coptic (the language of Christian Egypt), Arabic, Ethiopic, and, finally, English and European languages. *The Contendings of the Apostles,* translated into English from Ethiopian at the turn of the century, offers yet a further tradition. In a manuscript entitled "The Preaching of Judas Thaddeus in Syria," Jude and Peter, the impetuous apostle himself, set off across the desert together for a stunning unfolding of miracles, temptations, and achievements.

First they meet an old man plowing his fields whom they ask for a bit of bread. After he departs to get some, Jude takes over the reins of the oxen and plows thirty furrows; Peter blesses the baskets of seed "and in that same hour the seed sprouted, and the ears became full of wheat." The old man returns and, overcome by the miracle, falls at the apostles' feet and asks to follow them. Peter replies that this is not necessary, but tells him to spread the word of their entrance into the city "for our Lord Jesus Christ calleth unto us [to do so]."

When the magistrates see the old man with an ear of green corn from the field plowed by the apostles, they question him sternly. "Satan defiled the hearts of the magistrates with an evil intent" and they plot to mock and ward off the "sorcerers" by placing a naked harlot at the gates of the city.

At the sight of her, Jude begins to pray:

> "I beseech Thee to send Michael the Archangel, and to let him suspend this woman in mid-air by the hair of her head until we have entered into the city; and when we desire to come forth do Thou bring her down again [to the ground]."

Immediately, the woman is carried up into the midst of the air by the hair of her head. She reveals the magistrates' plot, cries out for God's mercy, and repudiates her life of whoredom, crying out: "Come, O ye young men whom I have corrupted by my fornications, and repent, and make supplication unto the Apostles of God on my behalf, that they may show mercy upon me."

As Jude and Peter pray for strength against their foes, Michael the Archangel descends, drives away the evil spirits that had afflicted the souls of the people, and brings the woman back down to earth. Jude and Peter preach "throughout the highways of the city," baptizing all, and sending the repentant harlot to minister in the church.

> "And they healed the sick, and they opened the eyes of the blind, and the dumb spake, and the deaf heard, and the lame walked, and they cast out devils, and they raised the dead, and at length all

the people of the city believed and entered into the knowledge of God, Whose Name is most glorious."

These events only stirred Satan's wrath. Soon after, Jude and Peter encounter a young man, dispatched by the devil himself, "who asks the road to salvation." When the fiery Peter tells him to give away all his possessions, he leaps upon Jude and asks him if he agrees. Jude answers that it is easier for a camel to pass through the eye of a needle than for a rich man to enter the kingdom of heaven. Furious, the young man chokes him, almost to death—"had it not been for the power of God, Who kept his eyes from starting out of his head through the pain of the rich man's grip upon his neck." Presently, a camel and a needle merchant happen by and the apostles ask for God's help. "In that same moment the man, together with his camel, went in through the eye of the needle."

The young man relents and, tearing his garments, bows down to the apostles, begging forgiveness and offering all his possessions for them to divide among the poor. The apostles agree, and again, after baptizing the city, they build a church, appoint bishops and priests, and even write a Gospel and a book of commandments.

> "Thus was the work of making them believe performed by our Lord Jesus Christ; and immediately after they had made their confession of faith Thaddeus died, on the second day of the month of Hamle [July]."

In a postscript to the legends, the twelve apostles and seventy-two disciples question Christ about their own salvation and are told they will pass bodily into heaven on the last day. But the apostles have a question:

> "What shall be the reward of the man who putteth his confidence in our prayer, and celebrateth the commemoration of us,

and causeth the book [of our acts] to be written?' And again Our Lord said unto them, 'Whosoever shall put his confidence in your prayers, and shall celebrate the commemoration of you, and shall praise your sufferings, shall pass with you boldly [into heaven] at the last day.'"

After his death, Jude's path is paved by word of his deeds on earth and by the hectic and even ghostly trail of his relics. War, pillage, and plain cupidity take their toll, but two general routes emerge by which his relics seem to have made their way to the modern world, one from the dry isolation of Edessa by a murky east-west path through Syria to Constantinople. How exactly, we do not know, although a fifteenth-century Ethiopian document records one such translation to the Byzantine capital on August 5 of an unrecorded year under the direction of Constantine "the Just." An entire church was consecrated to house the newly arrived fragments, says the text.

A second trail wanders from the north in Armenia to the holy capital, but Jude's forearm is hidden by Dominican friars and later brought to their general in Rome.

Along each of these routes springs up devotion to Jude himself: the East Syrian liturgical and devotional impact accounts for the prominence given the King Abgar correspondence in medieval Ireland and England; the Armenian migration headed southward into Cilicia (now in western Turkey), then northward into Galicia in East-Central Europe.

The belief that a saint can intercede with the Deity on behalf of any wretched soul who seeks his help is central to the development of Christian liturgy, traditions, and spirituality. It is a belief in miraculous power, and, as in the case of Jude and other early martyrs, many believers invested some saints with more of this influence—this ability to answer prayers—than they do others. An image or relic of the saint—and its specific wonder-working powers—enhanced a sense of the continuing presence of some long-dead martyr or confessor and was the focal point of his capacity to communicate with the living.

The translation or removal of a saint's body from one place to another began around 360 A.D., at least in the East, and gave rise to saints' special days and the ascription of their protecting power to a particular community. The process itself, one of great solemnity, emphasized the miracles of the saint so honored, and indeed it was expected that even more miracles would be manifest at the time the saint's body was removed to its shrine. By the Middle Ages, the church had systematized its saints and assigned each of them to a category in the hierarchy such as Apostle, Martyr, Confessor, or Virgin.

The classic tradition of pilgrimage began flourishing in the fourth century with St. Helena's reported discovery of the True Cross in Jerusalem. One journeyed to pray at the site of a relic—some fragment of a blessed one—whether relics of the first class (by which was meant a saint's corporeal remains) or of the second class (representative objects that at some point had come into contact with the venerated one). In essence, the cult of the saints grew out of the veneration of the holy dead.

Today, these are more often separated from the saint's actual body. Once the Vatican had conceded authenticity to a relic, a new church could be dedicated with the holy remains or fragment embedded in its altar. Pilgrims at medieval shrines sought to bear away with them some part of the saint's beneficent influence, and because this mysterious emanation was deemed to be present in the very oil that burned in lamps around the tomb, they would carry samples of it home in special *ampullae,* or oil flasks, much as they do at various Jude shrines in America to this very day.

Shortly after the coronation of Charlemagne in Rome on Christmas Day, 800 A.D., Pope Leo III presented the new emperor, an ardent relic collector, with the remains of several (perhaps six) of the apostles, including the heads and other major body parts of Sts. Simon and Jude. Charlemagne took them to Toulouse in southern France, thus opening Jude's way to the West. It is reasonable to infer that this proved a catalyst for the composition of special mass prayers in honor of Simon and Jude. In fact, from around 800 A.D. on, prayers for this feast, and those of other apostles previously omitted, began appearing in various sacramentaries used in France, Germany, and Italy. The conversions of whole nations to Christianity and the expansion of saints' cults greatly stimulated the demand for relics. By the late ninth century, apparently throughout western Europe, people were offering prayers to Jude, especially on October 28. And as relics gained ground, so too did devotion to the presences behind them.

The connecting link between East and West is Charlemagne, who deposited the relics at the great Church of St. Saturninus in Toulouse (Tolosa), a culminating station on the *via Tolosana,* the great pilgrim route southward across France. As Western Europe's population increased, the need for ever more churches made itself felt: competition for pilgrims rose to new ecclesiastical heights. Today, although aged narrow streets still wind through the Toulouse's ancient heart, and a dozen great churches still soar heavenward, the city's reputation rests on its aspiration to a more secular heaven—that of its aerospace industry. But a thousand years ago, all medieval Christendom venerated it as the ultimate treasury of relics, a terraced pile of spires giving endless material form to the one true faith. And among the greatest of the treasures it offered to the eyes of the pious was the greater part of the body of St. Jude, a claim genteelly disputed by the chagrined keepers of St. Peter's in

Rome. In any case, not only had Charlemagne contributed many saints' bodies to its sacred riches, but the Crusaders had bestowed upon it an array of treasures won from the tragically beckoning East: wood from the Manger, a stone from the Holy Sepulchre, a thorn from the Crown, a piece of the True Cross, and in 1366 the body of that dazzling intellect of the Middle Ages—St. Thomas Aquinas. Twelve superintendents and seventy-two guardians sworn to the most solemn of oaths kept watch over these blessed prizes.

After the cathedral's restoration in 1097, Pope Callistus II dedicated an altar to Sts. Simon and Jude, within which were reverently laid their relics. Grand state processions rich with pomp and pageantry and attended by ambitious royalty pressed to be near the priceless treasures.

Rich details of the relics are offered by Monsignor Paul Guérin, chamberlain to Pope Leo XIII, who records in the nineteenth century that Jude's head was in Toulouse: "The heads of the two Apostles are enclosed in two busts of gilded wood, placed with the other reliquaries in a large cupboard at the entrance of the apse. Their bodies are to be found in a single reliquary of wood, resting onan altar in a Roman chapel dedicated to them."

Despite this certainty that the sacred heads were safely ensconced in Toulouse, the Bollandists have recorded testimony dating from the seventeenth century that Jude's head had come to rest in Cologne at the Church of St. Mary in Capitolio. They sought to resolve this and similar discrepancies by arguing that what is said to be the head or body of a given saint often represents a mere fragment thereof. As the adroit investigator of the relics of Cologne put it: "I made out from one part what could be called an arm or the head."

Other Jude relics then in play included that undisclosed part of him placed on the breast of St. Bernard at his burial in

Clairvaux, only to be moved later to an undetermined part of France when the French mystic was disinterred to be installed in his own shrine. The sack of Constantinople in 1204 flooded the West with a headlong plunder of saints' parts, so we can only guess over how many dusty medieval roads were scattered Jude's earthly remains. His shoulder blades, and those of Simon, too, wound up at a Benedictine abbey in Prussia, long since leveled, and from there, like so much on Jude's trail, they vanish into the dark. An American writer, obviously tired of the scholar wars, summed it up nicely: "To philosophers, the theological question seems to come down to an idiot standing at a crossroads shouting, 'He went thataway.' And somehow contriving to point down all four roads at once."

Germany, also threaded by pilgrim multitudes that must have seemed a nation in themselves, fashioned a special cult around Jude. The Emperor Henry III offered the ultimate liturgical compliment by dedicating a church to Simon and Jude at Goslar in 1049, possibly because his birthday fell on their feast day. At any rate, Pope Leo IX himself consecrated the church with the help of seventy-three cardinals, bishops, and abbots.

More than any one facet of Jude's life on earth, the story of his encounter with King Abgar has endured over the centuries. With Jude came the rich and lasting Eastern influence upon the church that manifested itself in Spain during the fifth to seventh centuries in the "Mozarabic liturgy," traceable in large part to Byzantine sources. The East Syrian influence that had thrived at Edessa—derived from Semitic-speaking Christians—could readily be discerned in the rites of the Spanish church. The Syrian liturgy used the famous letter of Christ in the Divine Office for Lent. While there is no detailed record of the Office readings in Spain during this period, the chatty fourth-century abbess Egeria, who journeyed to Edessa from the Spanish province of Galicia, commented to her guide that the letter was a familiar document in her native land.

Far more tantalizing is the effect of Spain's Mozarabic liturgy on the Celtic Rite of Ireland, which, carried by Irish monks or wandering scholars, infiltrated the liturgy of Anglo-Saxon England, at least up until the eighth century. At the court of Charlemagne, anyone knowing Greek was assumed to be Irish: this was before the Vikings came. Christ's letter to Abgar was well-known in Ireland and translated into the national language. Prayers, hymns, and poems addressed to Jude were part of the early Irish liturgy; further versions of the legend appeared in Norse, Danish, and Anglo-Saxon.

A look at the *South English Legendary* contradicts the assertion that Jude's popularity faded in the Middle Ages. This extremely popular collection of saints' lives reprises the Abgar story and further emphasizes that Thaddeus and the apostle Jude were one and the same: powerful evidence that in the Middle Ages, the story of Christ's letter and Jude's visit was universally believed. A sixteenth-century book of saints based upon readings in the Brigittine Order's Sion Abbey includes a passage on the Abgar legend for June 20, just a day after the Byzantine calendar's commemoration on June 19.

> "The feast of Saint Abgar a confessor and king of Edessa unto whom our Saviour wrote an epistle and therewith sent him the very image of his own face . . . after his resurrection he sent the apostle Thaddeus to teach him the faith and baptize him . . . and all of his people."

Moreover, Christ's letter to Abgar not only appears to have been included in the Divine Office, but by the nineteenth century cottagers in Shropshire were hanging framed copies of it over their doorways—just as people in Edessa had eight hundred years before. Some even wore the letter as a holy charm to protect them "against lightning and hail, and perils by sea and land, by day and by night and in dark places."

Legends and relics, powerful clues, point the way of Jude's path, and in art, one masterpiece especially: the Mandylion, that miraculous piece of linen on which Christ imprinted His face and that Jude later delivered to King Abgar. The miraculous likeness embarked on its own strange journey from the old to the new worlds amid the clash of armies and the ferocious superstition that it held a power no man had ever possessed. From Edessa through the Middle Ages and onward, the devout and the covetous saw ownership of the Mandylion as a necessary charm.

Of the copies made, one (perhaps several) found its way to Constantinople; others were surrendered as ransom to the invading Arabs. Shortly after the Byzantine capital fell, copies of the Mandylion and possibly the letter, too, began turning up in Italy. The Venetians claimed to have brought a picture of the holy cloth to Rome and presented it to the Church of St. Sylvester, where as late as the seventeenth century a scholar asserted it was the very image that Jude had carried to Abgar. On the other hand, the Genoese insist that it is they who had custody since they were given the picture in the fourteenth century and enshrined it in their Armenian-rite church of St. Bartholomew.

Against this backdrop dappled with shadows of hope and despair, Thomas Hardy wrote his most controversial and often misunderstood novel *Jude the Obscure,* the darkly brilliant tale of young Jude Fawley, who dares to hope for a better life but is brought down in disaster and despair by uncrossable class barriers and his own moral frailty. Hardy never mentions the saint, but there is no mistaking his motive in choosing the name of the patron of impossible causes. The saint's particular authority is also clearly relevant to Jude's forlorn hopes of gaining entrance to the great university of Christminster, the barely disguised Oxford. Hardy gently signals the reader as he describes "a young man of obscure origins," but the most obvious clues to his symbolism surface during Fawley's nighttime passage through the streets of Christminster. Prowling "down obscure alleys," Jude marvels at the majesty of the hallowed buildings—relics in themselves—the city's rich history, and the exalted personages who trod these same streets:

> "Jude began to be impressed with the isolation of his own personality, as with a self-spectre, the sensation being that of one who walked but could not make himself seen or heard."

He eventually returns to his "obscure home," falls asleep, and dreams about the great men who have attended the university. Among these "spectres," writes Hardy, is one who once mourned Christminster as "the home of lost causes"—imparting a strong connection indeed between the two Judes. What's more, the spectre of the dream is actually Matthew Arnold, who, in his *Essays in Criticism* (1865), actually thought lost causes to be part of Oxford's attempts to civilize. He writes:

> "Adorable dreamer, whose heart has been so romantic! Who hast given thyself so prodigally, given thyself to sides and to heroes not mine, only never to the Philistines! *Home of lost causes* [emphasis added], and forsaken beliefs, and unpopular names, and impossible loyalties!"

Hardy's light-handedness, his confidence in hinting the connection to another never-named Jude who, alas, will not be called upon, highlights the legend of the saint itself, for this is the framework of devotion and myth within which he fashions his bleak story. Hope will not be allowed to redeem.

To those who contend that little is known about Jude, we must answer that in the final analysis, in the last learned text,

Jude does not make his presence felt through history, or iconography, or folklore, but by his endless indirect manifestations to the millions who catch his invisible hand as a first desperate clutch in their stretch toward God.

Even the Russians claim Jude as their evangelizer, asserts one of their principal church historians. A rare and important Byzantine exhibit at New York's Metropolitan Museum of Art in 1997 featured a splendid mosaic of "St. Thaddeus," on loan from a museum in Kiev. It was rescued from one of the city's great churches that was destroyed by the Communists in the 1930s. There are no precise explanations for this sustained fervor other than suggestions that Jude may have gone as far north as Scythia, that ancient name for a great part of European and Asiatic Russia. The fact remains that among the Slavic peoples as a whole, interest in Jude has flourished. "Thaddeus" is still a common Christian name among Poles especially (the Polish national epic is *Pan Tadeusz,* and Warsaw, Illinois, is named after the poem "Thaddeus of Warsaw"). This devotion derives from the immigration of Armenians to the Galicia region of southeastern Poland by the fourteenth century, as well as from an earlier and separate Russian cult of Jude.

As some Slavic nations fell under the Habsburg monarchy, it was inevitable that Thaddeus would become a popular name in Central Europe, and a recurring figure in its art. Leaving some clues, but characteristically never enough, Jude passes from the shadows of the first century, through the medieval twilight, and into the modern world, all the while manifesting a solid presence among persecuted believers, those, for example, who suffered for their faith behind the Iron Curtain. "The Cult of St. Jude Thaddeus in Czechoslovakia," a study by Dr. Ludvík Němec, reports that at least fifty-seven churches and chapels in Bohemia, Moravia, and Slovakia had been dedicated to Jude by the twentieth century, at least two of them dating back to the thirteenth century. In Slovakia, the popularity of the apostle is due at least in part to the Jesuits' active promotion of the Jude cult. Such tenacity became part of the Jude landscape right up to and through the Nazi conquest and as the Iron Curtain fell. Understandably, Dr. Němec dedicates his book to Jude in gratitude for a "special favor"—not a miracle, though it may have seemed like one to him at the time—as Jude guided him in his "escape from a Czechoslovakian Communistic 'paradise.'" So the book itself, like those piercingly simple notices of gratitude in the newspapers and the flowers and notes heaped on Jude altars, is an articulation of deep gratitude, an ex-voto acknowledgment of merciful intercession.

Dr. Němec captures for us one particularly telling detail from his country's turbulent history—perhaps one of the "meaningful coincidences" that seem to slam together as one passes into Jude's orbit. In 1918, at the end of World War I, Czechs and Slovaks won their independence from the old "dual monarchy" and established a new republic. In Prague, the country's first president, Tomas Garrigue Masaryk, proclaimed the birth of Czechoslovakia a "day of liberation": October 28, Jude's feast day.

The legacy of Jude is reflected even in the writings of today's president of the Czech Republic, Vaclav Havel, a man of letters and a defender of human rights. His reflections appear in "St. Jude's Journal," a newsletter published by the national Jude shrine in Chicago. In a thoughtful analysis of how Jude works, as if in implicit rebuke to the prayer-in-the-slot, miracle-on-demand approach, he writes, "Hope is definitely not the same thing as optimism. It is not the conviction that something will turn out well, but the certainty that something makes sense, regardless of how it turns out." Jesus laid it down clearly that His kingdom was not of this world.

There is no precise itinerary of Jude's critical journey, no straight line he traveled that we can authoritatively score onto a map. For example, in India, Jude's history is typically cloudy and perhaps even spurious. Still, he is held in high regard and evokes veneration among the six million Syro-Malabars and other "Christians of St. Thomas" whose ancestors are believed to have been converted by the latter apostle on his mission along the Malabar Coast. Here, scholars find confusion: the names and legends of Jude and Thomas interlock. Some place them as companions in Edessa even before they traveled India. Various ancients write of Thomas's shrine in Edessa, maintaining that a Christian merchant brought his martyred corpse back from India to be buried. Others contend that Jude and Thomas are one and the same person, Jude Thomas. Stoking the flames of argument is a copy of the famous letter to Abgar. Found in a cave outside Edessa, it refers to "Thuds that is Thomas." In any case, Indian devotion to Jude was not home-grown, but apostolically imported and planted firmly enough to outlast the old world. Not only are shrines to both Jude and Thomas to be found in India today, but the Syro-Malabar liturgy is deemed a branch of the East Syrian liturgy that flourished in Edessa. This may explain how faith in Jude held its own after twenty centuries amid the subtle and powerful Hinduism practiced by the surrounding scores of millions.

Here, too, traces of the Abgar tradition survive. An English writer reported in 1895 that he saw a copy of the famous Edessa letter in English on "a roughly printed sheet" and learned that it had wide circulation among certain classes of Eurasians in the Indian empire who wore it as protection against fever. Obviously, the Judean tradition of Edessa and the resulting recognition of Jesus by Eastern potentates had spread to the southwestern corners of the subcontinent, as it did wherever Christianity was propagated, from the cottages of Britain to the remote gray ledges of Iran.

Lebanon offers an example of longtime devotion to Jude, an allegiance that has remained strong with many of its emigrants. In the last half of the twentieth century, the late comedian Danny Thomas is, of course, the figure most widely associated with Jude, mainly for his founding of St. Jude's Children's Hospital in Memphis. Mr. Thomas sought Jude's help when he was down on his luck and soon his career rebounded. Another Lebanese, Jamie Farr, known to millions as the cross-dressing Corporal Maxwell Klinger in the hit TV series *M*A*S*H,* dedicated his autobiography to Jude for a similar reward of faith. Down on his luck and living in a grubby basement apartment, the discouraged actor began stopping at a local church in Los Angeles to light candles at the Jude statue. The turning point came soon enough. He won a part in the film *The Greatest Story Ever Told*—playing St. Jude Thaddeus!

A candle also burns for Jude in the mountain village of Zahlé in Lebanon's Beka'a Valley. From Beirut, this peaceful spot is a rigorous two-hour ride on the road to Damascus. Sitting atop a steep hill overlooking the Nahr al Berdaouni River, Zahlé is a wine-growing area with narrow winding lanes and houses made from the native stone. Many here are Eastern Catholics (Melchites), like Therese Karam Maalouf, who has built a shrine to St. Jude in front of her apartment building on Housh Al Zarani Street. The fifty-five-year-old mother of two acquired the statue in 1952 when her sister brought it on a visit from her home in Sao Paolo, Brazil, where Jude is a most popular saint and where, indeed, three Roman Catholic churches are dedicated to him.

Mrs. Maalouf is a petite henna-haired woman whose deep and expressive facial lines suggest the warmth and fortitude of her people. As a Lebanese Christian, she is part of a tapestry of tradition that goes back very far in these mountainous parts, where for centuries Lebanon's minorities have fled to escape persecution, whether from Christians or non-Christians. Every day she lights candles at the twelve-foot white marble shrine decorated with a plain wooden crucifix and fresh white gladioli. At night, electric candles take up the task. The statue depicts Jude wearing a green cassock and red shawl, carrying the halberd in his left hand and a book in his right. Above an alcove sheltering the statue, he is remembered in Arabic:

> "St. Jude, a relative of Jesus and a disciple, was
> called Thaddeus for his honesty and faithfulness.
> He was martyred at the hands of the Persians
> on the 28th of October 69 A.D."

Below the altar table, another carved inscription reads:

> "You, who carried the Evangile to the farthest
> places on earth, engraved it on our hearts so
> we could live it."

Standing before the shrine, Mrs. Maalouf holds a Jude novena booklet rendered into Arabic from Brazilian Portuguese. The nine different prayers for each day of the novena all emphasize Jude as a saint of influence because of his close relationship—perhaps even kinship—to Christ. An accompanying biography reports that he converted many pagans and that after his martyrdom and burial in Babylonia, his body was moved to Jerusalem, then to Toulouse at the behest of Charlemagne in 800 A.D., and finally to St. Peter's in Rome.

"He has granted many of my wishes," says Mrs. Maalouf, explaining how she and her family began invoking Jude for good health and the usual family needs. Her friends pray, too, she adds. One of them, a Lebanese banker, had been married for ten years, but was still childless. After praying to Jude for a month, his wife became pregnant and gave birth to a son. The father kept his promise to have the boy baptized in a church dedicated to St. Jude in Sao Paolo.

So far, Mrs. Maalouf has collected roughly two thousand dollars in cash donations for the St. Jude church she hopes to establish in Zahlé. Contributions are dropped in a little box in front of the homemade shrine. She has great faith that one day the church will be built.

In non-European Spanish-speaking countries such as the Philippines, Mexico, Cuba, Costa Rica, Chile, Peru, and other Central and South American countries, Jude is hardly a stranger. Though little has surfaced on Jude devotion in Mexico, a fascinating document has lain for years unnoticed in the rare-book stacks of California's Sutro Library: a Jude novena in Spanish dated 1702. Its sixteen worn and precious pages bear witness to how deeply established the saint was in what was once the heart of the Aztec realm, and places him on America's doorstep much earlier than imagined. The preface, written by a Franciscan priest, describes how the novena "came to light" at the request of the Royal Convent of Jesus Maria in Mexico. But it is the *motivo*—the reason for the novena—that documents Jude's popularity. Significantly, however, there is no hint in any of the prayers in this lengthy novena that Jude specialized in hopeless causes. The earliest reference to this connection (mentioned in chapter 1) appears by 1826 in the Acta Sanctorum. Nevertheless, this Mexican document certainly attests to the power of Jude's impact.

"Given that the devotion to the Glorious Apostle Saint Jude Thaddeus is so extended and general, and so that his devout have news of his life and miracles . . . the novena will be distributed by days and also according to the petitions that are helpful to our salvation and our needs.

The text cites Jacobus de Voragine, the thirteenth-century Dominican archbishop of Genoa whose *Golden Legend* of saints' lives enjoyed enormous popularity in the Middle Ages. It recounts the King Abgar story in prayers and lessons for the third day, followed over the succeeding days by the story of Jude and Simon at the court of the king of Persia and their eventual martyrdom by idol worshipers. The style is graphic in its innocence. "A big storm came with lightning that destroyed the temple and burned the witches. When the king knew of this he sent for the sacred corpses . . ."

This early novena of New Spain undoubtedly belonged to some library of one of the many religious orders—as the church was, in fact, responsible for all education. By the mid-nineteenth century, the Mexican government had confiscated all valuable church property, books and all. Anticipating this, some of the faithful had purchased many of the libraries, giving convents and monasteries at least a little working money now that their rents were rattling in the generals' pockets. Adolph Sutro, a great benefactor of California, bought up whole collections from those who had sought to preserve these treasures.

Slowly and inevitably, century by century, the ancient peoples and forgotten lands touched by the apostle's journeys would pass on a collective and unbroken golden chain of Judean hope to a new world that would in turn continue this ever-unfolding devotion. Forgotten saint? Not really. Even after the ruinous aftermath of World War I in 1918, Jude had already taken hold at Vilsbiburg in Bavaria as the monarchy collapsed and socialism arrived to change the face of Europe. Jude's name and, more important, his presence infiltrated the lands of a new world waiting to be born, beginning to dare to hope. Forging these links to the modern world meant coming to America, where he arrived just in time, soaring into pervasiveness from below the grass roots.

There is no hard date for Jude's arrival in America, but his sturdy popularity found a perfect fit in this culture of boundless optimism, quest, and, most of all, hope. Under other skies, it is Jude of the Mandylion in whom there is intense belief, but here in America he has taken on a new sphere of actuality: as the Jude of Opportunity. Making the transition from the old world to the new, with little fanfare but accelerating speed, he essentially was borne to America on the immigrant tides of the last century. "Give me your tired, your poor"—and he shipped with them.

As early as 1830, a church was dedicated to Jude in Blairsville, Pennsylvania, possibly the oldest of his parishes in the United States. In 1926, Czech-American newspapers were reporting that the nucleus of devotion to Jude in America was St. Joseph's Orphanage in Lisle, Illinois. Children there collected the building stones for a grotto set in the fields surrounding a nearby Benedictine abbey. It was consecrated in 1929, the year of the Great Depression, when devotion to him drove deep roots into the stony soil of deprivation. Thousands visited the grotto, thought to be the first Jude shrine in America. That same year, two more shrines rose, both in Chicago, one dedicated by the Dominicans at St. Pius Church, and another by the Claretian fathers as a "national" Jude shrine at Our Lady of Guadalupe Church; both operate as major Jude centers to this day.

St. Anthony Mary Claret, a Spanish-born Jesuit and archbishop, founded the Claretian order in the early nineteenth century, and by 1911 their missionaries working in Chile built a Jude shrine that served as one of the foci from which the devotion spread throughout South America. So, when Claretian priests arrived in Chicago in the 1920s, they brought with them a natural faith in the power of Jude. The initial surge to the devotion began largely among laborers at nearby steel mills devastated by job cutbacks and smothered by the Great Depression. Led by Father James Tort, they prayed for construction of a shrine on the southeast side of the city. Father Tort's own devotion went back to his chance discovery of a St. Jude prayer card in a pew of the small mission church in Prescott, Arizona, where he was previously assigned. After the first Chicago novena, word of Jude's works spread. European and South American immigrants poured into the North American cities, bringing their devotion to Jude with them. During World War II and the drawn-out war in Vietnam—times of extremity—Jude's popularity exploded. Today, several hundred thousand petitions are received every year at the Chicago shrine, whose parishioners are now 99 percent Hispanic. *The Voice of St. Jude,* a journal published by the Claretians, is a catalog of answered prayers, the stories and happy endings of those who asked for Jude's help. In the reflection of one thousand votive lights, a reliquary on the side of the altar holds a piece of Jude's tibia, or shinbone, sent from Rome years ago. Meanwhile, the saint's forearm—the precious relic believed to have been preserved through the centuries by Armenian and then Italian Dominicans—lies in St. Pius's Church, encased in silver, its forefinger and thumb extended "as in a benediction." Five times a year, under guard, it is exposed for veneration.

Jude had become an integral figure in the landscape of the spirit. If Mary and the postwar definition of her carnal Assumption met the longing for deliverance from the Cold War, especially from 1945 to 1970, then Jude, in his quiet, low-profile way, captured the private and personal loyalty of the frightened and despairing.

In the years after World War II a school of Jude stories surfaced across the country:

- An American businessman, after seventeen months in a Hungarian Communist prison camp, is suddenly escorted to the Austrian frontier and freedom. Why? Because his wife and two young sons had persevered in prayer. "Knowing that St. Jude Thaddeus was called the 'saint of the impossible,'" she recalled, "we besieged him with prayer to move the powers of the earth to secure my husband's release."

- An inmate of Joliet Penitentiary composes words and music for a hymn to Jude and sends it to the Chicago police department's St. Jude's League for their annual picnic.

- Ripley's "Believe It or Not" syndicated column had this item: "Between 1948 and 1956 Jack O'Leary estimated he had hiccuped 160 million times. He tried many remedies, but all in vain. Finally, in desperation, he prayed to St. Jude. His hiccuping stopped."

- After lying alone for days on a deserted battlefield during World War II, a gravely wounded American soldier cries out St. Jude's name. Within minutes, a medical team arrives.

- One woman sums up what so many have reported: "I was faced with a grave and apparently hopeless situation. I asked the intercession of St. Jude and after that a series of extraordinary coincidences took place in which there was an answer to my prayers."

Again, these are described as coincidences, a point aptly addressed a half-century ago by William Temple, Archbishop of

Canterbury: "When I pray, coincidences happen. When I stop praying, coincidences stop happening."

Devotion to Jude, in its simplicity, its directness, found modern expression in art and poetry. Kathleen Norris, an American novelist of the 1950s who was devoted to Jude, begins her "Prayer to St. Jude" bemoaning the past confusion of his name with that of the traitor Judas Iscariot and declares, "We, seeing more clear, concede thee what was thine." She then imagines Jude (cousin to Jesus in this context) making his way home after the Crucifixion. Like the other apostles, except John, he had fled before the Roman swords. Alone, he encounters friends, including the Virgin Mary, who just witnessed the death of her son:

> ". . . Oh, thou, the sad day done,
> Taking the homeward road
> To thine obscure abode
> In the long shadows of the setting sun,
> To meet the frightened crowd
> Sobbing aloud,
> With thine Aunt Mary silent in their midst,
> Leaning upon
> The faithful arm of John;
> Saint Jude, who didst
> Join them in unbelief
> And utter agony of grief,
> And in a voice of pain and terror cried:
> 'Saw'st thou—and thou—
> Saw'st thou indeed my Cousin crucified?'. . . "

The poem richly evokes a most possible vision of Jude's movements and even his personality on the last day of his Lord's life. Profound imaginings—culled from a cloud of legends and a few facts—are all we have to describe him as a living apostle. Similarly, depictions of him in art, where imagination has run the gamut in the scattered plethora of mosaics, paintings, wood panels, stained glass, and sculptures in the world's museums and churches, have not confined him to a look, a persona, or even a certain era. Artists see him through the kaleidoscope of the ages, a man of glass parts, shifting, redesigning, rearranging, adapting his colors to the situation at hand.

Two traditions seem to dominate, one holding that Jude and Simon were the Lord's cousins, as St. Matthew's Gospel reports, and thus depicting them as young. Another tradition suggests that they are two brothers who mingled among the shepherds to whom the angel and the heavenly host revealed the birth of the Savior; as grown men at this event, they must be depicted as old men when they are apostles half a lifetime later. In Greek art, Jude and Thaddeus are contrasting figures, Jude a young man, Thaddeus old.

There are scores of the varying examples. A Perugino at the Marseilles museum depicts a seated Virgin holding Christ in her arms, and before her throne two lovely undraped children with glories round their heads bearing the names Simon and Thaddeus. A sixteenth-century limewood altarpiece by Daniel Mauch, *The Holy Kindred,* at a church in Bieselbach, Germany, shows Mary of Cleophas and Alphaeus, Jude's presumed parents, with three chubby toddlers and an infant, probably our hero. A similar painting by Strigel exhibited at the Denver Art Museum places the infants Jude and Simon in their mother's lap. Rubens paints Jude as a handsome, clean-shaven young man; Ribera presents him as a Christ-like bearded figure—this painting is in the Prado in Madrid; a Borgognone of him can be seen at the Metropolitan Museum in New York; and he appears in a panel by Simone Martini at the National Gallery in Washington.

A bearded, much older Jude looks down in profile from the great Dome of the Crossing in St. Peter's basilica, appearing barefoot and "big-chested," as his other name, Thaddeus, suggests. In the Vatican museums, a stern, elderly Jude stares out of dark deepset eyes from a sixteenth-century piece created in the workshop of the Zuccari brothers, one of whom was named Taddeo. Another Vatican treasure, *The Martyrdom of Simon and Jude,* a fifteenth-century Italian oil-on-board platform section, depicts the two men seconds before they are executed against a background of the moon and sun symbols of Mesopotamian pagan belief and ritual. The conversion of King Abgar has its place as a motif of Judean art in an altarpiece by Borrassa at the Museum of Vich, north of Barcelona, and in a painting by Benso in Genoa. Polish artists especially have left a Judean mark in this century. For example, Jozef Mehoffer, in his window of the twelve apostles for the Fribourg Cathedral in Switzerland, depicts Jude not in the usual unadorned cassock and cloak but in rich clothes of medieval cut.

As artists advanced their vision over the years, the defining character of each of the twelve apostles has evolved, climaxing in Leonardo da Vinci's sublimely artistic and psychological study of *The Last Supper.* The master followed the tradition that depicted Simon and Jude as elderly brothers. Here, da Vinci plumbs the essence of each man, especially Jude, capturing it for an arrested and eternal moment. As the apostles wrangle over their places at the table for the doomed passion feast, Christ gives them a lesson in humility: "Let him who is the greatest among you become as the youngest, and he who is the chief as the servant." Jude and Simon take the last two seats farthest away from Jesus and to His left. Looking at the painting, Jude is second from the end on the right, between Simon on his left and Matthew on his right. Soon, Jesus is telling the group that one in their midst will betray him. The impetuous

Matthew, with outstretched arms, seems to be asking "Do you hear what He says?" The aged Simon displays his bewilderment with upturned palms, while Jude, the slightly stooped wise man, reflects the same question, but temperately, his right hand raised in unspoken entreaty to Simon. It is a marvel within a masterpiece that da Vinci, divining Jude's identity, places him at the end of the table, obscure, silent, but his whole body expressing unspoken consternation, concentrating gravely on the tragic and inconceivable development at hand: his namesake's betrayal.

Still, for all its genius and beauty, art does not really capture Jude. All it can do is excite our imagination and make us aspire to a subjective idea of the saint. The whole corpus of paintings, sculpture, and poetry devoted to Jude cannot add up to the sense one gets from a single Jude event. Could we expect art to capture him when his essence is that nothing can? We can trace his relics, his scattered members, but his power comes out of nowhere. If a Martian landed on earth today, it could not work out Jude's theme though it might readily conceptualize from art the powerful figure of Peter the fisherman, a burly man with a net, or St. Francis, a gentle man among his birds. Jude figures in art, as in so much else about him, as guesswork: old man, young man, handsome, so-so, baby, corpse. His is an utterly dispersed image offering as many manifestations as he has skills. The man of a million masks.

Jude's entire reputation is rising *because* of his very illusiveness. While politicians, film stars, and sports greats elbow for ever wider, ever more fleeting attention, behaving as if their actions and opinions count, Jude wafts above the roaring crowd, dodging the spotlight. Nobel Laureates and entrepreneurs die in obscurity, having changed the world. So it is with Jude. Here we have the classic man recognized only after the event, sensed but not heard, doing his job and moving on, defined only by his speed and impalpability.

Under stress, Americans discovered their national saint: democratic, daring, understated, resourceful, "one of the boys," supremely well suited to becoming the particular saint of this age. Can there be any doubt that he is responding to the impossible in the country that put a man on the moon? The land where pushing the edge of the envelope is a national pastime? At last he has found a place for himself. His earlier journeys, mighty as they were, paralleled the lives of the other apostles, as did his earthly fate: Jude, a man of the desert, a matter-of-factly naturalized saint, has quickly taken up the American approach. A man for the global village, he is a modern-day activist, a saint of action lost in the crowd whose after-death history can only be reconstructed from his quiet deeds. What's more, in the American tradition, he did it his way—no charismatic advocates, no organized tours to the St. Jude crypt in Rome, just dissolving into his mysterious pervasiveness with singleness of purpose and a rugged individualism of the spirit that made his arrival here a homecoming.

"The fascinating stories are the ones where a person has gone through a real tragedy," says Father Mark Brummel, C.M.F., director of Jude's shrine in Chicago. "Say a husband has died and the wife feels all alone. Suddenly she and others who have suffered similar losses feel helped in dealing with the situation through prayer. Suddenly something is totally different in their lives, and they are able to cope. Their situation isn't any different than before, but they are now able to handle it from a personal standpoint—and that, I believe, is the result of prayer. It is not a charismatic-type devotion. We don't find any crutches lying around the alter. It's much more of a silent kind of inner conversion. And they are increasing."

This observation confirms what many in the more sedulously avant-garde clergy are often too timid, or too "modern," to entertain: that devotion to saints in general has increased in spite of the warnings sounded by the Second Vatican Council of 1963. The mere mention of the council raises a point sheepishly debated in some church circles, and one that is worth a brief digression. Vatican II's statements on devotion to saints drew fire from those who saw the admonitions against "abuses" as an attempt to back away altogether from the cultus of the church's finest human witnesses and to diminish their very place in Catholic theology.

Lumen Gentium, one of the conciliar documents, announced:

> "This council urges all concerned to remove or correct any abuses, excesses or defects which may have crept in here or there."

Moreover, the *Constitution on the Sacred Liturgy* (1963), which the council laid down as the official formulation of liturgical discipline, made another precautionary point:

> "The practice of placing sacred images in churches so that they be venerated by the faithful is to be maintained. Nevertheless, their number should be moderate and their relative positions should reflect right order. For otherwise the Christian people may find them incongruous and they may foster devotion of doubtful orthodoxy."

Fair enough. Except that some liberal liturgists and theologians mistook the fresh air coming through the open window for a firestorm sent to consume all imagery as idolatrous. Statues disappeared overnight. Rosary beads were suspect in some quarters. Latin became a truly dead language. And saints took a back pew, or at least that's what alternative liturgists, with their guitar playing and endless singing, thought had happened. While the sophisticates labored to get the saints out of Catholicism, Jude weathered the storm, making friends with millions of non Catholics.

By 1994, the new catechism of the Catholic Church came to the rescue with its clear restating of the saints' unique place in the church. One line in particular throws a penetrating light upon the grounds of Jude's resurgence: "The saints have always been the source and origin of renewal in the most difficult moments in the Church's history."

Unclerical and uncategorical, our man explodes on the scene at a time when clerical presence and authority are facing dire challenges. One could argue that as the clerisy regroups, the whole order of organized Romanism does, too—not that the church is no longer powerful or united, holy, and apostolic, but that it has shifted to taking on new issues, such as abortion and genetic engineering, and settling old ones, such as rehabilitating Galileo after three centuries. Jude was never encouraged in catechism classes or in church garden circles, perhaps because he seemed to pale alongside Peter and Paul.

In one sense, a certain establishment discomfort that keeps him at arm's length seems to reinforce his very portability and resourcefulness. He is still the "man on the case," much like a private eye, and suggests the appeal of a television drama, perhaps that 1950s series *The Millionaire,* in which the emissary of an unseen philanthropist, John Beresford Tipton, each week showed up at the door of a needy soul and gave away a million dollars. A Judean figure to the rescue, arriving precisely on the doorstep of those who have never heard of him. In the Judean universe, such things "just happen": unmediated miracles arrive on a whisper. He comes on the spur of the moment, just as when Thomas dispatched him to deliver the Jesus letter to Abgar, in itself pure Judeana, and unique in Catholic culture. In the modern world, he usually penetrates people's lives by backing into them, or, as with Adam Stolpen, literally comes up from the floorboards.

High above the canyons of Manhattan, Adam, a successful businessman and art collector, is reflecting on the last month's events in his eclectically furnished seventy-second-floor apartment (this is, as a matter of fact, around the time that the Pullaras are planning their novena bus trip to Baltimore). Over dinner, the subject of a religious revival in the country comes up, and within minutes Adam has launched into his own story of the ubiquitous but elusive saint, hitching me to another unexpected link in the Jude chain.

"I remember sitting in the Westport, Connecticut, railroad station waiting to pick up my son, and seeing a short item in the classified section of the *Westport News,* something about if you're having problems, say the following prayer to St. Jude aloud three times. So there I was, a practicing and believing Jew, sitting on my suitcase in the station mumbling this prayer. I knew Jude was the patron saint of lost causes because I'd gone to a Catholic law school, Georgetown, and I remember hearing friends saying, 'Oh, God, there's an exam tomorrow and I'm not ready for it. I think I'm going to light a candle to St. Jude.' Believing in saints or apostles is incompatible with my faith. So your St. Jude, to me, is in all probability a divine prophet. I call him a saint the same way we call Joshua, Jesus, or Jesus, Joshua. At that moment in the station I was thinking about—I think it was Spinoza who said he believed in all religions because one of them might be right."

At that point Adam was entangled in an embittered divorce—house, fortune, child custody all at stake. Within days of the depot invocation, an iconographical scholar from New York University was examining one of Adam's paintings when suddenly her eye went to another work bought for a song from an old estate in Westport five years earlier. Since Adam and his then-wife had a deal not to display any painting that the other disliked, it had been consigned to a basement. When they parted, Adam hung it in his Manhattan bedroom: a beardless, radiantly holy figure gripping a spearheaded battle-ax—a halberd. The visitor took in its full serene power. "My goodness," she gasped, "so that's where the Van Dyke St. Jude is!" Van Dyke is known to have produced several series of apostles, only one them now complete, and it is virtually certain that he painted not just one but several portraits of Jude. And, rather specially, he did not set out to paint iconographic, or hagiological "types" but highly individual portraits. The halberd, of course, particularizes Jude in representations of the saint as the instrument of his martyrdom.

In the next few months, Adam's wife agreed to a settlement. He won custody of his daughter and son and bought a new home, which entailed pulling up stakes once more. When the movers pulled a couch away from the wall, lying on the floor was a St. Jude chain letter discarded months before and totally forgotten. "I didn't connect the railroad station incident and the painting right away, but the letter did it. David Ben Gurion had the right line, 'Anyone who doesn't believe in miracles isn't a realist.'"

A few weeks after telling his story, Adam sends me the wrinkled chain letter. The cover note simply says, "With faith, all things are possible."

Fired by American ingenuity and sensing the nation's postwar association of Catholicism with patriotism and morality, Hollywood perfected the secular canonization of Jude with the release of *Come to the Stable* in 1949. Once I learned that the screenplay actually had a factual basis—from the earlier-mentioned conversation with Pia Lindstrom—further investigation had to be undertaken. Where did Jude fit in at the mysterious Regina Laudis abbey around which the film is based?

In search of the answer, we are driving up to Connecticut on a bright spring Sunday, Pia at the wheel, Maria Cooper in the jump seat filling me in on what to expect at the abbey. She and Mother Dolores are old friends. In fact, it is through their efforts that Patricia Neal, once romantically involved with Gary Cooper, found a temporary home at Regina Laudis, where she mustered the strength to write her memoir of torments public and private. If Hollywood has a spiritual annex, this is it.

As we travel deeper into the countryside, I try to organize what I know so far: two nuns from France come to Bethlehem, Connecticut, to set up a hospital in fulfillment of a sacred promise made during the war when their own hospital faced destruction. Penniless, but beguiling in their energetic innocence, they are sure of Jude's help on this impossible mission. They kneel to bury a St. Jude medal on the very spot where their community will be established. Unable to resist Hollywood's preference for juxtaposing the sacred and the profane, the script calls for a notorious gangster to donate the property.

"Here's a medal of St. Jude to protect you," Sister Margaret says to the wisecracking bookie who works for the capo she has just conned into donating land for the hospital.

"Looks like a bum slug to me," he mutters after she leaves, and casually drops the medal in a gumball machine. Crash! All of them come tumbling out. Just a small example of what Big Jude can do.

The key scene has the unblinking sisters kneeling in the snow on their New England hill: "Dear St. Jude, patron of the impossible of our holy endeavors. Here on this lonely hilltop, with the help of Our Lord and His dear servants, we will build your hospital."

A talk with Celeste Holm, who portrays the tennis-playing Sister Scholastica, had added another piece to the puzzle. At seventy-seven, the former movie star remembered that at the time of shooting she was fully aware the film was based on a true story, but did not get around to visiting the real-life convent until twenty-five years after the film was released, and then quite by accident.

"My husband took me for a drive up to a resort in Connecticut. On the way the back I looked at the map and saw a place called 'Bethlehem.' I knew the convent existed, but I didn't know exactly where."

The Judean quality of this last observation was hard to miss.

"So I called there. 'Mother Superior's been waiting for you,' said the voice on the other end, and we were asked to lunch. I didn't know they were cloistered. We sat there and ate boiled fish and potatoes while they watched us through a grille . . . sort of startling. I said to Dolores, 'Can you get loose anywhere?' And she said, 'Yes, in the chapel.' You know, she went into retreat there before her planned marriage. It was *exactly* like the set. They had rebuilt the convent. I had never heard of Jude—I'm not Catholic. It's a good thing we had a Jewish director because everybody else was Catholic."

"Was Jude in the original story?" I asked.

"Well, I don't know. Clare Boothe Luce wrote the screenplay from the original story and sent it to Loretta."

Mrs. Luce, wife of the founder of Time Inc., diplomat, woman of letters, and an ardent Catholic convert, typified the Fulton J. Sheen–style faith of that time. Her biographer, Sylvia Morris, told me that Mrs. Luce had picked up the story from a

Look magazine freelance writer, and that the screenplay had gone through a few revisions. Exactly what kind, she didn't know.

We turn into the spacious grounds. I can only speculate which design came first, the architect's or Twentieth Century Fox's—art and life melting into each other. The Abbey of Regina Laudis functions as a 360-acre working farm where sheep, pigs, cows, and assorted dogs and cats have free run. The forty-three cloistered nuns work as farmers, bakers, gardeners, painters, sculptors, and whatever else is required. They prosper here as part of a quasi-secular fairy story, like the Von Trapp family. It is a passion play with a happy ending. Dolores Hart, who played opposite Elvis Presley in *King Creole,* had been on her way to a shining film career when she joined the Benedictines of the Strict Observance at Regina Laudis six weeks before her wedding day in 1958. The mills of showbiz gossip have whirled for forty years trying to come up with plausible reasons for her choice.

The fragrance of honeysuckle envelops us as we cross the stones from the beaches of Normandy paving the entrance. Water scatters from a little fountain—that rushing sound that is now a stage cue for entering Jude territory. After touring the farm with the still-lovely Mother Dolores, we keep our appointment with the monastery's Lady Abbess, Mother Benedict Duss, so luminously portrayed on-screen by Loretta Young. Seated in front of a large picture of General George C. Patton—the most arresting souvenir of her earlier life—she tells her story. Although born in America, she studied and took her vows abroad and entered the religious life in Jouarre, outside Paris. War followed and with it the occupation of France. In the summer of 1944—fifty-two years ago—amid the harmonies of Vespers, she heard the rumble of armor. Dashing next door to a twelfth-century bell tower and climbing the spiral staircase, she saw an army of great power bearing down on the unprotected town. At first, filled with dread, she believed it to be the vengeful Germans, but then, suddenly, she saw an American flag. At that moment, she said, "I felt something for the United States that I had not felt before," whereupon she vowed to return home one day and bring a house of her order to America.

Now, at age eighty-six, her tired blue eyes radiate the patience she must find to entertain my questions. As she speaks, across the way a bell tolls, lending dramatic overtone to what was already unfolding as a movie within the movie. She reveals a trove of vivid details, slowly, meticulously, and I am ashamed of my growing impatience. Finally, at the point where she acquires the land for her convent (not a hospital, and without the help of the underworld), and the first building is to go up, I blurt out: "Lady Abbess, what was on the medal you buried?"

"Why, it was a St. Benedict medal," she says matter-of-factly, "the founder of our order."

A sizable quantity of air went out of the suspense balloon floating over our group. I should have known. It had just seemed too pat—un-Judeanly pat. And yet, in another Judean sense, and for commercial reasons, it adds up. All those screenwriters and that Jewish director knew a star, and a star theme, when they saw one. Benedict just couldn't have cut it. No wonder *Come to the Stable* earned seven Academy Award nominations—including one for best story.

Of the Jude addition, Lady Abbess says firmly: "Totally fictitious."

One cannot fault her respect for truth. Still, a credit line—if only as creative consultant—should go to Jude for the key role he played in drawing attention to the story of Regina Laudis. The rushing water had thrown me off. Once more, it is apparent that there is something in the Jude experience that discourages discovery of who he really is. Once again, he is one jump—or whatever it is, a sort of spiritual knight's move—ahead of the fastest, sliding down a side passage to do his work and fading into the crowd. Jude may be a star, but he is not a celebrity. No, it would have been too obvious, too direct, for Jude to have been part of the real story. One might say it is simply not his style.

Maria tries to cushion my disappointment. "I once saw a Xerox copy of a letter my father sent to Hemingway apologizing for what Hollywood did to *For Whom the Bell Tolls,*" she says sympathetically.

Before leaving, we drop by the gift shop to inspect the monastery's produce: bread, cheese, honey, jam, soap, face cream, a few souvenirs of the Virgin. Suddenly, knowing it before seeing it—what at first was only a glimpse out of the corner of my eye—a lone statue of Jude seems to rise from the dimness of an obscure corner, as though he had seen me first and stepped back. So he is here, after all, half-hidden in shadow, prodding my imagination to pick up the sound of saintly laughter.

SAN FRANCISCO

"Laudare, Benedicere, Praedicare"
(To praise, To Bless, To Preach)

Motto of the Dominican Order

ONCE I KNOW ALL THE TEST RESULTS, I GET IN touch and say, 'Come in. We need to talk.' On my way to the office I'm in a state of terror when there is a person waiting who must be told he's tested positive. I usually meet him in the lobby, take him to my room, make sure he's seated comfortably, give him the results in a monotone—and let him take it from there. Suddenly, we're in an alternate universe."

The soft voice speaking such hard words belongs to a forty-eight-year-old "HIV antibody counselor"—a spirit of deliverance for some, a dark angel for too many. A picture of St. Jude hangs on his bulletin board at the Oakland blood bank where he works, although he never raises the subject with his clients—even the ones who must hear a dread diagnosis. "I just bounce off what the client says next. You see, Jude is always part of my spiritual and psychological preparation for meeting with a confirmed positive client. I've found a useful ally in difficult circumstances."

The counselor, C. M., has not reconciled his own beliefs (he defends birth control and recreational sex) with those of the Catholic faith in which he was raised. Nevertheless, he is sold on the power of Jude as he confronts the AIDS epidemic as his way of life, breaking the news, absorbing the agony. A few years ago a friend in Chicago sent him a Jude calendar and, like a tennis player psyching himself up for the key set, he has used it as a source of strength.

"It's given me an added confidence that I'm not doing this alone," he says. "I was still a lapsed Catholic and there was still an emotional tug. I started bringing St. Jude into my private meditations. He's clearly the saint of lost causes. It's not an intellectual thing. It's more like when you want the light on, you go for the light switch. In counseling, it's hard not to be inadequate, and I wanted to be the best, so I invited Jude to be the counselor. He isn't the flawed person here. I'm an instrument of St. Jude. Even though the clients don't know masses are being said for them, I believe there is a spiritual carryover that illuminates their way."

Shock is always there, he says, especially among women who have had an affair a few years before and didn't perceive themselves as part of a risk group. "This better not be AIDS, or I'm going to faint dead away," one of them told C. M. She didn't. He knows that in virtually every case people are a lot braver than they expect themselves to be. Three days later it's a different story, when shock gives way to the choking depression that is AIDS' faithful companion.

Unlike the typical Jude follower, C. M. is reticent to discuss his experience of the saint; he has not placed any "Thank You St. Jude" ads in the newspapers or talked him up among friends or strangers. "It's like Native American healing," he says lightly. "It loses its efficiency once divulged to another."

C. M.'s "clients" are never far away. Across the fog-shrouded bay, the siren beauty of San Francisco still lures gold-seekers with impossible dreams, adventurers with exaggerated hopes, and hedonists with a conscience dictated only by weather, a place where plants are called "flowering eucalyptus" and "star jasmine," where sea and sky meet in breathless, well-publicized spectacle. Some say this city is a caricature of where we are going. The undulating streets have offered a new Barbary Coast to those who drift here, people who catch on fast to the realization that when you live atop a crack in the earth, you resign yourself to just about anything. If there is a price to pay for gentle winds and sweet living, the ultimate one is exacted here, the epicenter of a plague that has redefined hopelessness for all time, cruelly and for staggering numbers. This is where AIDS drove its beachhead into America, a place where happiness is practically compulsory—from the cloying repetition of "Have a good day" to where Tony Bennett left his heart. The dirty little secret is that legions of the desperate are walking these golden streets wondering how the dream could end. What could be more bitter than this juxtaposition of oppressively positive California-ism and the looming certainty of withering death? The very genius of the place is mocked by the horror of AIDS. It begs for happy endings, to which Jude is no stranger.

Surrounded by this misery, San Francisco has played a major role in the continuing study of the connection between body and spirit and of the larger nature of illness. In the spring of 1996, doctors at the California Pacific Medical Center in San

Francisco decided to weigh the intangibility of prayer and the power of hope in a controlled double-blind study of twenty gravely ill AIDS patients chosen at rigorous random. A team of twenty faith healers, provided only with photographs, first names, and in some cases T-cell counts, prayed for half the patients (and not for the other half) for at least an hour every day for ten weeks. The patients were not told to which group they had been assigned. Dr. Elisabeth Targ, clinical director of psychosocial oncology research at the center, described the results as so "encouraging" that a follow-up study of one hundred more patients was planned. The search for a point at which spirituality and healing intersect is no longer seen as an echo of Freud's "regression to primary narcissism," but as a cutting edge of medicine.

In another experiment, at San Francisco General Hospital in 1988, born-again Christians prayed for half of 393 patients chosen at random in the coronary-care unit. To eliminate any placebo effect, they were not told the reason they had been selected. The result: those not being prayed for were five times as likely to require antibiotics and three times as likely to develop complications than those for whom prayers were offered.

L'ultima che si perde e la speranza (The last thing we lose is hope) say the Italians. For the sick and dying, hope is implicit in their prayers, and the embodiment of that classic renewing virtue (of course, impalpable) is Jude. I am the doorkeeper of your last hope, he murmurs. It is an iron belief of the thousands of sorrowing souls who yearly throng his San Francisco shrine—the Shrine of the West—which is housed in St. Dominic's Church, named after the thirteenth-century founder of the Dominican order. The church sits grand as any Gothic cathedral, its blunt majesty arresting the attention of casual strollers who come upon this massive presence in Pacific Heights. During its 125 years at the intersection of Bush and

Steiner streets, St. Dominic's has been rebuilt or restored at least four times, twice because of earthquakes. During the 1989 disaster, tremors coursed through its stones, cracking the lantern tower and shaking religious decorations from the ceiling beams like autumn leaves. In the aftermath, workmen found one of them, a small anchor—symbol of hope and part of Jude's iconography—lying untouched in the fallen plaster. Once the reconstruction was finished, parishioners had it mounted in a plaster square and presented to Father Thomas James Hayes, the shrine's affable director, who deems it one of those "interesting coincidences." The anchor is proudly displayed in his office, along with a Jude shrine constructed from magazine photos by a devout man at the California veterans' home in Napa Valley. Then there's the painting by Miguel Diaz, a young man who recovered from a serious illness after his father prayed to Jude; the statue donated by a man dying of AIDS; and the statue given by a man whose entire house was destroyed by fire, except for the figure itself—a common occurrence in the lore of saints and strange coincidences. Facing Father Hayes's desk is another Jude statue, resolute in all its chipped beauty, the scarred survivor of a tremor that sent it crashing to the floor. Relics all, that speak to the faith of this very age.

The St. Jude shrine evolved during the Great Depression—a hopeless time indeed, most assuredly in need of miracles—after one of the priests set up a small Jude statue near the chapel of the Virgin. By 1935, St. Jude novenas were part of the church's ritual, and in 1953, the devotion—as usual, ever expanding—found a permanent home in a Jude shrine constructed in the north side of the nave, where it stands today. By the 1960s, the shrine's popularity had reached beyond the parish and the West, drawing millions to worship in person or to present their petitions by letter.

A dozen priests and three brothers live and work here, four of them assigned to the shrine: Father Terrence Reilly, who retains his Bronx accent and has spent twenty-five of his forty-three years as a priest counseling troubled boys; Father Felix Cassidy, a native San Franciscan, forty-seven years a priest and missionary, known for his singularly sweet nature and the time he saved a man from drowning at a Dominican mission in Mexico; Father Gregory Anderson, born and raised a Baptist, who wound up baptizing his mother and grandmother into the church; and Father Thomas Paul Raftery, ordained forty-six years ago, a canon law specialist and former theology professor.

St. Jude and the Dominicans share a long and intimate history, at least as far back as the fourteenth century when the order tried to keep alive the reunion of the Armenian and Catholic churches, which had split on theological grounds in the sixth century. This reunion, lasting from 1198 to 1375, saw the formation of a native Armenian order, the Friars of Unity. Founded in 1320, it adapted Armenian monasticism to the Dominican rule, and was later incorporated into the Dominican order. Fleeing Muslim persecution, the Armenian Dominicans settled in Smyrna (now Izmir) in Asia Minor, a very Greek seaport in western Turkey that was part of the Ottoman Empire.

As discussed earlier, Armenia, possibly the oldest Christian country, has from the earliest times claimed that Jude perished there and that his followers, after exhuming the body from a secret grave, sent part of it to Rome. However, in the manner of the times, they kept a forearm, entrusting it to the Smyrna monastery. Eventually the relic was sent to the Dominicans in Turin, and, finally, in this century, to the Dominican St. Jude shrine in Chicago, where it remains.

A Dominican priest for thirty-eight years in an order traditionally known as Domini Canes ("the Hounds of the Lord") for its zeal and preaching skill, Father Hayes has seen it all in

Jude's territory: the devout, the superstitious, the doubtful, the faithless. He is a merry man with a penchant for Mark Twain. Short and stocky of build, his small mustache shadowed by a prizefighter nose, he cuts through the crowds like a gentle cannonball, a trifle absentminded to the world in his certainty of God's grace.

When he started overseeing the Jude devotion eighteen years ago, he had no idea that so many people were so profoundly influenced by the "forgotten saint," or that whenever somebody brought up the saint's name, somebody else would pipe up with a Jude story to prove how unforgotten he really is. "They had Jude in their thinking, Jude in their baggage," he says. Nowadays, it is likely that the story will be one about AIDS, and usually the result of a lifestyle in direct, if not hostile, opposition to the doctrines of Rome.

"There are a great number who find the shrine helpful to them," reflects Father Hayes. "First, one has to ask how they fit in with the teaching of the church. Right? That's the first hurdle. For those who can't accept it—or think that the church is against them—they're gone. They're not going to be turning to St. Jude. But those who believe the church does care or really is sympathetic—they'll be open to St. Jude, and we do get those."

Robert Thomas fits this description, simple in his abiding faith, deeply human in his straying from church teaching, movingly complex in his resignation. He was diagnosed HIV positive in 1987; by 1995 he had had meningitis and three bouts with pneumonia. Toxic reactions forced him to quit chemotherapy, and potent drugs that replaced it attacked him as well as the disease. Born a Catholic, he was attending mass, receiving communion, and even praying to St. Jude when he was diagnosed.

"I absolutely stopped any sexual activity whatsoever at that point," he says. "AIDS was my dragon. I was either going to be attacked and consumed, or domesticate it and put it on a leash and bring him into the village. I kept asking people connected with the shrine to remember me. I knew Jude was going to be there."

Robert is hard to forget. Handsome at forty-eight, blonde and tall, he uses his edgy wit to mock his condition, to find absurdity where many see only despair. Like so many homosexuals with AIDS, he has a good friend and former partner caring for him who is also HIV positive, but asymptomatic. Robert is very popular, enormously likable. A native San Franciscan, he ran a travel agency for twenty-eight years and stayed on the job until deep into his illness. Jude is an important part of his day.

"I recite the St. Jude prayer every morning. He's part of my ritual. He's also included in the afternoon when I can't make it to the shrine. A lot of power comes from being connected with this particular saint. I don't think the world really understands or recognizes it—and I don't know why—as much as they recognize St. Anthony, St. Ignatius, or others—I don't think he's come into his own yet.

"It's not on my agenda to ask to win the lottery—I never say, 'Save my life.' I say, 'Help me through this ordeal, You who listen to those and answer those prayers of people who go through heavier ordeals than mine.'

"No, no—what will be here is going to happen. I just want to have some dignity with it all and some connection. It's not easy, especially when you go to your friends' funerals, like I did three weeks ago.

"There is a certain level of comfort, of peace, that comes with devotion to this particular saint for people who have a terminal illness. I've seen desperate people with a terminal illness come to that shrine and witnessed them coming away feeling renewed, restored, and with hope that whatever ordeal they have to go through, Jude will not lose them. Their devotion is so strong that they are not going to be left without that assistance. I'm not quite sure whether I would say that Jude has helped me deliberately, but in a quiet, silent way he gives me that sense of peace and strength and comfort that I seek at the shrine.

"In the beginning I couldn't deal with being a recipient of help, spiritual or practical. I denied it the first time I had pneumonia. Now I'm a recipient and whoever wants to give me any type of encouragement, I welcome it. This came so gradually, I can't even tell you. Gradually, sort of like this whole process I'm going through of being symptomatic now—a phase of the journey—and there was nothing abrupt about it. It was very smooth. I've had St. Jude to go to throughout."

It is just after evening mass in spring, during one of the four annual Jude novenas. Father Hayes is patrolling the crowds that invariably gravitate to Jude's resplendent altar, his white robes gleaming in the light of 1,200 candles (3,000 on Jude's feast day) burning in green filigree coasters. In Rome itself Jude's altar does not blaze so brightly. He is represented in a traditional life-size statue, bald and long-bearded, green cloak over white tunic, holding a medallion on which the face of Christ is imprinted—a reminder of the Mandylion—and cradling a thick staff at his side. Polished cherry wood paneling embraces the marble altar. Stained-glass windows on both sides recall his iconography: a ship in full sail, a symbol of the church; a halberd and club, instruments of martyrdom; a carpenter's square, symbol of the building trades, which Jude may have practiced; and a shepherd's crook, the sign of Christ the Good Shepherd and the pastoral authority and mission of the apostles.

Father Hayes pauses to check the flowers and to see that the prayer books and calendars are neatly stacked. Every few steps, someone catches his arm or eye and stops to chat: a Filipino woman and her husband come for more Jude oil; a young Hispanic woman presents a photograph she took of the altar, convinced that a beam of light shooting down from the statue is a divine message ("You had your finger over the lens," Father Hayes says dryly); a middle-aged woman is anxious to show him a strange letter she has received. "Too chainlike," he tells her. "Ignore it." Meanwhile, in a scene I will see repeated throughout the week, a man, a woman, young or old, will grab Jude's foot, looking up into his face in earnest prayer, hanging on for dear life. Many fervent kisses have worn down the plaster foot, which, a few years ago, had to be replaced.

Every day of the novena, a man in his forties, almost totally bald and alarmingly thin, walks slowly around the church, taking communion, then stopping at the Jude altar. A large wooden crucifix hangs from a black ribbon resting on his concave chest. The expression is peaceful, but he wears "the look" I came to recognize in the mid–1980s while reporting stories on the first wave of AIDS casualties. In Vietnam it was called the "thousand-yard stare," the look of a soldier long in combat, eyes fixed on an invisible dread.

"I'm praying for patience and perseverance," says Jim Lenartz, not long ago a fallen-away Catholic. "One afternoon I saw the church and went in, and a year or so later I was back to the faith. This is the last call to give something back to the world."

Jim was born in Michigan and worked as a medical transcriber, a job he has had to give up. In 1984, he tested positive for HIV, and about a decade later began feeling the depths of illness and the temporary highs of recovery associated with his disease. Like Robert Thomas, he says he does not pray for a cure—even though he is certain that his chronic hepatitis was healed through St. Jude. Sometimes Jim's courage fails him—

when he's feeling very sick or confronting the likelihood of death. But his devotion does not waver; he leaves novena cards in buses and restaurants.

"I pray to find out what lessons I should learn. For patience and perseverance. I don't look for a cure through him because I know death is an inevitability. This is a terminal disease. Thanks to Jude, I got over chronic hepatitis. I would not be comfortable praying for a cure. Who am I? I don't feel comfortable asking for miraculous means. I pray to find out what lessons I should learn, not to despair, and for patience, knowing it will pass.

"For awhile I felt the church had nothing to say. Here in San Francisco it's not politically correct to be in the church. The gay community used to be inclusive, but now you have to fit in. I don't fit in. It's trendy. Some people who really are against the church are the same ones who run down to Catholic Charities for financial help and housing.

"Many gays, all they do is blame. We're too busy with this. We have to get beyond this. There must be a spiritual awakening, a new age of nondenominational psychic healing. For lots of gays, AIDS has awakened a spiritual hunger. They don't go to the Catholics because of the church's stand on homosexuality. Who needs their approval? I don't need approval to be gay. They're still stuck in blaming and approving, just where they were twenty years ago.

"My nephew had a friend who wanted to be a Catholic. I talked about the faith with him. He lives in a flat and has to move. What will happen? I prayed to St. Jude that he would calm down. He prayed to Jude and found a wonderful house for rent. He feels his prayers have been answered.

"Another friend needed a place to stay. His roommates are druggies. He's not a Christian—nothing—he's just moved out and is staying with his girlfriend. Sure enough, he found a clean and sober roommate. His chances are very good, but he has the trendy notion that it's not cool to be Catholic. I prayed for him to St. Jude every day—I generally keep him busy—and eventually he decided to give Jude a break. I ask him for just about anything, but one must always say *if God wills it*. With my prayer life, I think I get results, but I think twice about what I ask. The clearer you are in your petition, the easier it is to be heard. He takes away the clouds so I can see clearly."

At the time of my interview with Jim, he was awaiting approval to enter the Dominican Third Order, a fraternity of laymen and women who live secular lives, but assist the Dominican order in preserving and propagating the faith. By the summer of 1996, he had been accepted.

Jude has drawn many afflicted with AIDS close to him. Why this is so may be partly traceable to his very facelessness. The stigma that AIDS bestows, the sense of shame many sufferers may feel, seem to be subsumed in the elusiveness of Jude. Going to him instead of to saints with pronounced identities is like confessing your sins to a priest behind a grill rather than meeting him face-to-face. Anything but high profile by nature, Jude's persona, his essence, occupies the quiet end of a saintly spectrum that includes Paul, the dynamic and even overbearing preacher; Peter, the swashbuckling sailor who lost his nerve at the crucial moment; and St. Teresa of Ávila, the mystical yet outspoken intellectual. Jude is the workmanlike spiritual mechanic, the one who does his job and moves on. Approaching him takes no energy and is as secret as shouting in a cave for help. Jude is not interested in the humiliation of being messily cut down in one's prime, or in the cold, triumphant judgment so many of the told-you-so chorus would be willing to pass. There is no discussion about how the facts of AIDS stack up against his record or reputation, no overwrought emotional debate of how you got it, no gleeful moralizing—only Jude, cool, practical, not offering a solution, but so often seeming to provide one.

How Jude works theologically, without metaphoric drama, is a subject Father Thomas Paul Raftery, the novena preacher, addresses on day two. This is a no-nonsense priest, a former professor of theology ever on the lookout to confront superstition where there should be sound doctrine. The church is crowded for a Monday morning, with candles glowing, a fragrance of roses lifting from the Jude altar, and worshipers clutching their novena booklets. Looking out over the splendid, familiar scene, Father Raftery reads the Gospel, in which Jesus talks about what will happen to the apostles after His Crucifixion and even after His Resurrection. Fifty days later, the apostles are sequestered in the Upper Room, on their own, in confusion and fear for their lives. Not until the Holy Spirit descends on them, just as Jesus has promised, do they find the courage to go out into the world. Then they are ready to bear witness, to take their message to the ends of a hostile earth. All but one will die a martyr.

"You know one of the things about devotion to St. Jude that you must understand is that . . . St. Jude is not really the one who helps us, but he is the one through whom we approach the Lord. And he is a particular patron for very difficult, desperate, even, as we say, hopeless cases. However, we have to remember that the one we are calling upon is God, and St. Jude is the channel through which we approach God and ask for His help in these particular cases. . . . This is what devotion to St. Jude is all about. We are asking for the spirit of God to come and to inspire our lives and through the intercession of St. Jude we ask for that spirit. This is what St. Jude wants."

After mass, I wander over to the throng before Jude's altar, an unending stream, the hopeful mingling with the desperate, but all reaching out to the mysterious presence. I wonder how many have considered Father Raftery's crucial distinction, or even care. Do they see Jude as a channel, an intercessor, one through whom we approach the Lord, *and not the one who helps us himself?* Their suffering and trusting faces suggest that this distinction may be of no great consequence to them. Jude is Jude. He listens, and his listening makes things happen.

A woman in a black coat and scarf kneels before the statue, weeping, dabbing at her eyes. Another woman approaches, embraces her, tries to console. What is her desperate cause—a sick child, a drunken husband, a lost job, a dying lover? Every Jude altar in the world echoes with such plangent questions.

Ed Suever is in church, too, a retired man who has a two-foot statue of Jude "anchored in concrete" on the lawn in front of his house on Euclid Avenue. An avid six-day-a-week bike rider, he suffered a staph infection in his left knee some years ago, and it took six surgeons to save his leg. "If it weren't for Jude, I wouldn't have a leg."

Early next morning, the city's golden glow has dissolved into steady rain. A ghostly mist out of the sea masks the great span of the Golden Gate. Fourth-century Constantinople, a city that also honored Jude, had its Golden Gate, too. Three arches formed the state entrance for the high and mighty visiting this splendid capital of the Roman Empire. Built on its own seven hills, Constantinople rose above the sea, ringed by three walls and overlooking the gilded church domes and grand palaces that made it the heart of Byzantine learning and a bastion of Christianity.

Grayness is all on this day. Humidity seeps into every crevice. People shift uncomfortably in the pews at St. Dominic's, sticking to their plastic raincoats, wrestling with umbrellas. Father Raftery derives the theme of his sermon—how a community sees itself—from Jesus' discourse at the Last Supper, the night before the Crucifixion: "Love one another," he says. "By this, will all men know you are my followers."

Heads snap up at the sound of the word *love*, and the page-turning and coughing seem to evaporate in the echoes of the thought. This "new commandment"—the essence of Christianity—permeates the Master's response to Jude's famous, and only, question at this, their last meal together. In short, God doesn't need publicity; love will be your ID badge.

If anything has tested this new commandment at the end of the second millennium it is the scourge of AIDS. How a community sees itself—whether the homosexual community or the particular town or city in which its members live—has tested true charity. In San Francisco, the sheer numbers of ailing and dying young men have carried it beyond the individually tragic to the darkly epic, pervading and altering the atmosphere of what so recently was set on being the most lighthearted city in North America. New and powerful drugs continue to arrive, none of them yet the magic bullet the world awaits.

"Love one another," repeats Father Raftery. "And that is what we try to create here at St. Dominic's."

That very evening I would see this claim put to the test at an HIV-AIDS support group in a church parlor. But the hours leading up to this event hold some surprises, and, as this is Jude territory—a land of the unexpected, the curiously coincidental—not out of character. I am about to run a gauntlet of people who, in the tradition of Judean encounters, have stories to tell.

Michele Alioto surprises me. I had noticed her in church during the week. At this moment she is talking to Father Hayes, who soon introduces us. The striking blonde daughter-in-law of the late Joseph L. Alioto, former mayor of San Francisco, has been a friend of the shrine since her girlhood and throughout her twenty-nine-year marriage to Joseph M. Alioto. At fifty, she is still girlishly pretty, with large blue eyes, old-fashioned poise, and a knockout figure. What could she want of Jude? But Mrs. Alioto, like most of us, has had her own cross to bear. Fifteen years ago, Michela, one of her four children, fell off a ski lift. Spinal damage transformed a cheerful young lady into a paraplegic.

"I never said 'why me?' I always felt there was a reason," recalls Mrs. Alioto. "At first I was furious and went through all the emotions, but I never felt defeated by it at all. She didn't either.

"I made a lot of novenas after the accident. I'm convinced that the prayers that I said for my daughter, the prayers she said for herself, and the prayers that surrounded her life growing up had everything to do with the person she has become. I think her life has been a real miracle. She's just an extraordinary young women.

"It's very powerful, praying to Jude. I have an affinity, I can't put it into words. When things get very tough he usually comes through. I've really had a lot miracles in my life. The accident was very difficult on all of us, especially Michela's sister. But I think all of us really felt that something great would come out of it."

Indeed, something already has. The Aliotos founded the American Paralysis Association, with which Christopher Reeves is now very involved. And Michela, at twenty-eight, won the Democratic congressional primary in California's first congressional district, the state's largest, which runs from the North Bay up to the Oregon border.

"If she wins," says her mother, "she'll be the youngest woman ever elected to Congress, and the only one ever in a wheelchair."

Just before parting, she volunteers: "My daughter took the confirmation name 'Jude,'" something her Republican opposition might have considered. Michela lost the election by fewer than ten thousand votes, hardly a lost cause for one so young and courageous.

A damp wind sweeps the parking lot as the rain subsides. It blows loud enough to muffle what I thought might be someone calling my name. The second time it comes through loud and clear. A robust middle-aged woman with short dusty-blonde hair has overtaken me. Before the simplest pleasantries can be exchanged, she is spilling out her tale, as though time is running out, as though the sooner she gets it out, the sooner she can forget. It had unfolded twenty-seven years ago in a place that for many Americans seemed a truly hopeless cause.

"I don't want to tell you my name because I feel this is a personal thing. My husband and I went to Vietnam together in 1969. He was a veterinarian and I was a nurse. Both of us went out into the field, he would take care of the working dogs. My husband—he's dead now—was supposed to go out with me this day, but he was called back to Saigon and so I went out alone to the field hospital in the Mekong Delta. Normally, we'd go out for a couple of weeks and then stay in Saigon for two weeks, back and forth. They gave you that break, because otherwise you just couldn't handle it. That night I had just gotten off duty. You never really got undressed because you were on duty all the time, so you'd take a little snooze on an empty bed, which is what I did.

"Meanwhile, the Vietcong had attacked the hospital and were burning it out. I kicked out the window. Two young troopers beside me were hurt, so I threw them out the window and we scrambled. They didn't know we were alive. We were out in the bush for about fifteen days, waiting for them to find us. We knew the Cong were around, and they had dogs, too . . . and I knew that if they got us, that would be it.

"I kept saying, 'Please, St. Jude, let me die in my own country. I know I'm going to die here—but please St. Jude let me die in my own country.' I knew we didn't have a chance. The guys would sneak back at night into the medical compound to get cans of water that weren't burned. I figured like I was in hell already. But they—our guys—found us. In fact, they thought we were VC at first. They were flying us all over the country for treatment—as you can see, I have the burns. Everyone had been killed. I was in the hospital for a long time with internal bleeding. Anyway, after they picked us up, I said, 'St. Jude, I will sing your praises for life.'

"I take no credit for this. It's part of my life now. I have scars from the burns, and very bright sun still gives me headaches— it brings back memories. Every day, before I go to bed, I say thank you. And I go to Jude novenas at least once a year. If you're in a tough spot, this is the man to call. He will put your petition up."

When I press for her name, she says, "Call me Carol. I just wanted you to tell my story." She pulls her windbreaker around her and walks slowly away.

Back at my hotel, Patricia Mitchell is on the telephone. She works in the admitting department of the University of California Medical Center, where she has seen the whole spectrum of AIDS. One of her patients was the dying man who gave his St. Jude statue to Father Hayes. Some are looking for a quick fix, she says, others just want spiritual help, strength to carry out God's will.

"If they're not cured, they know the Lord had a different purpose," Patricia says shakily. "Some families care more than others. Some AIDS victims are buried from their homes. One gay priest had them coming to church, but he burned out. They're all dead. It's almost as though they're out of mind."

From the tone of her voice, it is apparent that the daily grind of the disease has drawn her, too, into its dark orbit of exhausted suffering. Indeed, Patricia has her own private hell.

She endured a difficult marriage for eighteen years until her husband left her with their two children, ages twelve and thirteen. She developed severe allergies, dropping from 106 to 82 pounds.

"I remember the trees blooming in May and August, and I couldn't come out of the house. My immune system was shot and I could only handle a half-dozen foods. In October of 1984 I saw a 'Thank you St. Jude' ad in the *San Francisco Chronicle*. I made the novena on November 4 and began to feel pretty good. I started eating, and after three months, eating almost everything. I went back to work—and I wasn't sick anymore. My doctor, a Jewish man, said, 'Tell me that story,' and I told him about it. I gave him a Jude medal and Jude oil. I'm not sick anymore, and every day I have to thank St. Jude and remember what he did and spread the devotion. He's always with me. He's always a part of me."

Arriving at the shrine in the evening for the support-group session, I encounter Chuck Landis sitting on the stone steps. He tested positive for the AIDS virus in 1988, one year after his partner, an Episcopalian, died from a brain tumor. Chuck was born and raised a Lutheran and describes himself as spiritual but not religious. He has become an Episcopalian, largely, he says, because of the influence of two Third Order Dominicans who founded the HIV-AIDS support group at St. Dominic's.

Straining his voice above the rush-hour traffic, he says, "I give them credit for my devotion to the Episcopal church." A dozen people show up for the support-group session in a small parlor off the church's main office. Jim Lenartz, still wearing his cross, is there, looking edgy and sad. So is Robert Thomas, who arrives a bit late, tanned, dimpled, wearing chinos and a green checked shirt that matches his sunken eyes. A Franciscan, Brother Karl; a Dominican in blue jeans from Germany; Raymond, a regular group member; another Jim; and three women who have experienced AIDS through others, usually a dying friend. Brian, the moderator or "facilitator," does a "check," asking each person for a psychological and medical update. Desperation is not spoken here; instead, resignation, even peace, each frame of mind demanding an understatement that only highlights the deeper meaning of this communal sorrow. "OK" becomes a codeword, masking great pain, but telegraphing determination enough to carry on. Hope invites reinforcement, just as Milton says: "What reinforcement we may gain from hope. If not, what resolution from despair."

Jim: I'm having a kind of dark night of the soul. Last week was hard. But I'll be OK.

Rejane: One of the tenants in my building died of AIDS, alone, and it shook me up.

Raymond: Three friends died in the past two weeks, another just had surgery. I understand he's OK although he doesn't answer the phone. I'm doing OK.

Don: Last night I had spasms in my back, and this morning I tried to get up, but I couldn't because I had such pain. I called the doctor and he told me to soak in the bathtub.

Robert leans forward to speak for the first time, and everyone is immediately cheered. His voice is thin and weak.

Robert: I'm recovering from this last setback. I couldn't have done it without the dedication of this group, coming to me on a daily basis, calling me, bringing me the sacrament, weeding my rose beds. It's been wonderful. My doctor told me that my success in getting back to being comfortable is good nutrition. I'm still preparing my own food, a full meal four times a day— that's the key. And I've gained eight pounds (APPLAUSE).

I've got ten more to go, and I think I'll feel, well, anyway . . . I *hope* to be here every other week.

Moderator: I hope so, too.

Robert: One of the bonuses is going to the shrine, frankly. When I first came into the church, I didn't realize there was a shrine to Jude. I was born and raised in San Francisco, and all I remember was the image of Jude, perhaps from catechism. But I started meeting people here, participated in the novenas. I even brought my godchild to a novena here when she was eight. Now she's fifteen, and she comes every year and we go together. I think, physically, people will get relief, the acceptance will ease the pain. But there's a lot of mystery to it.

Jim L.: Oh, I don't know. I've just been getting more and more discouraged. I'm not having as much hope as I've been having. . . . My case is advancing . . . Now they're giving me Andriomycin, which is really heavy-duty. I slept for two days straight. My whole body aches . . . I feel as though the insides of my legs are on fire. Just a lot of weird things. If I walk a few blocks, I feel like I've run the marathon. My legs want to fall off. It's just a drag, just a drag. And when I go through this, I feel that God—Jesus—walks away and is not there for me until I'm feeling better again and feel that connection again. But I force myself to pray and try to go to mass every day. I pray every night. I do it. I just do it. My spiritual life is all I have left. And I know that I'm not getting better. I'm just very frustrated with this whole scene.

His voice cracks. The room is dead silent.

Jim L. (continuing): Sometimes I want to give up . . . You know, for me, the way I look at it is, I don't really pray that I get over this, or that there's a cure. So I invite you, if you pray for me, to pray that I have the strength to accept God's will for me. That's all there is. It's like I'm trying to take everything back and do it my way. But it's not about my way. It's that God wants me to learn from this process. But it's very hard. He's not letting up. It's like, would you please give me a break? "No" is the answer, for whatever reason, and I don't need to know the reason. It's just hard to accept sometimes—having AIDS.

The last two words ring with an eerie finality.

Robert: Certainly this isn't the first time that you have felt discouraged?

Jim L.: This is the longest-lasting event.

Robert: I can identify with this—as many can. I have severe allergies to many of the drugs, so every time I'd take a new one, I prayed to Jude that I wouldn't have a severe reaction. It's difficult to remember how you felt you when you started to feel better because we concentrate on the present moment of discouragement and of health. However, if you can, ask the Lord for it. Ask the Lord for that gift. Certainly He's the one who is giving us the gift of recovery and better health. The connection is there and yours is very strong, Jim. I know that your devotion is very, very strong. For me to see you discouraged is OK, it's part of the process, but I would like you to shorten the amount of time. Drugs aren't going to work. They didn't work on me a lot of the time. There will be something that will make you feel more like yourself. Do you know what I'm saying?

Jim L.: I do. Thank you.

Everyone seems to be staring at a distant point in space, weighing the argument. "Let's talks about how AIDS challenges us spiritually," suggests the moderator in a whisper. It is as though everyone present is listening hard for a secret clue, a hidden key, an untried path.

Jim L.: For myself I know where I'm at in my prayer life. I'm asking for the humility to accept, for patience, for perseverance that I can stay connected spiritually. That's all that really ultimately matters to me. I have that, and I feel much more comforted, and it's OK to be sick.

Moderator: Why is that important to you?

Jim L.: Coming from years of destructive self-abuse, a destructive lifestyle, I'm finally getting it that God loves me and that I'm deserving. In a certain respect, I feel chosen, and I have something to give back. That's why I'm still here.

Richard: What do you mean chosen? Chosen to have AIDS?

Jim L.: No, chosen to be aware of God's love for me. I feel that there's a reason for all this happening, and that the reason I'm still alive is that He wants something from me in return.

Richard: I don't agree with the whole thing that AIDS is a gift from God, and it's a way for us to test our spirituality and all that bullshit. There's nothing good about AIDS. I don't find anything good about it. It hasn't made me a better person.

Jim: Has it made you a worse person?

Richard: No. Some people feel AIDS is an invitation to become more loving or more accepting of God's will in your life. I haven't found that in my life. It's affected my spirituality in the sense that I'm more confused. It's just created more grayness, more ambiguity, more questions in my life than I had before.

Jim: Do you try to find answers to these questions, or do you just sit with them?

Richard: I just sit with them—I walk with them; I feel as though I'm on a journey . . .

Jim L.: Sounds like enough to me. It sounds spiritual.

Richard: It goes back to your feeling that God has abandoned you, especially in times of despair when you feel you are alone. I can totally identify with that. I mean we can all sit here and say, "Oh, no, God's with you, He's carrying you at this moment," but that's just platitudes at a time when you're really feeling despair.

Robert: On the other hand, you can't do this alone. You can't have AIDS by yourself. It doesn't work. If you have a supporting community, as fortunately I do, God is working through them. He is putting people in touch with me. His love radiates through them. Their good works are an expression of their love for me. I believe that absolutely. At first it was rhetoric to me, and I thought, OK, it's kind of like going through a St. Jude novena and bringing it off by rote, not really getting into it. But there's a moment when that devotion becomes spiritual. It comes from you guys. It comes from the world that's coming to me.

Jim L.: I agree with that very much. God does speak to us through other people. If you really listen, we can get something from other people that applies to our spirituality. I need the spirituality and love of all those around me.

Jim: What you said really hits me. I was a member of the parish choir when I found out I had AIDS two years ago. I went into a spiral and I really thought that God had deserted me—it was awful. I went back to the choir after a couple of months and back to church, and the people and the choirmaster were wonderful to me. Their love for me, and His love for me, and their help kept me going every Sunday at the practice. I believe that that was God. And since that happened, so many people—my parents—well, my father died last month and I found out that his last words that last afternoon were that he was worried about me.

Moderator: A lot of times we get so caught up in ourselves, we don't want anyone going through that pain and emotion with us. But opening yourself up and accepting people's love— which, to me, is the language of God—allows people who are giving to give. You have to get beyond the stigma of AIDS to really benefit spiritually from it or you die alone. And a lot of people choose to do that. But that's not my way.

It's difficult knowing the outcome of the disease. If I didn't know that . . . (*LAUGHTER*) I know one day it's going to be me. There's no doubt in my mind about that. Some days I feel like I can't deal with it anymore, you know. I'm not even forty yet, and all my friends are dead. That's crazy. I just turn it over to God . . . I just turn it over to God, not my doctor or this person or that. And if God wants me get up in the morning, then He's going to give me the energy to do that. If He doesn't, that's OK, too, God must want me to stay in bed. It's very humbling. We often think we're in control of our lives, and we're often told, with AIDS, that, you know, *we* did it. Obviously, I don't see it that way. People have all sorts of diseases, some they caused themselves, some not. It's all part of God's plan, and we don't necessarily have to understand it.

Robert: Without any cure there is an inevitability of death . . . We've lost about fourteen people in this group. I'll never forget the friend who said at a funeral, "I'm next." I didn't know how to respond. He probably was next, but my human nature went into denial, and I said, "Oh no, Ernie, not necessarily." I'm bringing this up only to tell you that it is inevitable right now.

But there's no doubt about it that medicine is really trying to relieve us. We're not the first generation to suffer a plague. Let's face it. Let's make it as easy on us as possible. Let's not make it a rigid battle between life and death. I've just reached a place where I can think about death. The Dominicans got me to this place—because their way is to look for the truth, and in this case the truth is the inevitability of death. These men here in this community are God's work for me. They can really sit down and say death is inevitable, and, unfortunately, yours is going to be earlier than most. That's OK, really. Really. I'm not afraid of it.

Moderator: It's true we all have to die—physically.

A closing prayer, and all embrace, some for the last time, as the good-natured warmth of the room holds them intact.

It is difficult to fathom the faith of these men who must face their own mortality, charting their time left by the grisly progression of T-cell counts and viral loads. New medicines can only prolong life as the search for that magic bullet goes on. Understandably, some argue that death's nearness has driven them back to Jude, to hope, or simply to recognition of a forgiving God. The question is, why some and not others? And how does one account for the strength so many have found?

The exhausted hearts, beating lighter, the hands reaching out with a strange confidence in that small parlor, offer just a snapshot of the long shadow AIDS has cast in a place so sure of its beauty, in a world already locked in moral and cultural struggle. Fundamental questions are asked, not only of medicine, science, philosophy, and religion but of how far patient and "fellow man" are willing to muster charity, respect, and a modicum of hope. This is where Jude thrives, insinuating himself among the weary, acting as a catalyst in the realm of hope. He is the man of the moment, an abnormal saint for an abnormal age in this "time of testing," as Camus calls his evocation of a city ravaged by bubonic plague. His Father Paneloux asks, "Who would deny everything?" in such a time, where religion is not everyday religion but the hour for practicing the greatest of all virtues: that of the "all or nothing." Extremity being God's—and Jude's—opportunity requires finer mettle, greater risks, uncommon courage. It is one thing to proclaim to a support group that you are "OK"; it's quite another to sweat out the daily terror alone in your room. Not one of the many people I encountered with the virus or the disease would admit to praying for a cure, a miracle. Yet I can easily imagine that in some dark hour, in a flash of desperation, more than one had rattled the heavens crying out for just that. Doesn't Jesus Himself, facing death, do the same? Agonizing in the garden of Gethsemane just hours before His Crucifixion, He sees what tortures lie ahead—the mocking crowds, the lash, the nails, the bitter gall—but knows it is all to be inseparable from His mission in the world, to the whole process of man's redemption, yet He still cries out to His Father, "Let this cup pass from me."

Dennis Heberling says he is not asking for a miracle, and yet he felt compelled to possess a relic of St. Jude. A former deacon in the Lutheran church, Dennis grew up in Richland, Pennsylvania. He served as a Navy corpsman with the U.S. Marines in Vietnam and battled alcoholism afterward. A machinist by trade, Dennis lost his job and made his way to Phoenix, finding work one week after his unemployment insurance ran out. By 1988, Dennis and his companion, Steve, had joined the Malta, a local AIDS outreach organization that handles more than one thousand cases a year. "I've stopped counting the number of funerals," says the group director, Father Joseph O'Brien, another Dominican.

Steve died in 1993, and Dennis, still mourning, is himself afflicted. With no prompting, Dennis decided that he wanted a relic of Jude—not an easy acquisition in these days of more rigorous Vatican standards. But by the fall of 1996, he had received a tiny fragment that looks like bone—or, more likely, something believed to have come into close contact with the saint during his life—from Rome, via the Dominican network.

"I asked Father O'Brien if it would be possible for me to lay my hands on a first-class relic of St. Jude. He said he thought it possible through his connections. The only stipulation is that after I die it goes back to him. I'm not a Catholic. I was born and raised Lutheran, and after I quit drinking, I became a deacon in a high liturgical Lutheran church. We did mass like Catholics did it pre–Vatican II. I like the pomp and circumstance. We had the smells and bells. My walls are full of icons and angels. Everybody thinks I'm Catholic. A Catholic lady asked where my reliquary is. She was a volunteer at Malta when my lover was alive. She and Steve and I became very close. I'm a very private person—now I have only one extremely close friend and he doesn't have much time either. I pick all these young ones and then they die on me.

"I want the relic because I do the rosary, I do the stations of the cross. I have my own little altar built atop a bookshelf. I burn incense a lot. Just having the relic would make me feel it would be a pleasure to get up because I have a part of a saint.

"I never prayed to Jude before, but I lived with a retired Brazilian who had been an entertainer all his life, and he was always praying to Jude, not always for the right things . . .

"I thought it was sort of strange when they unofficially announced that St. Teresa of Ávila was the patron saint of AIDS patients. My automatic pick would have been St. Jude, for the hopeless. I wasn't miffed—just confused. She had worked with sick people, but Jude automatically came to mind. Being raised a Protestant, I don't believe I need a saint to be an intercessor for my prayers, but I don't see any harm in it either. When I was a kid I was brought up to think that this was idol worship—but it's just a help in devotions.

"I don't want a miracle. I was diagnosed in early 1988 and the last three guys I've been involved with have been eight to ten years younger than I, and they're dead. The one I'm taking care of right now is thirteen and a half years younger than I, and he has two T-cells. He's wheelchair-bound outside of his apartment and he gets fevers, sometimes four to five days out of the week. He won't even permit me to come over unless—I made him agree—his temperature stays at 103 for more than an hour. Then I go over to try to reduce it; otherwise he goes to the hospital.

"My last lover who died—we were together almost eight years—had such a zest for life. He had three hospital trips, and each time the doctors said, 'You won't be taken home from here.' All three times I took him home. Six months before he died he went into dementia. The miracle to me would have been to give the rest of my days to him—and have me take his place. But you can't work with God that way. It's His way or no way.

"To tell you the truth, I'm tired. When I was twenty, I went through Vietnam. I was on a Medivac helicopter . . . anywhere from Chu Lai to the DMZ, and I'm sure we got into Cambodia. MAG 16. Marine Air Group 16. First Marine air wing, about a mile or two outside Danang. We picked up the wounded off the battlefield. We went in when they were receiving fire. My nickname after three months of flying was "Magnetass." I volunteered, straight into the Navy from school. I was suicidal and I couldn't do it myself, so I thought

I'd let the gooks do it. I couldn't accept my sexuality. I came back from Vietnam a total alcoholic.

"Wanting a relic is deeply personal. Even though I say I don't look for a miracle, or I don't want a miracle, I would hope that by my having AIDS I'm helping other people, and I guess that's my mission. I think I'm looking for some strength to keep going, to accept what I have to do with another person, and get over the dying.

"I wrote the Jude shrine in Baltimore and got the pamphlets and an eight-inch statue of Jude. I already had a three-inch pewter one. I have books on saints, but really not much is written about Jude.

"What interests me is that he's the forgotten saint because of the close resemblance his name has to Judas Iscariot. It's unfair that just because his name resembled Judas's, people didn't want to pray to him, so he ends up the patron saint of hopelessness, which I do think is fitting. I've been a loner most of my life, too.

"I pray to Jude, asking for strength to go on, and I'm no longer suicidal. I've heard of Jude since I was a boy. There was a Catholic boy who lived upstairs from us and my mother said I shouldn't spend too much time with them because they're idol-worshipers. I wear the AIDS ribbon every day and a guardian-angel pin on the other collar. If anybody asks me about being disabled, I tell them it's my way of doing what I can."

By his own admission, Dennis has lived and loved hard, and, as with all of us, not always wisely. Some may judge him harshly; apparently Jude has not. But the turbulent rapids of his life and the deep strong current of devotion to Jude are typical: the unanticipated, but not perhaps unpredictable, meeting of the underdog saint and a tired man craving hope, reaching out in the dimness for Jude's anchor.

By day four of the novena, Father Raftery is discussing miracles and the "discernment" of them. Once more, he emphasizes the unending obligation entailed by service to the God of truth: that of carefully distinguishing fact from fantasy in devotional prayer. He describes how the apostles, "still groggy" and trying to adjust to suffering, death, and the Resurrection, waited for the Holy Spirit promised by Jesus, who would bestow on them great gifts: the ability to cure, to heal, to speak in all the languages of the world. "We need to recognize which gifts come from the Holy Spirit and which do not," he says slowly, gearing up for his point. "At Lourdes, for example, medical experts study the 'so-called miracles' to see if they have natural causes. When they don't find natural causes, they do not proclaim a miracle, but simply say we have no explanation.

"For example, if somebody has a cancer, and it suddenly disappears on the spot on a visit to Lourdes, it may be the *speed* of the recovery that cannot be accounted for by virtue of natural causes. And so the church is very careful in discerning what is the word of God and what is not."

It is clear that Father Raftery, mid-novena, is cautioning Jude's many present followers to avoid warping devotion into superstition, or, at least, to remember that Jude, fully an object of reverence and devotion, is an intercessor only, not the Lord God Himself. Caution on this point cannot not be emphasized enough. In fact, the shrine sends out a red-alert letter at least once a year, warning against chain letters that promise great bounty if the recipient sends a certain number of copies to others. Break the chain, and you invite dire consequences.

"They should be disregarded and ignored," Father Hayes gently scolds. "God doesn't deal with people in this way." It is a crucial distinction to one who runs a shrine that each year receives sixty thousand letters, a million dollars in contributions, and an incalculable tide of worshipers.

Seated in his office, drawing thoughtfully on a good cigar, he elaborates:

"Here, St. Jude is very much 'theologically fumigated,' as he should be. This is one of the things that we do. We're 'theological fumigators.' That's what I call it. We're trying to clean it up. They get crazy ideas; superstitions; say this nine times, blah, blah, blah; and even worse than that, or more deeply rooted, is the idea that if I do this, God will do that. If I do this, Jude has to do that. This is a deal. I made this deal. It's like going to the supermarket. You put your money down, and you get your groceries. That is not what the relationship between God and man and the communion of saints is all about.

"The communion of saints is a peculiarly Catholic notion. It's inimical to Protestantism: there you're on your own; we don't need any saints. Go directly to God—or, well, you can bring Jesus in, He's God. And then it's 'but you don't need Mary, or the saints. Deal with God.' Then you don't need the church. And the result of all that is that everybody's lost, shipwrecked.

"I think people identify their own obscure situations with Jude. In their desperation or difficulties they feel loneliness—loneliness and alienation—and so they identify with Jude, who is on the outside, one of the Twelve, but nobody knows much about him. I think they identify with that: this is for me. I like to amplify on that by looking at the Gospel and Jude's question at the Last Supper: why is it, Lord, that you do not tell the whole world about all this, but only speak to us? In other words, this would be great, everybody should know this. And that's the thing. So people come and say Jude will help them deal with their cause, and he'll be a good intercessor, and they feel that they should spread the word around, too. Make his name known. I really don't know where that idea came in: he's forgotten, make it known. You know, 'publication must be promised.' Well, I think it was an effective preacher's way somewhere, some way, sometime, of saying, Write your congressman, do this, do that, emphasize the power of prayer and let everybody know about it.

"Then there are the papers with petitions that are stuck in the statue. They are a natural phenomenon in people's religious sensitivity; they want to be in touch with their deity, not that Jude is a deity. Sometimes a lot of people oversimplify it to the point of distortion. But their basic sentiment is good, and their sentiment is basically Catholic. They're OK at root, but their manifestation or expression, or the way they understand it, is mixed up. I think that brings discredit on devotion and turns off a lot of people, but then again, a lot of people are comfortable with it. But I think we have to make an effort to, as I say, 'theologically fumigate' it.

"God works through Jude, just as God works through secondary causality all over the place. He does not immediately cure you of your headache. He sends you to a doctor who prescribes the right medicine, or gives the right analysis so that you're able, and by very natural means, to come to a healing. Obviously in some of these things there are no natural means. Some of them are directly supernatural, I am sure, but not everything is that way, nor should we expect it to be.

"For example, my grandmother died in Sacramento, and I went home for the funeral. It was in an old church, where you have to open the windows by hand, and it was hot and stifling, so the windows were open. As the priest ended mass, a burst of wind slammed the windows shut—so loudly that everybody stopped and looked. When we left the church, there was no wind outside. I was impressed. What is this, I thought, a message? Is this the angels saying, Good-bye, we're taking over now. Was it the exit of the spirit?

"So you see, this is how people get started, and they build on that—and then legend develops. Even in the Gospels, Jesus Himself is not saying, 'I've proved to you that I am who I am, so you better believe in me.' He just lays it out, and you still have to make *the* jump—the leap of faith—don't you? You can accept it or not. The evidence is there, the motives of credibility, the teaching, but if you don't want to, you don't have to. Some don't, but for those who do, it's reasonable, depending on their nature and their situation. Some can be quite adamant, and they want everybody else to listen to them, and on this is built devotion."

Pausing, in a halo of smoke, Father Hayes falls silent, as though weighing the profound implications of his analysis. One does not hear a lifetime of confessions, write years' worth of sermons, spend untold hours in prayer and not confront these matters with the patient comprehension of human nature that such experience confers. He speaks with wonder still of that unending parade before Jude's altar, "devout, and not devout, every nation under the sun," of all ages and all faiths, each driven by his own private dream or torment to the specialist in impossible causes.

"People feel lonely," he continues, "Catholics and not, and want to be part of something. We always want heroes. The people want to hear about Jude, a role model and hero. I don't think people consciously go around the church in order to approach Jude, like an end run. Some may feel that the church is too alien, too big, too powerful, whatever, for them. Do they say, 'I'll be satisfied just with St. Jude'? Perhaps. But I don't think it's a substitution, the best one could do. In most cases, it's more of a humble thing, that they're not worthy or deserving, and that God doesn't want anything to do with them.

"Some said after Vatican II that devotions would be gone. We'll be rid of those things. No more. No way: they've increased, not decreased. Also, of course, the percentage of senior citizens has much increased, and as one gets older one expects to hold onto old things, while the young are off looking for and doing something else. We get a significant number of young people, but I think many more would be involved if they had the opportunity to be linked with Jude.

"Jude is of the people more than he is of the hierarchy. That's part of the appeal. He's one of ours, whereas St. Peter would belong to the priests."

Father Hayes chuckles subversively, adding, "although that may be stretching it a bit." Leaning into his desk, he seems to be thinking aloud as he continues.

"All the apostles are shadowy figures. Mary, too, something mysterious about her movements: Why did she follow Jesus around? Where did she go after the Resurrection? Where did she die? Anybody associated with the life of Christ—this is my thesis—is submerged in 'I must decrease. He must increase.' Like John the Baptist—out of the picture. Their role is to shed light on Christ, and that's why St. Jude's question is very appropriate: 'Why don't you tell the rest of the world? Why just tell us?' The mystery lends to the legend. The whole purpose was to push Christ."

There it is, the most logical yet somehow obscure legacy of the apostle Jude. What Robert Thomas had said in the support group immediately comes to mind: how these eminently practical men, much like the apostles themselves, had sat down and shown him how to look for the truth—in his case, the pulsating nearness of death; in mine, the meaning of Jude's riddle. Things finally begin to fall into place. Father Hayes goes on:

"Many have commented on the criteria for picking an apostle. Frankly, it's a job description they would have flunked today. St. Paul is hard to get along with. Peter was a vacillator, he goes this way and that way. Judas was a traitor and a thief. And Jude—Jude is a shadow in the background. We don't know a lot about him except that he's there. And that is the whole point, because that, par excellence, is what the apostle is supposed to do—although I'm not trying to put words in the mouth of the Lord Jesus.

"Jude asked the question and Jesus said, 'Look, you've seen it. You've seen me. You've heard me. You know all there is, the Holy Spirit—I'm going to send the Paraclete to come as a guide to teach you—and you are the ones who are going to tell the people, go and tell the whole world. That's what an apostle is. You do the talking.' And that's the answer to Jude's question."

It is time to press him on the key issue—what everyone wants to know from everyone else, but especially a man of God: "Have you ever had a case where there was no explanation, and you, personally, thought it was a miracle?"

"Oh yes," he replies, with no hesitation. "Where there's no explanation—I mean it's more of a miracle—it's more reasonable to expect a miracle at work here than to deny the facts, to be oblivious to the facts of the case.

"I've seen answers to prayers where I would like to think that it's St. Jude answering. The thing that comes to mind is— well, you've heard about the restoration of this church. There was a period of time when we didn't know if we were going to make it or not. I remember going outside—now see, I can't verify this because it's too iffy, too tentative, but I can say this much about it—and seeing a man who was looking for one of the priests. And I said I'd help him, and as we walked, he said, 'How's it coming?' meaning the project. And I said, 'Well, to tell you the truth, it's not going too well. It's difficult. We're just going to have to hope and pray.' Well, he was going through some personal difficulties, health and so forth, so in the course of the discussion, I did two things: I said, 'We'll both pray. You pray for this and I'll pray for that. And I'll get you the priest you want.' Well, as a result of that, this brought people on board. He introduced people to the problem—people who must remain nameless—who, I think, were very instrumental in getting us over the hump in the restoration of the church. He didn't do it himself. He was a contact person. He went to A, who went to B, and because of C, D did something."

"Just a chance conversation?"

"You say 'chance conversation.' I don't really know."

The magnetic pull of the Shrine of the West continues to draw multitudes of the weary into its field of silent, invisible, yet somehow very powerful Judean happenings. Fragments of the sermons and stories of novena week linger in the air.

Jude is at work here. There is no great display of might, or pomp, or legend to advertise his worth. You do not wait for the day he will hover above the city, as did Michael the Archangel, mightiest of the hosts of God, over Rome of the Dark Ages when a fearful plague raged below. Alighting on the crest of Hadrian's mausoleum, he sheathed his sword, dripping with blood—and the pestilence vanished. That is how, they say, the emperor's tomb came to be called Castel Sant' Angelo.

You will not find people claiming to have seen the "forgotten saint" poised over the Golden Gate; such behavior, even in imagination, has never been part of his "profile." And yet, paradoxically, it is here in this American paradise that Jude slides more intensely into focus, perhaps because of the dire need for his intervention and his affinity for extremity. In Urfa, his legend survives from the old world, even as heavy machinery scours away the last traces of the city of his earthly life. In Rome, a majestic spiritual tent, he is present in ceremony and tradition, albeit occluded by the city's own eagerness to grab center stage. But here, at the geographical center of advanced technology, in future-racing America, Jude is on call, right down to the softest prayer, the smallest hope. Once lost himself—on the map and in history—he is found among those lost who, accepting their solitariness, take refuge in his invisible presence. From East to West, from the first century to the brink of the twenty-first, his message vibrates in the hollow reaches of the unanchored modern world.

He is no Coast Cult hero, no feel-good craze. In this state of extremes, the Jude reality—mysterious, yet distinct—is truly present, not relying on the wonders and essences of Edessa, nor even the resonant authority of Rome, but on the willingness to ask difficult questions of another hand-me-down belief.

Where grief is not in fashion—if not in bad taste—where cheerfulness is a religion, where being "in charge of your life" is an art form, all too many have had to admit that none of the above applies. Just as the apostles, confused and afraid, sought to fathom God's plan in the aftermath of Golgotha, so, too, do the shaken seek answers, repeatedly disappointed yet endlessly resuming the quest. And just there, amid shadows and disappointments—in the promised city of America, as pervasive and noiseless as the fog drifting in to enshroud its vaunted beauty—Jude thrives, and so does hope.

EPILOGUE

THE JOURNEY HAS BEEN LONG, THE STREAM OF stories brought forth by Jude's name more than any reporter could ask. Beyond imagining, his active presence in the lives of so many, his concrete manifestations, stirred up the wind and filled the sails of this expedition. Gradually, we discover, as I did one violet Roman evening, that Jude is the pursuer even as he withdraws, that he hunts his hunter by retreating. In the end, he is the consummate spiritual strategist, an embodiment of how the struggle makes the saint. To know this fully, we must complete the journey and thus come to realize that it is also the pilgrimage that makes the pilgrim.

From vanished Edessa to haunted Rome to the pulsing streets of America, we cannot remain unchanged walking in the steps of the rising saint of the age. Beyond the scant facts of the record, it is easy to see him as fearless, loyal, ferociously patient, and—true to his name—big hearted. Not simply a saint, but a spirit who cast his bright shadow over a trail of inexplicable wonders worked in virtue of One greater than he. The quest over, we are left with a chaos of impressions, a yearning of the heart that brings home the simplest of truths: that "journeys end in lovers meeting." There, standing at the crossroads, Jude waits in the twilight, watching for an outstretched hand, listening for a whisper of his name:

Most Holy Apostle, St. Jude Thaddeus. . . come to my assistance in this great need. . . Amen.